THE BONHAMS DIR

THE
BONHAMS
DIRECTORY

The Collector's Guide to
Care, Restoration and Repair

compiled by
Tim Forrest

assisted by
John Kirkwood

Kyle Cathie Limited

First published in 1991 by
Kyle Cathie Limited
3 Vincent Square London SW1P 2LX

ISBN 1 85626 047 X

Introduction copyright © Sir Roy Strong 1991
This compilation copyright © Bonhams 1991

A Cataloguing in Publication record for this title is available from the British Library

Tim Forrest is hereby identified as compiler of this work in accordance with
Section 77 of the Copyright, Designs and Patents Act 1988.

Printed and typeset by Butler & Tanner, Frome and London.

Contents

Important notice to readers

Acknowledgements

Many thanks to the staff of Bonhams for their encouragement and support, especially:

Helen Grantham
Odile Jackson
Heather Mann

How the Directory works

Each section of the book contains alphabetical lists of restorers and services in the following order:

England   –   by county

Ireland   –   by county (North/South)

Scotland   –   by regions

Wales   –   by county

The Collectors' section lists each subject in the same way and is followed by musical instruments.

Arms and Armour are followed by Sporting Equipment under each subject.

Lighting, Display and Suppliers are followed by Specialist Booksellers.

Contributors

Sir Roy Strong is renowned as an art historian and writer. He is a former Director of the Victoria and Albert Museum.

David Dallas is a dealer specialising in Old Master and later paintings. He has worked at both Christie's and Phillips, and is now a consultant to Bonhams.

Eric Knowles is well known from his television appearances on the Antiques Roadshow. He is Director of the Porcelain Department at Bonhams.

Christopher Claxton Stevens is a Director of Norman Adams Limited, leading dealers in eighteenth and early nineteenth century furniture. He is treasurer of the Regional Furniture Society.

Brand Inglis is a specialist dealer in silver based in Belgravia. He is a past President of the British Antique Dealers Association.

Sheila Landi was head of Textile Conservation at the Victoria and Albert Museum before becoming a consultant. She is the author of the *Textile Conservators Manual*.

Nicholas Pickwoad is adviser to the National Trust on book conservation and a visiting professor at Columbia University.

Alexander Crum Ewing is head of the Collectors Department at Bonhams.

Peter Horner is head of the Musical Instruments Department at Bonhams.

Philip Saunders is Editor of *Trace* magazine, which specialises in the listing of stolen works of art.

Diddi Malek is Manager of the Valuations Department at Bonhams.

Introduction

Loving care is not only required by human beings, but also by the objects around them, above all those precious things, either inherited or purchased, which fall into that ever-expanding bracket of collectibles. During the thirty years of my life spent in museums, few revolutions have been greater than the emergence of conservation departments as integral and respected sections of any well-run institution. It has been a slow process beginning in the post-war years and only attaining momentum after 1960. Out of it has emerged a whole new profession which has lifted the art of the conservator and the restorer to new heights, but which has also brought its own problems.

For those who use this book to be fore-warned is to be fore-armed because not everything in that world is so determinate as it appears from the outside. What is heartening is that its practical do-it-yourself guidance to the care of the objects in your possession is unanimous. Don't expose watercolours or textiles to strong light or they will fade, don't hang a panel painting over a radiator or it will split, are two typical basic tips. Once we move beyond those dictates of common sense we can quickly enter a different and difficult world with more complex parameters. This is often the result of the change from the old craftsman-conservator to the new, scientifically qualified degree-trained specialist. As the latter takes over, this division of attitude and approach is fast disappearing but it's still there. I suppose that the basic rule for any owner is not to part with anything until you know what is going to be done to it, and then only to someone who will provide you with a written record and, if relevant, photographs of the work in progress with a 'before' and 'after' print.

It is important to remember that a conservator doesn't know everything. The input of the academic expert is of equal importance. The historical sources, both written and visual, need also to be taken into account in the restoration of an object. In the case of a piece of upholstered furniture, for example, much of its effect will have been achieved through the textile component long since gone. What to put back can provide major interpretive challenges calling for many disciplines.

Many areas of conservation too are rent by disagreement. I remember, for instance, an enormous file dedicated to a long-standing battle between two schools of textile conservation. I wish that I could say that I understood what it was all about but it was so sated in technical jargon that it has remained a mystery to me to this day. I was just cast in the role of luckless referee between two entrenched schools of practice engaged in permanent trench warfare.

But that is enough on the pitfalls. I wrote about them on the basis that it is better to know than not to know and that it is better to be safe than sorry. Now the reverse side of that coin is extremely positive, stemming from the spread of conservation awareness through society. To own an object is like owning an animal; it brings with it responsibilities. Perhaps a better analogy would be a houseplant. Unless it is tended and watered, given air and light, fertilised and repotted and protected from the cold, its leaves will turn brown and wither, eventually they will fall off and the plant itself will die. Any object undergoes a similar if more protracted slide downhill over longer periods of time. The trouble with objects as against animals or plants is that that process is often so slow and so imperceptible that it can pass unnoticed. Cleaning the glass on a framed drawing is a healthy reminder of just what is in the air. One can remove the cloth and find it caked in black, a salutary indication if one is needed of what is accumulating on your pictures and textiles.

Don't rush into conservation. So often when one generation inherits from another it goes through the family heirlooms as though dealing with a bagwash. It is far more prudent to take stock and make a plan with expert guidance stretching over several years. Good conservation and restoration is not cheap but it is a sound investment. Work out an A and B list in terms of urgency. If things are in a bad way, seek immediate advice on preventive first aid. A planned programme should give you sustained delight, for an object put into sound order is more often than not as satisfying as acquiring something new.

Do remember to open even the most rudimentary file. Put into it any information you have on an object and just pop in the restorer's report and any photographs which were taken. A later generation will thank you for being able to know what was done to a particular piece. Often this is vital, for what was done might have to be undone in the light of subsequent knowledge.

What you don't want to feel at the end of this exercise is that you are inhabiting a museum in which no form of normal daily existence can be lived. Balance is essential. Some conservationists are so extreme that they would have you close the shutters and curtains in favour of a preserving everlasting murk. It is important if life is to go on that conservation is borne in mind when arranging a house from the outset. An embroidered silk hanging might look marvellous in a sunny room, but only if you're prepared to let it be reduced to a heap of shredded rags in a few years. So it is always a good idea to start off by working out which are your most vulnerable pieces and the reasonable precautions demanded for their survival. Look for places which meet that but which also set it off to advantage. Then you can move on and place the less valuable items.

Never lose sight of the fact that you inhabit a home. Nothing can be so unwelcoming to your guests as to be warned off from sitting on a prominently placed antique chair because it is too fragile. Or to create an atmosphere in which a visitor feels that his slightest movement will decimate the Worcester porcelain. Also, if you have domestic help, it is not only unwise but unfair to expect them to cope with dusting and cleaning vulnerable objects. The Meissen should be safely displayed and any handling be the province of the owner. I well remember the hostess who snapped at a guest who leaned back on a Chippendale chair whose back promptly fell off: 'That'll be several hundred pounds to repair and it's ruined its value.' That is no way to make friends.

Perhaps the most rewarding aspect of restoration and conservation is that it makes an owner truly appreciative of the intricacies of the creative act. In excess of any other approach one is made to share in the technical processes which went into the making of a particular piece, leaving one amazed at such skills. This is an exciting voyage of learning and discovery. It is also one which has made me not only respectful of those who created a piece but of those who had the skill to return it to its pristine state. I always found any contact with restorers and conservators immensely enjoyable and certainly greatly enlightening. It is after all thanks to their skills that we are able to pass on the huge heritage of art works from the past in good shape into the twenty-first century.

Roy Strong
July 1991

Oil Paintings, Watercolours, Prints and Drawings, Framing

Thirty years of improvements in conservation technique have led to a greater understanding of the condition of pictures. Accurate recognition of their quality, and thus their worth in every sense, is affected by how much of what we see is by the original artist. A picture, the surface of which has been abraded and then retouched by a poor restorer, gives one a general sense of design but lacks the subtlety and refinement of touch which allows us to enjoy and distinguish the hand of one painter from the next.

There are two basic causes for the alteration of a picture's state: the natural and the unnatural. Let us first deal with the natural.

In the case of watercolours and, to a lesser extent, oil paintings, subjection to light is a crucial factor. Whether light is transmitted by waves or particles it equals heat. Heat has an effect on the chemical structure of the pigments which give colour to the paints and if they are altered the balance of the picture changes. Tinted drawings and watercolours hung for recent generations in direct sunlight will become a combination of pale pink and brown. The indigo blue goes pink, the gamboge (yellow) disappears and the other dyes fade, leaving only vestigial smudges over a pencil outline. Until the 18th century these were kept in portfolios.

Oil pigments fade too and, in the case of lapis lazuli (blue), can become granular and fall off or produce bloom like a plum. Humidity has a bearing. Watercolours, drawings and prints were made, traditionally, on paper made from a highly acidic wood pulp, which turns brown and brittle with time and the inevitable exposure to air. Little brown spots of mildew called 'foxing' occur and in extreme cases other fungi can grow on the surfaces of paper. Paper may also absorb acid from the pine back-boards to show the grain and knots, like an early photographic experiment. Oil paintings tend to be primed with a layer of gesso (water-soluble plaster) over the size (glue which covers the

1

canvas). This can swell and blister in damp conditions and cause the paint to bubble and blow off, much as it does on a window frame painted in spring before the wood has exhaled its winter rain.

Old and bowed watercolour frames are susceptible to the incursions of silver fish, which relish the sugar in watercolour size and honey and gum arabic (used as media) and are perfectly prepared to digest the covering pigments in pursuit of their food. Thunder flies can squeeze between even the most seemingly air-tight occlusions and it is their starved bodies that leave disfiguring stains. To date, framers have found no cure for their invasions.

Against the ravages of some of these natural enemies various protections have been devised. No picture should be subjected to light exceeding 50 'Lux' (equal to perhaps a 40-watt bulb) which is the agreed museum standard. Oils on wood should be humidified at a similar level to furniture to prevent warping and preclude fungal growth. All works on paper should be mounted on acid-free Conservation Board, both between the image and the glass and the image and the back-board. Whenever possible, the paper (support) of the drawing or watercolour should be deacidified by a highly competent conservator of works on paper.

In my opinion, the greatest damage perpetrated to pictures historically has been committed out of ignorance by those owners and dealers who have entrusted their 'cleaning', as it once was known, 'restoration' latterly and 'conservation' currently, to those incompetent to carry out the work sympathetically. Works on paper can and have been bleached by those who were not cognizant of the chemical complexities. But I am thinking more of oil paintings and tempera paintings when I strike this alarming note. Log, coal and nicotine smoke have formed, over the centuries, yellow and brown layers of matter on top of or fused with the varnish on many oil paintings, which masks and distorts the true colours of the picture underneath. Often people have not realised that the solvents used to break down dirty varnish will dissolve certain soft pigments, especially organic dyes – brown, black, yellow, green and certain reds. The whites and some blues are made of harder metallic oxides but have suffered, in many instances, from being cleaned more often than the rest of the picture, perhaps because the 'expert' could always get a result from the lighter bits!

One thing is certain; the softening effect of the cleaning solvent, combined with the abrading effect of moving the fluid over the picture's surface, has often led to the paint layer being worn away. This is true even when a painting is in the best of hands.

The lining or re-lining of canvases onto new strengthening supports is a further minefield. Lining onto a substance of similar strength and type is the only acceptable course; thus canvas onto canvas, not cotton-duck or worse still panel, metal or board. The right pressure and heat must be applied to prevent the paint layer being crushed or burnt. Only organic adhesives, the action of which can be reversed, should be used to fix a battered old canvas to a new one. The use of plastic glues or the wrong wax can be irreparably damaging.

In short, I would suggest that cleaning is carried out as infrequently as possible and that conservation (that is, in my field, the consolidation of a painting in a critically dangerous state of preservation) is carried out alone and then only by someone who has undergone modern and rigorous training in the correct techniques. Graduates of the Camberwell School of Paper Conservation or the Courtauld Institute in London, those trained at Gateshead, the Hamilton Kerr Institute in Whitlesford, Cambridge and members of the Association of British Picture Restorers are recommended. Try to choose someone who specialises in working on oil paintings if you have one in need of conservation, or a watercolour specialist for a watercolour rather than a general picture restorer. There is just too much to learn to be an expert in all four subjects covered here. If in doubt consult your local museum.

I can touch only on some problems which arise if you wish to protect and appreciate pictures. The lesson of the past is that too many great works of art, owned by well-intentioned people seeking only to have them 'restored' to their former glory, have been literally loved to death. It is our responsibility to house these treasures, whilst being able to enjoy them as thoughtfully as we are able and to entrust their conservation only to those who are competent to preserve them. Moreover, if there are financial constraints which preclude the best work being carried out, to do nothing is vastly better than to do the wrong thing.

David Dallas

ADAM GALLERY
13 John Street, Bath, **Avon BA1 2JL**
TEL   0225 480406
OPEN   9.30–5.30 Mon–Sat.
Specialise in consolidation, restoration
and cleaning of oil paintings and
cleaning, defoxing and conservation of
watercolours and drawings and framing.
PROVIDE Home Inspections. Free
Estimates. Collection/Delivery Service
by arrangement.
SPEAK TO Paul or Philip Dye.

DAVID A. CROSS GALLERY
3A Boyce's Avenue, Clifton, Bristol,
Avon BS8 4AA
TEL   0272 732614
OPEN   9.30–6 Mon–Fri; 9.30–5.30 Sat.
Specialise in restoring oil paintings,
watercolours and prints of all periods.
PROVIDE Home Inspections. Free
Estimates. Chargeable
Collection/Delivery Service.
SPEAK TO Jo David.

THE FRAME STUDIO
2nd Floor, 14 Waterloo Street, Clifton,
Bristol, **Avon BS8 4BT**
TEL   0272 238279
OPEN   10–6 Tues–Sat.
Specialise in restoring oil paintings and
watercolours.
PROVIDE Home Inspections. Free
Estimates. Chargeable
Collection/Delivery Service.
SPEAK TO Graeme Dowling.
Member of the Guild of Master
Craftsmen.

GEORGE GREGORY
Manvers Street, Bath, **Avon BA1 1JW**
TEL   0225–466055
FAX   0225 482122
OPEN   9–1, 2–5.30 Mon–Fri; 9.30–1 Sat
           By Appointment.
Specialise in cleaning and restoring old
prints

PROVIDE Home Inspections. Free
Estimates.
SPEAK TO Mr. H. H. Bayntun-Coward.

INTERNATIONAL FINE ART
CONSERVATION STUDIOS
43–45 Park Street, Bristol, **Avon
BS1 5NL**
TEL   0272 293480 or 293988
FAX   0272 225511
OPEN   10–5.30 Mon–Sat.
Specialise in conserving and restoring oil
paintings, murals and painted ceilings.
PROVIDE Home Inspections. Free
Estimates. Chargeable
Collection/Delivery Service.
SPEAK TO Miss Alexandra Deck.
This firm has worked at Wilton House,
the Foreign Office and The Queen's
House, Greenwich.

ANTHONY REED
94–96 Walcot Street, Bath, **Avon
BA1 5BG**
TEL   0225 461969 or 0272 333595
OPEN   9–6 Mon–Sat.
Specialise in cleaning and restoring oils,
watercolours and prints. He also
restores picture frames and does gilding.
PROVIDE Home Inspections. Chargeable
Estimates. Chargeable Local
Collection/Delivery Service.
SPEAK TO Anthony Reed.
Member of the IIC.
SEE Furniture.

K. A. WHEELER
4 Bayswater Avenue, Westbury Park,
Bristol, **Avon BS6 7NS**
TEL   0272–423003
OPEN   9.30–1, 2–5.30 Mon–Fri.
Specialise in conserving and restoring
fine prints, watercolours and drawings.
PROVIDE Free Estimates.

4

SPEAK TO Keith Wheeler.
Member of the Institute of Paper
Conservation and the UKIC.

LIEUT. COL. R. L. V. ffrench BLAKE
D.S.O.
Loddon Lower Farm, Spencers Wood,
Reading, **Berkshire RG7 1JE**
TEL   0734–883212
OPEN   By Appointment.
Specialise in restoring oil paintings,
church hatchments, as well as repairing
gesso frames, calligraphy picture
labelling and high class copying of
Dutch flower paintings, marine pictures
and winter landscapes.
PROVIDE Home Inspections. Free
Estimates. Chargeable
Collection/Delivery Service.
SPEAK TO Lieut. Col. ffrench Blake.

THE COLLECTORS' GALLERY
8 Bridge Street, Caversham Bridge,
Reading, **Berkshire RG4 8AA**
TEL   0734 483663
OPEN   10–5 Mon–Fri; 10–4 Sat.
Specialise in conserving and restoring
18th and 19th century oils and
watercolours.
PROVIDE Home Inspections. Free
Estimates. Collection/Delivery Service
by arrangement.
SPEAK TO Helen Snook.
SEE Furniture.

GRAHAM GALLERY
Highwoods, Burghfield Common,
Reading, **Berkshire RG7 3BG**
TEL   0734 832320
FAX   071 930 4261
OPEN   By Appointment.
Specialise in restoring 19th and early
20th century watercolours and prints.

PROVIDE Home Inspections. Free
Estimates. Free Collection/Delivery
Service.
SPEAK TO John Steeds.

HERON PICTURES
High Street, Whitchurch-on-Thames,
Reading, **Berkshire RG8 7EX**
TEL   0734 843286
OPEN   10–7 Tues–Sat.
Specialise in cleaning and restoring oil
paintings and frames as well as gilding.
PROVIDE Home Inspections. Free
Estimates. Free Local
Collection/Delivery Service.
SPEAK TO George Duckett.

CHESS ANTIQUES
85 Broad Street, Chesham,
Buckinghamshire HP5 3EF
TEL   0494 783043
FAX   0494 791302
OPEN   8–5 Mon–Sat.
Specialise in restoring oil paintings.
PROVIDE Home Inspections. Chargeable
Estimates. Chargeable
Collection/Delivery Service.
SPEAK TO M. Wilder.

H. S. WELLBY LTD.
The Malt House, Church End,
Haddenham, **Buckinghamshire
HP17 8AB**
TEL   0844 290036
OPEN   9–5 Mon–Sat.
Specialise in the lining, cleaning and
restoration of oil paintings.
PROVIDE Home Inspections. Free
Estimates. Free Collection/Delivery
Service.
SPEAK TO Christopher Wellby.

CAMBRIDGE FINE ART LTD.
Priesthouse, 33 Church Street, Little
Shelford, Cambridge, **Cambridgeshire
CB2 5HG**
TEL   0223 842866 or 843537
OPEN   10–6 Mon–Sat.
Specialise in restoring oil paintings and
watercolours (1780–1950).
PROVIDE Free/Chargeable Estimates.
Chargeable Collection/Delivery Service.
SPEAK TO Ralph Lury.

ALAN CANDY
Old Manor House, 4 Cambridge Street,
Godmanchester, Huntingdon,
Cambridgeshire PE18 8AT
TEL   0480 453198
OPEN   By Appointment.
Specialise in restoring oils, watercolours
and prints.
PROVIDE Free Estimates.
SPEAK TO Alan Candy.

FRANK GOODINGHAM
Studio 3, Hope St Yard, Hope Street,
Cambridge, **Cambridgeshire CB1 3NA**
TEL   0223 410702
OPEN   10–6 Mon–Fri.
Specialise in restoring 18th and 19th
century gilded work including
composition or carved frames.
PROVIDE Home Inspections. Refundable
Estimates. Collection/Delivery by
arrangement.
SPEAK TO Frank Goodingham.
SEE Furniture.

A. ALLEN ANTIQUE RESTORERS
Buxton Rd, Newtown, Newmills, Via
Stockport, **Cheshire SK12 3JS**
TEL   0663 745274
OPEN   8–5 Mon–Fri; 9–12 Sat.
Specialise in restoring picture frames and
gilding.

PROVIDE Home Inspections.
Free/Chargeable Estimates. Free
Collection/Delivery Service.
SPEAK TO Tony Allen.
SEE Furniture, Silver.

HARPER FINE PAINTINGS
Overdale, Woodford Road, Poynton,
Cheshire SK12 1ED
TEL   0625 879105
OPEN   By Appointment.
Specialise in restoring 18th, 19th and
early 20th century British and European
oils and watercolours.
PROVIDE Home Inspections. Chargeable
Estimates. Free Collection/Delivery
Service.
SPEAK TO Peter Harper.

ART WORKS
54b Church Street, Falmouth, **Cornwall
TR11 3DS**
TEL   0326 211238
OPEN   By Appointment.
Specialise in restoring works of art on
paper.
PROVIDE Home Inspections. Free
Estimates. Chargeable
Collection/Delivery Service.
SPEAK TO Suzanne Nunn.
SEE Books.

TAMAR GALLERY (ANTIQUES &
FINE ART)
5 Church Street, Launceston, **Cornwall
PL15 8AW**
TEL   0566 774233 or 82444
OPEN   10–1, 2.30–5 Tues–Sat; Early
         Closing Thur.
Specialise in restoring and cleaning
watercolours of all periods.
PROVIDE Free Estimates.
SPEAK TO N. O. Preston.

TIMES PAST ANTIQUES
13 Chatsworth Road, Chesterfield,
Derbyshire
TEL   0246 234578
OPEN   9.30–5 Mon–Sat. Closed Wed.
Specialise in restoring oil paintings.
PROVIDE Home Inspections. Refundable
Estimates. Chargeable
Collection/Delivery Service.
SPEAK TO L. Lewis.

RITA BUTLER
Stour Gallery, 28 East Street, Blandford,
Dorset DT11 7DR
TEL   0258 456293
OPEN   10–1, 2–4 Tues, Thur–Sat; 10–1
        Wed.
Specialise in cleaning and restoring oil
paintings, watercolours, prints and
maps.
PROVIDE Home Inspections. Free
Estimates. Chargeable
Collection/Delivery Service.
SPEAK TO Rita Butler.
SEE Books.

GALERIE LAFRANCE
647 Wimborne Road, Winton,
Bournemouth, **Dorset BH9 2AR**
TEL   0202 522313
OPEN   8.30–1, 2–5.30 Mon–Fri; 9–1
        Sat.
Specialise in cleaning and restoring oils,
watercolours and prints and picture
frames. Gesso and composition
replaced, gilding as necessary.
PROVIDE Home Inspections. Free
Estimates. Free/Chargeable
Collection/Delivery Service.
SPEAK TO Pierre Lafrance.

MRS. CATHERINE MATHEW
Kiwi Cottage, Maperton Road,
Charlton Horethorne, Sherborne, **Dorset
DT9 4NT**
TEL   096 322 595
OPEN   9–6 Mon–Fri or By
        Appointment.
Specialise in cleaning picture frames to
leave the original gold, regilding where
new moulding has been applied or where
necessary.
PROVIDE Home Inspections. Free
Estimates. Free Collection/Delivery
Service.
SPEAK TO Catherine Mathew.
SEE Porcelain, Furniture.

THE SWAN GALLERY
57 Cheap Street, Sherborne, **Dorset
DT8 3QT**
TEL   0935 814465
FAX   0308 68195
OPEN   9.30–5 Mon–Sat; 9.30–1 Wed.
Specialise in cleaning works of art on
paper and restoring oil paintings.
PROVIDE Free Estimates.
SPEAK TO Simon Lamb.

S BOND & SON
14/15 North Hill, Colchester, **Essex
CO1 1DZ**
TEL   0206 572925
OPEN   9–5 Mon–Sat.
Specialise in restoring oil paintings.
PROVIDE Home Inspections. Free
Estimates. Free Local
Collection/Delivery Service.
SPEAK TO Robert Bond.
This family firm has been established 140
years and is run by the fifth generation.
SEE Furniture.

TERRY HILLIARD
The Barn, Master Johns, Thoby Lane,
Mountnessing, Brentwood, **Essex
CM15 0JY**
TEL   0277 354717
OPEN   By Appointment.
Specialise in restoring gilded picture
frames and carving and gilding including
making reproduction frames.
PROVIDE Home Inspections. Free
Estimates. Free Collection/Delivery
Service.
SPEAK TO Terry Hilliard.
Member of the Guild of Master
Craftsmen.
SEE Furniture.

RICHARD ILES GALLERY
10 Northgate Street, Colchester, **Essex
CO1 1HA**
TEL   0206 577877
OPEN   9.30–4.30 Mon–Sat.
Specialise in restoring 19th and early
20th century watercolours as well as
picture framing.
PROVIDE Free Estimates.
SPEAK TO Richard Iles.

MEYER'S GALLERY
66 High Street, Ingatestone, **Essex
CM4 0BA**
TEL   0277–355335
OPEN   10–5 Mon–Sat, Closed Wed.
Specialise in restoring oil paintings and
watercolours.
PROVIDE Home Inspections. Free
Estimates. Free Local
Collection/Delivery Service.
SPEAK TO Mrs. Meyers.
Member of LAPADA.

MILLSIDE ANTIQUE
RESTORATION
Parndon Mill, Parndon Mill Lane,
Harlow, **Essex CM20 2HP**
TEL   0279 428148
FAX   0279 415075
OPEN   10–5 Mon–Fri.
Specialise in cleaning and restoring
watercolours, prints and oil paintings.
Also do watercolour tinting of sepia and
black and white prints and restore
picture frames.
PROVIDE Home Inspections.
Free/Chargeable Estimates. Chargeable
Collection/Delivery Service.
SPEAK TO David Sparks or Angela
Wickliffe-Philp.
SEE Porcelain, Silver.

PEARLITA FRAMES LTD.
30 North Street, Romford, **Essex
RM11 2LB**
TEL   0708 760342
OPEN   9–5.30 Mon–Sat.
Specialise in restoring oil paintings,
watercolours and engravings as well as
picture framing.
PROVIDE Home Inspections. Free
Estimates. Free Collection/Delivery
Service.
SPEAK TO Trevor Woodward.

ELIZABETH POWELL
5 Royal Square, Dedham, Colchester,
Essex CO7 6AA
TEL   0206 322279
OPEN   9–5.30 Mon–Sat.
Specialise in conserving and restoring oil
paintings, watercolours, pastels and
prints.
PROVIDE Home Inspections, Free
Estimates, Free Local
Collection/Delivery Service.
SPEAK TO Elizabeth Powell.
Member of the IIC.

8

MRS JACQUELINE TABER
Jaggers, Fingringhoe, Colchester, **Essex CO5 7DN**
TEL   0206 729334
OPEN   9–6 Mon–Fri. Other times by appointment
Specialise in conserving and restoring oil paintings.
PROVIDE Home Inspections. Free Estimates. Collection/Delivery Service by arrangement.
SPEAK TO Jacqueline Taber.
Associate Member of the APBR.

ASTLEY HOUSE FINE ART
Astley House, High Street, Moreton-in-Marsh, **Gloucestershire GL56 0LL**
TEL   0608 50601
FAX   0608 51777
OPEN   9–5.30 Mon–Sat.
Specialise in cleaning and restoring oil paintings, watercolours and framing.
PROVIDE Free Estimates. Chargeable Collection/Delivery Service.
SPEAK TO David or Nanette Glaisyer.

DAVID BANNISTER
26 Kings Road, Cheltenham, **Gloucestershire GL52 6BG**
TEL   0242 514287
FAX   0242 513890
OPEN   By Appointment.
Specialise in restoring, colouring and cataloguing topographic prints.
PROVIDE Free Estimates. Chargeable Collection/Delivery Service.
SPEAK TO David Bannister.
SEE Books.

KEITH BAWDEN
Mews Workshop, Montpellier Retreat, Cheltenham, **Gloucestershire GL50 2XS**
TEL   0242 230320
OPEN   7–4.30 Mon–Fri.
Specialise in conserving and restoring all aspects of paintings.
PROVIDE Free Estimates. Home Inspections. Local Collection/Delivery Service.
SPEAK TO Keith Bawden.
SEE Furniture, Silver, Porcelain.

CLEEVE PICTURE FRAMING
Coach House Workshops, Stoke Road, Bishops Cleeve, Cheltenham, **Gloucestershire GL52 4RP**
TEL   0242 672785
FAX   0242 676827
OPEN   9–1 Mon–Fri; 9–1 Sat.
Specialise in restoring and conserving picture frames, oil paintings, watercolours, papers and prints as well as bespoke framing and decorative mounts.
PROVIDE Home Inspections. Free Estimates. Free Collection/Delivery Service.
SPEAK TO James Gardner.

JOHN DAVIES
Church Street Gallery, Stow-on-the-Wold, **Gloucestershire GL54 1BB**
TEL   0451 31698
FAX   0451 32477
OPEN   9.30–1, 2–5.30 Mon–Sat.
Specialise in restoring pictures in all mediums including oil, watercolour, tempera and pastel.
PROVIDE Home Inspections. Free Estimates. Chargeable Collection/Delivery Service.
SPEAK TO John Davies.

G. M. S. RESTORATIONS
The Workshops (rear of Bell Passage Antiques), High Street, Wickwar, **Gloucestershire GL12 8NP**
TEL   0454 294251
FAX   0454 294251
OPEN   8–5 Mon–Fri.
Specialise in restoring oil paintings and watercolours.

PROVIDE Home Inspections. Refundable
Estimates. Chargeable
Collection/Delivery Service.
SPEAK TO Mr. G. M. St.George-Stacey.
Member of LAPADA, Upholsterer's
Guild, Guild of Master Craftsmen,
Guild of Woodcarvers, Guild of Antique
Dealers and Restorers.
SEE Furniture.

A. J. PONSFORD ANTIQUES
51–53 Dollar Street, Cirencester,
Gloucestershire GL7 2AS
TEL   0285 652355
OPEN   8.30–5.30 Mon–Fri.
Specialise in restoring oil paintings and
picture frames.
PROVIDE Home Inspections. Free
Estimates. Free Collection/Delivery
Service.
SPEAK TO A. J. Ponsford.
SEE Furniture.

PETER WARD GALLERY
11 Gosditch Street, Cirencester,
Gloucestershire GL7 2AG
TEL   0285 658499
OPEN   9.30–5.30 Mon–Sat.
Specialise in restoring oils and
watercolours as well as framing and
mounting.
PROVIDE Home Inspections. Free
Collection/Delivery Service.
SPEAK TO Peter Ward.

JOAN A. LEWRY
'Wychelms', 66 Gorran Avenue,
Rowner, Gosport, **Hampshire**
PO13 0NF
TEL   0329 286901
OPEN   By Appointment.
Specialise in cleaning, conserving and
restoring pictures.
PROVIDE Home Inspections.

Refundable Estimates. Free Local
Collection/Delivery Service.
SPEAK TO Joan Lewry.

THE PETERSFIELD BOOKSHOP
16a Chapel Street, Petersfield,
Hampshire GU32 3DS
TEL   0730 63438
FAX   0730 63438
OPEN   9–5.30 Mon–Sat.
Specialise in restoring and cleaning oil
paintings, watercolours, picture framing
and restoring.
PROVIDE Home Inspections. Free
Estimates. Collection/Delivery Service
available.
SPEAK TO Frank Westwood.
SEE Books.

PRINTED PAGE
2–3 Bridge Street, Winchester,
Hampshire SO23 9BH
TEL   0962 854072
FAX   0962 862995
OPEN   9.30–5.30 Tues–Sat.
Specialise in cleaning, colouring and
repairing old prints and restoring oil
paintings and watercolours.
PROVIDE Home Inspections. Refundable
Estimates. Chargeable
Collection/Delivery Service.
SPEAK TO Jean or Christopher Wright.
Member of the FATG and the Institute
of Paper Conservation.

EDWIN COLLINS
Coltsfoot Gallery, Hatfield, Leominster,
Hereford & Worcester HR6 0SF
TEL   056 882 277
OPEN   By Appointment.
Specialise in restoring and conserving all
works of art on paper and also offer a
mounting and framing service.
PROVIDE Home Inspections. Free
Estimates.

SPEAK TO Edwin Collins.
Member of Institute of Paper
Conservation.

JAMES GRINDLEY
2 Fownhope Court, Fownhope,
Hereford, **Hereford & Worcester
HR1 4PB**
TEL   0432 860396
OPEN   By Appointment.
Specialise in restoring and conserving
works of art on paper, particularly
watercolours and prints.
PROVIDE Free Estimates.
Collection/Delivery Service by
arrangement.
SPEAK TO James Grindley.

HAY LOFT GALLERY
Berry Wormington, Broadway, **Hereford
& Worcester WR12 7NH**
TEL   0242 621202
OPEN   10–5.30 Mon–Fri or By
           Appointment.
Specialise in restoring paintings,
particularly 19th century ones.
PROVIDE Home Inspections. Free
Estimates. Chargeable
Collection/Delivery Service.
SPEAK TO Jane or Sally Pitt.

JENNINGS & JENNINGS
30 Bridge Street, Leominster, **Hereford
& Worcester HR6 9JQ**
TEL   05448 586
OPEN   By Appointment.
Specialise in conserving and restoring
gilded picture frames.
PROVIDE Home Inspections. Free
Estimates. Free/Chargeable
Collection/Delivery Service.
SPEAK TO Sabina Jennings.
SEE Furniture.

EUGENE B. OKARMA
Brobury House Gallery, Brobury,
Hereford & Worcester HR3 6BS
TEL   09817 229
OPEN   9–4 Mon–Sat.
Specialise in restoring old prints,
watercolours, oil paintings and frames.
PROVIDE Local Home Inspections.
SPEAK TO Mr. Okarma.

LEONORA WEAVER
6 Aylestone Drive, Hereford, **Hereford
and Worcester HR1 1HT**
TEL   0432 267816
OPEN   By Appointment.
Specialise in restoring and hand-
colouring prints.
PROVIDE Free Estimates.
Collection/Delivery Service sometimes
available.
SPEAK TO Leonora Weaver.
SEE Books.

WOODLAND FINE ART
16 The Square, Alvechurch, **Hereford &
Worcester B48 7LA**
TEL   021 445 5886
OPEN   10–6 Mon–Sat.
Specialise in restoring oil paintings and
watercolours.
PROVIDE Home Inspections. Free
Estimates. Free Collection/Delivery
Service.
SPEAK TO C. J. Haynes.
SEE Furniture.

BECKWITH & SON
St. Nicholas Hall, St. Andrew Street,
Hertford, **Hertfordshire SG14 1HZ**
TEL   0992 582079
OPEN   9–1, 2–5.30 Mon–Sat.
Specialise in restoring oils and
watercolours.

PROVIDE Home Inspections. Chargeable
Estimates. Free Local
Collection/Delivery Service.
SPEAK TO G. Gray.
See Furniture, Porcelain.

ST. OUEN ANTIQUES LTD.
Vintage Corner, Old Cambridge Road,
Puckeridge, **Hertfordshire SG11 1SA**
TEL   0920 821336
FAX   0920 822877
OPEN   10–5 Mon–Sat.

Specialise in restoring 19th century
paintings.
PROVIDE Home Inspections. Refundable
Estimates. Chargeable
Collection/Delivery Service.
SPEAK TO Tim or John Blake.
SEE Furniture.

CLARE GALLERY
21 High Street, Royal Tunbridge Wells,
Kent TN1 1UT
TEL   0892 38717
FAX   0323 29588
OPEN   8.15–5.30 Mon–Sat.

Specialise in restoring 19th and 20th
century oil paintings and watercolours,
framing service.
PROVIDE Home Inspections. Free
Estimates. Chargeable
Collection/Delivery Service.
SPEAK TO M. Ettinger.

FRANCES ILES FINE PAINTINGS
Rutland House, 103 High Street,
Rochester, **Kent ME1 1LX**
TEL   0634 843081
FAX   0474 822403
OPEN   9–5.30 Mon–Sat.

Specialise in conserving and restoring oil
paintings and works on paper. Framing
service for all mediums including early
samplers and needlepoint.

PROVIDE Home Inspections. Free
Estimates. Free Collection/Delivery
Service.
SPEAK TO Jeanette or Lucy Iles.

G. & D. I. MARRIN & SONS
149 Sandgate Road, Folkestone, **Kent
CT20 2DA**
TEL   0303 53016
FAX   0303 850956
OPEN   9.30–5.30 Mon–Sat.

Specialise in restoring prints.
PROVIDE Home Inspections. Chargeable
Estimates. Chargeable
Collection/Delivery Service.
SPEAK TO John or Patrick Marrin.
SEE Books.

W. J. MORRILL LTD.
437 Folkestone Road, Dover, **Kent
CT17 9JX**
TEL   0304 201989
OPEN   8–5 Mon–Fri.

Specialise in relining and restoring oil
paintings of all periods. They also make
both wood and composition period
frames.
PROVIDE Home Inspections. Free
Collection/Delivery Service.
SPEAK TO Mr. Barnes.

C. W. ALLISON & SONS
Hillview, Bilsborrow Lane, Bilsborrow,
Preston, **Lancashire PR3 0RN**
TEL   0995 40344
OPEN   10–5 Mon–Fri.

Specialise in restoring paintings, prints
and watercolours.
PROVIDE Home Inspections. Free
Estimates. Chargeable
Collection/Delivery Service.
SPEAK TO Richard Allison.
SEE Porcelain, Furniture.

DYSONS ARTS LTD.
87 Scotland Road, Nelson, **Lancashire BB9 7UY**
TEL   0282 65468
OPEN   9.30–5.30 Mon–Sat; closed Tues.
Specialise in cleaning, repairing and restoring oil paintings. Also mount and frame pictures.
PROVIDE Free Estimates.
SPEAK TO O. A. Davies.

BARBARA WILDMAN
9 Woodside Terrace, Nelson, **Lancashire BB9 7TB**
TEL. 0282 699679
OPEN   By Appointment.
Specialise in restoring oil paintings of all periods including relining. She also restores gilt frames, gesso work and gold leaf.
PROVIDE Home Inspections. Free Estimates. Chargeable Collection/Delivery Service.
SPEAK TO Barbara Wildman.
SEE Furniture.

JOHN GARNER
51–53 High Street East, Uppingham, **Leicestershire LE15 9PY**
TEL   0572 823607
FAX   0572 821654
OPEN   9–5.30 Mon–Sat. Sun By Appointment.
Specialise in restoring 18th and 19th century pictures.
PROVIDE Home Inspections. Free Collection/Delivery Service.
SPEAK TO John or Wendy Garner.
SEE Furniture.

THE OLD HOUSE GALLERY
13–15 Market Place, Oakham, **Leicestershire LE15 6DT**
TEL   0572 755538
OPEN   10–5 Mon–Fri; 10–4 Sat; closed Thur pm.
Specialise in restoring Victorian and Modern British oils, watercolours and antiquarian prints. They also offer a framing service.
PROVIDE Home Inspections. Free Local Collection/Delivery Service.
SPEAK TO Richard Clarke.
SEE Books.

BURGHLEY FINE ART CONSERVATION
Burghley House, Stamford, **Lincolnshire PE9 3JY**
TEL   0780 62155
OPEN   By Appointment.
Specialise in conserving and restoring easel paintings, wall paintings (oil on plaster), picture frames and gilding.
PROVIDE Home Inspections. Free Estimates. Chargeable Collection/Delivery Service.
SPEAK TO Michael Cowell.
Any work undertaken is fully documented.
SEE Furniture.

HOWARD & STONE CONSERVATORS
27 Pennybank Chambers, 33–35 St John's Square, **London EC1M 4DS**
TEL   071 490 0813
OPEN   9.30–6 Mon–Fri.
Specialise in conserving prints, drawings and watercolours.
PROVIDE Home Inspections. Free Estimates. Chargeable Collection/Delivery Service.
SPEAK TO Deryn Howard or Rosemary Stone.

PETER CHAPMAN ANTIQUES
Incorporating CHAPMAN
RESTORATIONS
10 Theberton Street, **London N1 0QX**
TEL   071 226 5565
FAX   081 348 4846
OPEN   9.30–6 Mon–Sat.
Specialise in cleaning, relining and
restoring oil paintings and repairing
gesso and composition frames.
PROVIDE Home Inspections. Refundable
Estimates. Chargeable
Collection/Delivery Service.
SPEAK TO Peter Chapman or Tony
Holohan.
SEE Furniture, Porcelain, Silver.

ALEXANDER LEY AND SON
13 Brecknock Rd, **London N7 OBL**
TEL   071 267 3645
FAX   071 267 4462
OPEN   8–6 Mon–Fri.
Specialise in restoring antique frames.
Also reproduction carving and gilding.
PROVIDE Home Inspections. Free
Estimates. Free Collection/Delivery
Service.
SPEAK TO Alexander or Anthony Ley.
SEE Furniture.

WILLIAM CHARLES MACKINNON
176 Park Road, **London N8 8JT**
TEL   081 340 6172
OPEN   9–6 Mon–Fri.
Specialise in conserving and restoring
both traditional and modern oil
paintings.
PROVIDE Free/Chargeable Estimates.
SPEAK TO Bill Mackinnon.

HARRIS FINE ART LTD
712 High Road, North Finchley, **London
N12 9QD**
TEL   081 445 2804 or 081 446 5579
FAX   081 445 0708
OPEN   9–6 Mon–Sat.
Specialise in restoring Victorian
paintings and Victorian picture frames.
PROVIDE Home Inspections. Free
Estimates. Free Local
Collection/Delivery Service.
SPEAK TO Clive Harris.

DEANSBROOK GALLERY
134 Myddleton Road, **London N22 4NQ**
TEL   081 889 8389
OPEN   10–5 Mon–Sat.
Specialise in framing and restoring oil
paintings and prints.
PROVIDE Home Inspections. Free
Estimates. Chargeable
Collection/Delivery Service.
SPEAK TO Anthony Edmunds.

THE CATTO GALLERY
100 Heath Street, **London NW3 1DP**
TEL   071 435 6660
FAX   071 431 5620
OPEN   10–6 Mon–Sat; 2.30–6 Sun.
Specialise in framing and restoring oils,
watercolours and pastels.
PROVIDE Free Local Collection/Delivery
Service.
SPEAK TO Mrs. G. Catto.

COLLERAN & CIANTAR LTD
17 Frognal, **London NW3 6AR**
TEL   071 435 4652 or 0895 56410
FAX   071 435 4652 or 0895 56410
        Open 9–5 Mon–Fri or By
        Appointment.
Specialise in conserving and restoring
watercolours, drawings, prints and
other items on paper.

PROVIDE Chargeable Home Inspections.
Free/Chargeable Estimates.
Collection/Delivery Service by
arrangement.
SPEAK TO Kate Colleran or Marcel
Ciantar.

JOHN DENHAM GALLERY
50 Mill Lane, **London NW6 1NJ**
TEL　071 794 2635
OPEN　11–5 Sun, Tues, Wed, Thur, Fri.
Specialise in restoring oil paintings and
works on paper and picture framing.
PROVIDE Home Inspections. Free
Estimates. Free Collection/Delivery
Service.
SPEAK TO John Denham.

JANE ZAGEL
31 Pandora Road, **London NW6 1TS**
TEL　071 794 1663
OPEN　9–6 Mon–Fri.
Specialise in restoring watercolours,
prints and gouache drawings.
PROVIDE Home Inspections. Refundable
Estimates. Chargeable
Collection/Delivery Service.
SPEAK TO Jane Zagel.
This workshop is included on the register
of conservators maintained by the
Conservation Unit of the Museums and
Galleries Commission.
SEE Books.

WELLINGTON GALLERY
1 St. John's Wood High Street, **London
NW8 7NG**
TEL　071 586 2620
OPEN　10–5.30 Mon–Sat.
Specialise in restoring oil paintings.
PROVIDE Home Inspections. Free
Estimates. Chargeable
Collection/Delivery Service.

SPEAK TO Mrs. Maureen Barclay or
Mr. K. J. Barclay.
Member of LAPADA.
SEE Furniture, Porcelain, Silver.

VOITEK
Conservation of Works of Art, 9
Whitehorse Mews, Westminster Bridge
Road, **London SE1 7QD**
TEL　071 928 6094
FAX　071 928 6094
OPEN　10.30–5 Mon–Fri.
Specialise in conserving Old Master
drawings, prints, watercolours and
works of art on paper.
PROVIDE Home Inspections. Chargeable
Estimates. Chargeable
Collection/Delivery Service.
SPEAK TO Elizabeth Sobczynski.

ALEXANDRA WALKER
4 Whitehorse Mews, 37–39 Westminster
Bridge Road, **London SE1 7QD**
TEL　071 261 1419
OPEN　10–6 Mon–Fri.
Specialise in restoring easel paintings of
all periods.
PROVIDE Home Inspections.
Free/Chargeable Estimates.
SPEAK TO Alexandra Walker.

CLAIRE GASKELL
32 St John's Park, **London SE3 7JH**
TEL　081 858 2756
OPEN　10–5 Mon–Fri.
Specialise in restoring prints, drawings,
watercolours, Japanese prints and
Indian paintings.
PROVIDE Home Inspections. Free
Estimates. Free Collection/Delivery
Service.
SPEAK TO Claire Gaskell.

SARAH JENNINGS
CONSERVATION OF FINE ART
Linnell Road, **London SE5 8NJ**
TEL   071 701 0866
OPEN   By Appointment.
Specialise in conserving and restoring
paintings in oil, tempera, fresco, on
copper, wood, plaster, board and canvas.
PROVIDE Home Inspections. Refundable
Estimates. Chargeable
Collection/Delivery Service.
SPEAK TO Sarah Jennings.

GREENWICH CONSERVATION
WORKSHOPS
Spread Eagle Antiques of Greenwich,
8–9 Nevada Street, **London SE10 9JL**
TEL   081 305 1666
OPEN   10–5.30 Mon–Sat.
Specialise in restoring oil paintings,
watercolours and prints.
PROVIDE Home Inspections. Refundable
Estimates. Free/Chargeable
Collection/Delivery Service.
SPEAK TO Richard Moy.
SEE Furniture.

RELCY ANTIQUES
9 Nelson Road, **London SE10 9JB**
TEL   081 858 2812
FAX   081 293 4135
OPEN   10–6 Mon–Sat.
Specialise in restoring oil paintings and
prints.
PROVIDE Home Inspections.
Free/Chargeable Estimates.
Collection/Delivery Service by
arrangement.
SPEAK TO Robin Challis.
SEE Collectors (Scientific Instruments),
Furniture, Silver.

GLEN'S ANTIQUE RESTORATION
Unit 134, 62 Tritton Road, **London
SE21 8DE**
TEL   081 761 5609
FAX   081 761 5609
OPEN   9–6 Mon–Fri.
Specialise in picture framing.
PROVIDE Home Inspections. Free
Estimates. Chargeable
Collection/Delivery Service.
SPEAK TO Glen Beckford.
SEE Furniture.

PETER ROBERT MALLOCH
75C London Road, **London SE23 3TY**
TEL   081 699 8754
OPEN   By Appointment.
Specialise in restoring oil paintings and
pastels.
PROVIDE Chargeable Estimates. Free
Collection/Delivery Service.
SPEAK TO Peter Malloch.

OSCAR AND PETER JOHNSON
LTD
27 Lowndes Street, **London SW1X 9HY**
TEL   071 235 6464
FAX   071 823 1057
OPEN   9–6 Mon–Fri.
Specialise in restoring 18th to 20th
century English paintings, watercolours
and drawings.
PROVIDE Home Inspections.
SPEAK TO Charles Glazebrook.

DAVID KER GALLERY
85 Bourne Street, **London SW1W 8HF**
TEL   071 730 8365
FAX   071 730 3352
OPEN   9.30–5.30 Mon–Fri or By
       Appointment.
Specialise in restoring and framing
decorative oil paintings 1750–1950,
particularly Scottish colourists.

PROVIDE Home Inspections. Free
Estimates. Chargeable
Collection/Delivery Service.
SPEAK TO David Ker or Miles Cato.

KING STREET GALLERIES
17 King Street, **London SW1Y 6QU**
TEL   071 930 9392 or 3993
OPEN   9.30–5.30 Mon–Fri; 10–1 Sat.
Specialise in restoring oils and
watercolours.
PROVIDE Home Inspections. Free
Estimates. Chargeable
Collection/Delivery Service.
SPEAK TO Hal O'Nians.

THE O'SHEA GALLERY
89 Lower Sloane Street, **London
SW1W 8DA**
TEL   071 730 0081
FAX   071 730 1386
OPEN   9.30–6 Mon–Fri; 9.30–1 Sat.
Specialise in framing 15th–19th century
maps and prints.
PROVIDE Home Inspections.
Free/Chargeable Estimates.
Collection/Delivery Service.
SPEAK TO Raymond O'Shea.

SHEPHERD'S BOOKBINDERS LTD
76B Rochester Row, **London SW1P 1JU**
TEL   071 630 1184
FAX   071 931 0541
OPEN   9–5.30 Mon–Fri; 10–1 Sat.
Specialise in restoring works of art on
paper including prints and watercolours.
PROVIDE Free Estimates.
SPEAK TO Mairi Salters.
SEE Books.

ARNOLD WIGGINS AND SONS LTD
4 Bury Street, **London SW1Y 6AB**
TEL   071 925 0195
FAX   071 839 6928
OPEN   9.30–5.30 Mon–Fri.
Specialise in conserving and restoring
period picture frames.
PROVIDE Home Inspections. Free
Estimates. Chargeable
Collection/Delivery Service.
SPEAK TO Michael Gregory.
Members of BADA, the Master
Woodcarvers Association and the
Society of Gilders.

MARIA ANDIPA ICON GALLERY
162 Walton Street, **London SW3 2JL**
TEL   071 589 2371
FAX   071 589 2371
OPEN   11–6 Mon–Fri; 11–2 Sat.
Specialise in restoring icons from all
Eastern European countries, Syria,
Egypt, Ethiopia.
PROVIDE Home Inspections.
Free/Chargeable Estimates. Chargeable
Collection/Delivery Service.
SPEAK TO Maria Andipa.

JOHN CAMPBELL PICTURE FRAMES LTD
164 Walton Street, **London SW3 2JL**
TEL   071 584 9268
FAX   071 581 3499
OPEN   9.30–5.30 Mon–Fri; 1–5 Sat.
Specialise in restoring oil paintings and
watercolours.
PROVIDE Home Inspections. Free
Estimates. Free Collection/Delivery
Service.
SPEAK TO Roy Hogben
Member of the Guild of Master
Craftsmen.
SEE Display/Lighting, Furniture.

P. DOWLING
Chenil Galleries, 181–183 Kings Road,
London SW3 5EB
TEL   071 376 5056
FAX   071 493 9344
OPEN   10–6 Mon–Sat.
Specialise in restoring antique pictures,
framing and mounting.
PROVIDE Free Estimates.
SPEAK TO P. Dowling.

GREEN AND STONE
259 Kings Road, **London SW3 5EL**
TEL   071 352 6521
FAX   071 351 1098
OPEN   9–5.30 Mon–Fri; 9.30–6 Sat.
Specialise in restoring antique frames
including gilding and veneer work. They
offer a picture framing service.
PROVIDE Free Estimates. Free Local
Collection/Delivery Service.
SPEAK TO Mr. Baldwin

MALCOLM INNES GALLERY
172 Walton Street, **London SW3 2JL**
TEL   071 584 0575
OPEN   9.30–6 Mon–Fri; Sat By
          Appointment.
Specialise in restoring oil paintings and
framing.
PROVIDE Free Estimates. Chargeable
Collection/Delivery Service.
SPEAK TO Malcolm Innes.
SEE **Lothian**

**FELIX ROSENSTIEL'S WIDOW &
SON**
33–35 Markham Street, **London
SW3 3NR**
TEL   071 352 3551
FAX   071 351 5300
OPEN   8.30–5 Mon–Fri.

Specialise in hand colouring prints.
PROVIDE Chargeable Collection/Delivery
Service.
SPEAK TO David Roe or Sylvie Schnabel.

COOPER FINE ARTS LTD
768 Fulham Road, **London SW6 5SJ**
TEL   071 731 3421
OPEN   10–7 Mon–Fri; 10–4 Sat.
Specialise in restoring oil paintings and
watercolours, framing.
PROVIDE Free Estimates.
SPEAK TO Jonathan Hill-Reid.

GILT EDGE
275 Wandsworth Bridge Road, **London
SW6 2TX**
TEL   071 731 7703
OPEN   10–6 Mon–Fri; 10–1 Sat.
Specialise in picture framing.
PROVIDE Free Estimates.
SPEAK TO Richard Pitt.
Member of the Guild of Master
Craftsmen.

PETER L. JAMES
681 Fulham Road, **London SW6 5PZ**
TEL   071 736 0183
OPEN   7.30–5.30 Mon–Fri.
Specialise in restoring lacquer, painted
and gilded frames.
PROVIDE Home Inspections. Refundable
Estimates. Chargeable
Collection/Delivery Service.
SPEAK TO Peter L. James.
SEE Furniture.

MICHAEL MARRIOTT LTD
588 Fulham Road, **London SW6 5NT**
TEL   071 736 3110
FAX   071 731 2632
OPEN   9.30–5.30 Mon–Fri.

Specialise in mounting and framing of prints.
PROVIDE Home Inspections. Free Estimates. Collection/Delivery Service.
SPEAK TO Michael Marriott.
SEE Furniture.

JOHN TANOUS LTD
115 Harwood Road, Fulham, **London SW6 4QL**
TEL　　071 736 7999
FAX　　071 371 5237
OPEN　　9–1, 2–5 Mon–Fri.
Specialise in making and restoring picture frames and gilding.
PROVIDE Free Estimates.
SPEAK TO Peter Copcutt.
This firm was established in 1913.

20th CENTURY GALLERY
821 Fulham Road, **London SW6 5HG**
TEL　　071 731 5888
OPEN　　10–6 Mon–Fri; 10–1 Sat.
Specialise in restoring oil paintings and bespoke framing.
PROVIDE Free Estimates.
SPEAK TO Erika Brandl.

SIMON FOLKES
Studio 6, 5 Thurloe Square, **London SW7 2TA**
TEL　　071 589 1649
OPEN　　By Appointment.
Specialise in restoring 15th–early 20th century oil paintings.
PROVIDE Home Inspections. Free/Chargeable Estimates. Free Local Collection/Delivery Service.
SPEAK TO Simon Folkes.
This workshop is included on the register of conservators maintained by the Conservation Unit of the Museums and Galleries Commission.

HULME FINE ART RESTORERS LTD
31 Palfrey Place, **London SW8 1PE**
TEL　　071 735 1218
OPEN　　8–6 Mon–Fri.
Specialise in conserving and restoring European Old Master and modern oil paintings. They also do in–house lining of paintings, transferring and panel work.
PROVIDE Home Inspections. Chargeable Estimates. Collection/Delivery Service by arrangement.
SPEAK TO Derek or Roger Hulme.
This is a third-generation firm.

LOWE AND BUTCHER
Unit 23, Abbey Business Centre, Ingate Place, **London SW8 3NS**
TEL　　071 498 6981
OPEN　　9.30–5 Mon–Fri.
Specialise in restoring Old Master, 19th century and Impressionist oil paintings.
PROVIDE Home Inspections. Free/Refundable Estimates. Free Collection/Delivery Service.
SPEAK TO D. C. Butcher.

SUSANNAH WATTS-RUSSELL
44 Lamont Road, **London SW10 0JA**
TEL　　071 352 4508
OPEN　　By Appointment.
Specialise in restoring oil paintings.
PROVIDE Home Inspections. Free Estimates. Free Collection/Delivery Service.
SPEAK TO Susannah Watts-Russell.

BATES AND BASKCOMB
191 St. John's Hill, **London SW11 1TH**
TEL　　071 223 1629
OPEN　　9.30–5.30 Mon–Fri and By Appointment.

Specialise in restoring works of art on paper, including prints, drawings, watercolours, gouaches, pastels, and photographs.

PROVIDE Local Home Inspections. Free/Chargeable Collection/Delivery Service.

SPEAK TO Debbie Bates or Camilla Baskcomb.

SEE Books.

REGENCY RESTORATIONS
Studio 21, Thames House, 140 Battersea Park Road, **London SW11**
TEL   071 622 5275
OPEN   9–6 Mon–Fri or By
         Appointment.

Specialise in restoring pictures and frames including carving and gilding.

PROVIDE Home Inspections. Free Estimates. Chargeable Collection/Delivery Service.

SPEAK TO Peter Curry or Elizabeth Ball.

RUPERT BEVAN
75 Lower Richmond Road, **London SW15 1ET**
TEL   081 780 1190
OPEN   9–6 Mon–Fri.

Specialise in restoring gilded picture frames.

PROVIDE Home Inspections. Free Estimates. Chargeable Collection/Delivery Service.

SPEAK TO Rupert Bevan.

SEE Furniture.

TREVOR CUMINE
133 Putney Bridge Road, **London SW15 2PA**
TEL   081 870 1525
OPEN   By Appointment.

Specialise in picture lining, antique frames and making gilt frames for 20th century pictures.

SPEAK TO Trevor Cumine.

SERENA CHAPLIN
32 Elsynge Road, **London SW18 2HN**
TEL   081 870 9455
OPEN   By Appointment.

Specialise in restoring gilded picture frames.

PROVIDE Free Estimates within the London area.

SPEAK TO Serena Chaplin.

Ms. Chaplin also runs gilding courses.

SEE Furniture.

MAURICE E. KEEVIL
60 East Hill, **London SW18 2HQ**
TEL   081 874 5236
OPEN   By Appointment.

Specialise in restoring oil paintings, murals and ceiling paintings.

PROVIDE Home Inspections. Free Estimates.

Fellow of the IIC.

PLOWDEN AND SMITH LTD
190 St Ann's Hill, **London SW18 2RT**
TEL   081 874 4005
FAX   081 874 7248
OPEN   9–5.30 Mon–Fri.

Specialise in conserving and restoring paintings.

PROVIDE Home Inspections. Free Estimates. Chargeable Collection/Delivery Service.

SPEAK TO Bob Butler.

They also advise on conservation strategy, environmental control and micro-climates for collections as well as installing, mounting and displaying temporary and permanent exhibitions.

SEE Furniture, Porcelain, Silver.

Paintings, Prints & Drawings

London–London

HAMISH DEWAR
1st Floor, 9 Old Bond Street, **London W1X 3TA**
TEL   071 629 0317
FAX   071 493 6390
OPEN   9–6 Mon–Fri.
Specialise in conserving and restoring oil paintings.
PROVIDE Home Inspections. Free/Refundable Estimates. Chargeable Collection/Delivery Service.
SPEAK TO Hamish Dewar.

HAHN AND SON LTD
47 Albemarle Street, **London W1X 3FE**
TEL   071 493 9196
OPEN   9.30–5.30 Mon–Fri.
Specialise in conserving and restoring oil paintings.
PROVIDE Home Inspections. Free Estimates. Free Collection/Delivery Service.
SPEAK TO Paul Hahn.
Established 1870.

DAVID MESSUM
34 St George Street, Hanover Square, **London W1R 9FA**
TEL   071 408 0243
OPEN   9.30–5.30 Mon–Sat.
Specialise in restoring and framing 18th century–modern day British paintings particularly Impressionists.
PROVIDE Home Inspections. Chargeable Collection/Delivery Service.
SPEAK TO Carol Tee.

PAUL MITCHELL LTD
99 New Bond Street, **London W1Y 9LF**
TEL   071 493 8732
FAX   071 409 7136
OPEN   9.30–5.30 Mon–Fri.
Specialise in the conservation and restoration of paintings and antique picture frames. They also supply hand-carved replica frames.
PROVIDE Home Inspections. Free Estimates. Chargeable Collection/Delivery Service.
Member of BADA, the Guild of Master Craftsmen, ABPR and the IIC.
SPEAK TO Paul Mitchell.

FENELLA HOWARD
14 Shaa Road, **London W3 7LN**
TEL   081 749 5656
OPEN   By Appointment.
Specialise in conserving and restoring 18th–20th century British and European oil paintings.
PROVIDE Home Inspections. Free Estimates. Chargeable Collection/Delivery Service.
SPEAK TO Fenella Howard.

C. J. G. GILDERS & CARVERS
Unit 10, Sandringham Mews, **London W5 5DF**
TEL   081 579 2341
FAX   081 571 9022
OPEN   10–5 Mon–Sat.
Specialise in restoring antique picture frames.
PROVIDE Home Inspections. Free Estimates. Free Local Collection/Delivery Service.
SPEAK TO Chris Gostonski or Richard Kosmala.
SEE Furniture.

THE CONSERVATION STUDIO
The Studio, 107 Shepherds Bush Road, **London W6 7LP**
TEL   071 602 0757 and 081 871 5075
OPEN   9–5 Mon–Fri.
Specialise in restoring items made from paper including Old Master drawings,

18th–20th century British and European watercolours and prints as well as Oriental prints and watercolours. Posters, wallpaper screens and 19th and 20th century photographs are also repaired

PROVIDE Home Inspections. Free Estimates. Chargeable Collection/Delivery Service.
SPEAK TO Norma McCaw.

DR. POPPY COOKSEY
Aston House, 8 Lower Mall, **London W6 9DJ**
TEL 081 846 9279
OPEN By Appointment.
Specialise in cleaning and restoring oil paintings, watercolours and picture frame repairs.
PROVIDE Home Inspections. Free Estimates in London. Chargeable Collection/Delivery Service.
SPEAK TO Dr. Poppy Cooksey.

ANTHONY BELTON
14 Holland Street, **London W8 4LT**
TEL 071 937 1012
OPEN 10–1 Mon–Fri;10–4.30 Sat.
Specialise in restoring paintings.
PROVIDE Home Inspections.
SPEAK TO Anthony Belton.
SEE Porcelain.

CLAUDIO MOSCATELLI
Flat 5, 20 Prince of Wales Terrace, **London W8 5PQ**
TEL 071 937 2877
OPEN 9–5 Mon–Fri or By Appointment.
Specialise in restoring oil paintings, relining, retouching, varnishing.

PROVIDE Home Inspections. Free Estimates. Chargeable Collection/Delivery Service.
SPEAK TO Claudio Moscatelli.

THE ROWLEY GALLERY LTD.
115 Kensington Church Street, **London W8 7LN**
TEL 071 727 6495
OPEN 9.00–5.00 Mon–Fri; 9–7 Thur.
Specialise in restoring antique picture frames, bespoke framing, gilding and veneering.
PROVIDE Home Inspections. Free Estimates. Free Collection/Delivery Service.
SPEAK TO A. J. Savill.
This firm was founded in 1898.
SEE Furniture.

COUTTS GALLERIES
75 Blythe Road, **London W14 OHD**
TEL 071 602 3980
OPEN 10.00–5.00 Mon–Fri.
Specialise in restoration of pictures and antique frames.
PROVIDE Home Inspections, Free Estimates, Free Collection/Delivery Service.
SPEAK TO Seabury Burdett–Coutts.
SEE Furniture.

RICHARD JOSLIN
150 Addison Gardens, **London W14 OER**
TEL 071 603 6435
OPEN By Appointment.
Specialise in restoration of oil paintings and watercolours.
PROVIDE Home Inspections, Chargeable Estimates, Chargeable Collection/Delivery Service.
SPEAK TO Richard Joslin.

PAUL FERGUSON
Unit 20, 21 Wren Street, **London**
WC1X OHF
TEL   071 278 8759
FAX   071 278 8759
OPEN   9–5.30 Mon–Fri.

Specialise in restoring carved and gilded picture frames.

PROVIDE Home Inspections by arrangement. Free Estimates. Collection/Delivery Service by arrangement.

SPEAK TO Paul Ferguson.

SEE Furniture.

BLACKMAN HARVEY LTD
36 Great Queen Street, **London**
WC2B 5AA
TEL   071 836 1904
FAX   071 404 5896
OPEN   9.30–6 Mon–Fri;10–4 Sat.

Specialise in repairing picture frames including replacement of lost details, gilding and restoration. Also restoration of works of art on paper and oil paintings on canvas and board.

PROVIDE Home Inspections. Free Estimates. Chargeable Collection/Delivery Service.

SPEAK TO R. M. Wooton Wooley.

HENRY DONN GALLERY
138–142 Bury New Road, Whitefield,
Greater Manchester M25 6AD
TEL   061 766 8819
OPEN   9.30–1, 2–5.15 Mon–Sat.

Specialise in restoring modern British oils.

PROVIDE Home Inspections. Chargeable Estimates. Chargeable Collection/Delivery Service.

SPEAK TO H. or N. Donn.

Mr Donn is Past Master of the FATG.

J. G. TREVOR–OWEN
181–193 Oldham Rd, Rochdale, **Greater**
Manchester OL16 5QZ
TEL   0706 48138
OPEN   1.30–7 Mon–Fri or By Appointment.

Specialises in restoring paintings.

PROVIDE Home Inspections. Refundable Estimates.

SPEAK TO J. G. Trevor–Owen.

SEE Furniture, Collectors (Musical Instruments).

HARRIET OWEN HUGHES
41 Bluecoat Chambers, School Lane,
Liverpool, **Mersyside L1 3BX**
TEL   051 708 6808
OPEN   By Appointment.

Specialise in restoring easel paintings (16th–20th century) as well as contemporary paintings.

PROVIDE Home Inspections. Chargeable Estimates. Chargeable Collection/Delivery Service.

SPEAK TO Harriet Owen Hughes.

Member of ABPR.

LYVER & BOYDELL GALLERIES
15 Castle Street, Liverpool, **Merseyside**
L2 4SX
TEL   051 236 3256
OPEN   10–30–5.30 Mon–Fri; Sat By Appointment.

Specialise in restoring and framing watercolours and prints.

PROVIDE Home Inspections. Free Estimates.

SPEAK TO Paul or Gill Breen.

SEE Books.

WELLINGTON CRAFTS (1980)
121A/123A St John's Road, Waterloo,
Liverpool, **Merseyside L22 9QE**
TEL   051 920 5511
OPEN   9.30–5 Mon–Sat.
Specialise in a full picture–framing
service.
PROVIDES Home Inspections. Refundable
Estimates. Chargeable
Collection/Delivery Service.
SPEAK TO Neville Hymus.
SEE Furniture.

COLMORE GALLERIES
52 High Street, Henley–in–Arden,
Solihull, **West Midlands B95 5AN**
TEL   0564 792938
OPEN   11–5.30 Mon–Fri; 11–4.30 Sat.
Specialise in restoring 19th and 20th
century oils and watercolours, picture
framing, gilding.
PROVIDE Home Inspections. Refundable
Estimates. Collection/Delivery Service
available.
SPEAK TO B. D. Jones.

**HAMPTON UTILITIES (B'HAM)
LTD**
15 Pitsford Street, Hockley,
Birmingham, **West Midlands B18 6LJ**
TEL   021 554 1766
OPEN   9–5 Mon–Thur; 9–4 Fri.
Specialise in restoring and repairing
picture frames including gilding.
PROVIDE Free Estimates. Chargeable
Collection/Delivery Service.
SPEAK TO B. Levine.
SEE Furniture, Silver.

JOHN HUBBARD ANTIQUES
224–226 Court Oak Road, Harborne,
Birmingham, **West Midlands B32 2EG**
TEL   021 426 1694
FAX   021 428 1214
OPEN   9–6 Mon–Sat.

Specialise in restoring oil paintings.
PROVIDE Home Inspections. Refundable
Estimates. Collection/Delivery Service.
SPEAK TO John Hubbard or David
Taplin.
SEE Furniture, Silver.

**THE HAMPTON HILL GALLERY
LTD**
203 & 205 High Street, Hampton Hill,
Middlesex TW12 1NP
TEL   081 977 1379
OPEN   9–5 Tues–Sat.
Specialise in restoring 18th–20th century
watercolours, drawings and prints. Oil
painting restoration is also undertaken.
PROVIDE Home Inspections. Free
Estimates.
SPEAK TO Robert Crewdson.

THE BANK HOUSE GALLERY
71 Newmarket Road, Norwich, **Norfolk
NR2 2HN**
TEL   0603 633380
FAX   0603 633387
OPEN   By Appointment.
Specialise in restoration of 18th and 19th
century oil paintings and watercolours
with emphasis on the Norfolk and
Suffolk schools.
PROVIDE Home Inspections. Free
Estimates. Free Collection/Delivery
Service.
SPEAK TO Robert Mitchell.
Member of LAPADA.
SEE Furniture.

LAWRENCE & CABLE
6 Merchants Court, St. Georges Street,
Norwich, **Norfolk NR3 1AB**
TEL   0603 632064
OPEN   9–5 Mon–Fri.
Specialise in restoring and conserving oil
paintings, watercolours, prints and
picture frames.

PROVIDE Home Inspections. Free
Estimates. Free/Chargeable
Collection/Delivery Service.
SPEAK TO Penny Lawrence or Tim Cable.
This workshop is included on the register
of conservators maintained by the
Conservation Unit of the Museums and
Galleries Commission.
SEE Furniture, Silver.

LEON LIDDAMENT
St. Seraphim's, Station Road, Little
Walsingham, **Norfolk NR22 6DG**
TEL   0328 820610
OPEN   By Appointment.
Specialise in restoring icons.
PROVIDE Home Inspections.
Free/Chargeable Estimates.
Collection/Delivery Service by
arrangement.
SPEAK TO Leon Liddament.

**WESTCLIFFE GALLERY AND ART
FRAMES**
2–8 Augusta Street, Sheringham,
Norfolk NR26 8LA
TEL   0263 824320
OPEN   9.30–5.30 Mon–Sat. Closed
       Wed.
Specialise in conservation mounting,
gilding, period frame restoration, oil,
watercolour and print restoration.
PROVIDE Home Inspections. Free
Estimates. Collection/Delivery Service
charges depending on distance.
SPEAK TO Richard Parks.

BROADWAY FINE ART
61 Park Avenue South, Abington,
Northampton, **Northamptonshire
NN3 3AB**
TEL   0604 32011
OPEN   By Appointment.

Specialise in restoring oil paintings.
PROVIDE Home Inspections. Estimates.
Collection/Delivery Service are all by
arrangement.
SPEAK TO Michael Robinson.

SAVAGE FINE ART
Alfred Street, Northampton,
Northamptonshire NN1 5EY
TEL   0604 20327
FAX   0604 27417
OPEN   9–5.15 Mon–Fri; 9–12.30 Sat.
Specialise in restoring oil paintings and
19th–20th century watercolours and
prints. They also restore picture frames.
PROVIDE Home Inspections. Free
Estimates. Free Collection/Delivery
Service.
SPEAK TO Michael Savage.

J. A. & T. HEDLEY
3 St Mary's Chare, Hexham,
Northumberland NE46 1NQ
TEL   0434 602317
OPEN   9–5 Mon–Sat; 9–12 Thur.
Specialise in picture framing.
PROVIDE Free Estimates. Chargeable
Collection/Delivery Service.
SPEAK TO D. Hall or W. H. Jewitt.
SEE Furniture.

**FLORENCE CONSERVATION &
RESTORATION**
102 Nottingham Road, Long Eaton,
Nottingham, **Nottinghamshire
NG10 2BZ**
TEL   0602 733625
OPEN   8–5 Mon–Fri; 9–12 Sat.
Specialise in cleaning and restoring oil
paintings, watercolours, pastels,
drawings, prints and photographs.
PROVIDE Home Inspections. Refundable
Estimates. Chargeable
Collection/Delivery Service.
SPEAK TO Ron Florence.
SEE Ceramics, Furniture.

BART LUCKHURST
The Gallery, 9 Union Street, Bingham,
Nottinghamshire NG13 8AD
TEL   0949 837668
OPEN   9–5 Thur; 9.–1 Sat or By
Appointment.

Specialise in restoring oils and
watercolours, relining and handmade
stretcher bars. He also restores period
frames and old photographs.
PROVIDE Home Inspections. Free
Estimates. Collection/Delivery Service
by arrangement.
SPEAK TO Bart Luckhurst.
Mr. Luckhurst is a founder member of
the Institute of British Picture Framers,
soon to be incorporated within the Fine
Art Trade Guild.

MARK ROBERTS
1 West Workshops, Tan Gallop,
Welbeck, Nr. Worksop,
Nottinghamshire S80 3LW
TEL   0909 484270
OPEN   By Appointment.

Specialise in conserving and restoring
European easel paintings and their
gilded frames.
PROVIDE Home Inspections. Refundable
Estimates. Chargeable
Collection/Delivery Service.
SPEAK TO Mark or Diana Roberts.
Mr. Roberts holds the Museum
Association Conservation Certificate.

ARTHUR & ANN RODGERS
7 Church Street, Ruddington,
Nottingham, **Nottinghamshire**
NG11 6HA
TEL   0602–216214
OPEN   9–5 Tues, Wed; 9–1 Thur, Fri;
9–5 Sat.

Specialise in hand–colouring, cleaning,
restoring and repairing
prints and paintings.

PROVIDE Home Inspections. Chargeable
Estimates. Free Collection/Delivery
Service.
SPEAK TO Arthur Rodgers.
SEE Books.

OLIVIA RUMENS
30 Corve Street, Ludlow, **Shropshire**
SY8 1DN
TEL   0584 87 3952
OPEN   10–5 Mon–Sat; closed Thur.

Specialises in conserving and restoring
oil paintings.
PROVIDE Home Inspections. Free
Estimates.
SPEAK TO Olivia Rumens.
Member of the IIC.

NICK COTTON FINE ART
Beachstone House, 46/47 Swain Street,
Watchet, **Somerset TA23 0AG**
TEL   0984 31814
OPEN   10–6 Mon–Sat.

Specialise in restoring and conserving
paintings, watercolours and drawings
from the period 1850–1991.
PROVIDE Home Inspections. Refundable
Estimates. Chargeable
Collection/Delivery Service.
SPEAK TO Nick Cotton.

CLARE HUTCHISON
1A West Street, Ilminster, **Somerset**
TA19 9AA
TEL   0460 53369
OPEN   10–5.30 Mon–Fri; 10–1 Sat.

Specialise in restoring antique picture
frames.
PROVIDE Free Estimates.
SPEAK TO Clare Hutchison.
SEE Furniture.

THE ANTIQUE RESTORATION STUDIO
The Old Post Office, Haughton,
Staffordshire ST18 9JH
TEL   0785 780424
FAX   0785 780157
OPEN   9–5 Mon–Fri.
Specialise in restoring antique and modern paintings.
PROVIDE Home Inspections. Free Estimates. Free Collection/Delivery Service.
SPEAK TO D. P.Albright.
SEE Carpets, Furniture, Porcelain.

VICTORIA DES BEAUX ARTS LTD
11 Newcastle Street, Burslem, Stoke-on-Trent, **Staffordshire ST6 3QB**
TEL   0782 836490
OPEN   9–5.30 Mon–Sat.
Specialise in cleaning and restoring 17th–19th century oil paintings and framing.
PROVIDE Home Inspections. Free/Chargeable Estimates. Free Collection/Delivery Service.
SPEAK TO Mrs. Bryden.

ROGER & SYLVIA ALLAN
The Old Red Lion, Bedingfield, Eye, **Suffolk IP23 7LQ**
TEL   0728 76 491
OPEN   By Appointment.
Specialise in restoring oil paintings on panel or canvas and miniatures.
PROVIDE Home Inspections. Free Estimates.
SPEAK TO Roger Allan.
SEE Furniture, Silver.

JOHN GAZELEY ASSOCIATES FINE ART
17 Fonnereau Road, Ipswich, **Suffolk IP1 3JR**
TEL   0473 252420
OPEN   By Appointment.

Specialise in cleaning, relining and restoring oil paintings, particularly 17th and 18th century English portraits. They do gilding and repairing of picture frames as well as making reproduction frames.
PROVIDE Free Estimates.
SPEAK TO Dr John Gazeley.
SEE Furniture.

NORTHWOLD GALLERY
206 High Street, Newmarket, **Suffolk CB8 9AP**
TEL   0638 668758
OPEN   10–5 Mon–Sat; closed Wed.
Specialise in restoring watercolours and prints. They also do framing.
PROVIDE Home Inspections. Free Estimates. Free Collection/Delivery Service.
SPEAK TO C. G. Troman.

PEASENHALL ART & ANTIQUES GALLERY
Peasenhall, Nr Saxmundham, **Suffolk IP17 2HJ**
TEL   072 879 224
OPEN   9–6 Sun–Sat.
Specialise in cleaning and restoring oils, watercolours and prints.
PROVIDE Local Home Inspections.Free Estimates. Free Local Collection/Delivery.
SPEAK TO Mike Wickins.
SEE Furniture.

BOURNE GALLERY LIMITED
31–33 Lesbourne Street, Reigate, **Surrey RH2 7JS**
TEL   0737 241614
OPEN   10–1, 2–5.30 Mon–Sat; 10–1 Wed.
Specialise in restoring 19th and 20th century oil paintings.

PROVIDE Home Inspections. Free
Estimates. Collection/Delivery Service
by arrangement.
SPEAK TO John Robertson.

DAVID EMBLING
45 Fairfield, Farnham, **Surrey GU9 8AG**
TEL   0252 712660
OPEN   8–1, 2–5 Mon–Fri.
Specialise in restoring lacquered and
gilded picture frames.
PROVIDE Home Inspections. Free
Estimates. Chargeable
Collection/Delivery Service.
SPEAK TO David Embling.
SEE Furniture.

KING'S COURT GALLERIES
54 West Street, Dorking, **Surrey
RH4 1BS**
TEL   0306 881757
FAX   0306 75305
OPEN   9.30–5.30 Mon–Sat.
Specialise in paper conservation and
restoration including engravings,
decorative and sporting prints.
PROVIDE Home Inspections. Free
Estimates.
SPEAK TO Mrs. J. Joel.
SEE Books.

LIMPSFIELD WATERCOLOURS
High Street, Limpsfield, **Surrey**
TEL   0883 717010 and 0883 722205
OPEN   11–3 Tues; 9.30–2 Thur–Sat.
Specialise in conserving , framing,
cleaning and restoring prints and
watercolours.
PROVIDE Local Home Inspections.
Refundable Estimates.
SPEAK TO Christine Reason.
They have applied for inclusion in the
Conservation Register of the Museum

and Galleries Commission. Also
undertake minor repairs to gilt frames,
although they prefer to concentrate on
cleaning of watercolours.

**MANOR ANTIQUES AND
RESTORATIONS**
2 New Shops, High Street, Old Woking,
Surrey GU22 9JW
TEL   0483 724666
OPEN   10–5 Mon–Fri; 10–4.30 Sat.
Specialise in picture framing.
PROVIDE Home Inspections. Free
Estimates. Collection/Delivery Service.
SPEAK TO Alan Wellstead or Paul
Thomson.
Member of the Guild of Master
Craftsmen.
SEE Furniture.

SAGE ANTIQUES & INTERIORS
High Street, Ripley, **Surrey GU23 6BB**
TEL   0483 224396
FAX   0483 211996
OPEN   9.30–5.30 Mon–Sat.
Specialise in restoring oil paintings and
watercolours.
PROVIDE Free Estimates. Free
Collection/Delivery Service.
SPEAK TO Howard or Chrissie Sage.
Members of LAPADA and the Guild of
Master Craftsmen.
SEE Porcelain, Furniture.

**S. & S. PICTURE RESTORATION
STUDIOS**
The Rookery, Frensham, Farnham,
Surrey GU10 3DU
TEL   025 125 3673
OPEN   10–6 Mon–Fri.
Specialise in restoring oil paintings,
watercolours and prints of all periods.

PROVIDE Home Inspections.
Free/Chargeable Estimates.
Collection/Delivery Service by
arrangement.
SPEAK TO Roy Skelton.

R. SAUNDERS
71 Queens Road, Weybridge, **Surrey
KT13 9UQ**
TEL   0932 842601
OPEN   9.15–5 Mon–Sat; closed Wed.
Specialise in cleaning and restoring oil
paintings and watercolours.
PROVIDE Home Inspections. Free
Estimates. Free Collection/Delivery
Service.
SPEAK TO J.B.Tonkinson.
SEE Furniture, Porcelain, Silver.

JOHN DAY OF EASTBOURNE FINE ART
9 Meads Street, Eastbourne, **East Sussex
BN20 7QY**
TEL   0323 25634
OPEN   10–5 Mon, Tue, Thur, Fri.
Specialise in cleaning, restoring and
relining oil paintings, particularly East
Anglian and Victorian Schools.
PROVIDE Home Inspections. Free
Estimates Chargeable
Collection/Delivery Service.
SPEAK TO John Day.

FIRELEAD LTD
Banff Farm, Upper Clayhill, Uckfield
Rd, Ringmer, Lewes,
East Sussex BN8 5RR
TEL   0273 890918
FAX   0273 890691
OPEN   8–5.30 Mon–Fri By
        Appointment.
Specialise in restoring oil paintings and
watercolours.
PROVIDE Local Home Inspections. Local
Free Estimates. Chargeable
Collection/Delivery Service.
SPEAK TO David Gilbert.
SEE Furniture.

GOLDEN FISH GILDING & RESTORATION
94 Gloucester Road, Brighton, **East
Sussex BN1 4AP**
TEL   0273 691164
FAX   0273 691164
OPEN   9–5 Mon–Fri.
Specialise in gilding and restoring picture
frames including carving.
PROVIDE Home Inspections. Free
Estimates. Free Collection/Delivery
Service.
SPEAK TO Marianne Hatchwell.
Ms. Hatchwell will also teach gilding
techniques.
SEE Furniture, Porcelain.

RPM RESTORATIONS
7 Hurst Close, Amberley, **West Sussex
BN18 9NX**
TEL   0798 831845
OPEN   By Appointment.
Specialise in paper conservation and
restoring watercolours, drawings and
prints.
PROVIDE Home Inspections. Free
Estimates. Free Collection/Delivery
Service.
SPEAK TO James Jacob.

STEWART GALLERY
48 Devonshire Road, Bexhill–on–Sea,
East Sussex TN40 1AX
TEL   0424 223410
FAX   0323 29588
OPEN   9–5.30 Mon–Sat.
Specialise in restoring 19th and 20th
century oil paintings and watercolours,
framing service.
PROVIDE Home Inspections. Free
Estimates. Free Collection/Delivery
Service.
SPEAK TO Mrs. L. Knight.

STEWART GALLERY
25 Grove Road, Eastbourne, **East Sussex BN20 4TT**
TEL   0323 29588
FAX   0323 29588
OPEN   9–5.30 Mon–Fri; 11–4 Sat.
Specialise in restoring 19th and 20th century oil paintings and watercolours, framing service.
PROVIDE Home Inspections. Free Estimates. Free Collection/Delivery Service.
SPEAK TO S. A. Ettinger.

SURREY PRINT WATERCOLOUR CLEANING COMPANY
Mockingbird, Spy Lane, Loxwood, **West Sussex RH14 0SS**
TEL   0403 752097
OPEN   By Appointment.
Specialise in cleaning and restoring of works of art on paper, particularly watercolours and prints.
PROVIDE Free Estimates. Chargeable Collection/Delivery Service.
SPEAK TO Ken Downs.

DAVID WESTON
East Lodge, Woldringfold, Lower Beeding, Horsham, **West Sussex RH13 6NJ**
TEL   0403 891617
OPEN   By Appointment.
Specialise in restoring composition frames and gilding and make reproduction composition frames.
PROVIDE Free Estimates.
SPEAK TO David Weston.

MACDONALD FINE ART
2 Ashburton Road, Gosforth, **Tyne & Wear NE3 4XN**
TEL   091 2856188 or 2844214
OPEN   10–1, 2.30–5.30 Mon–Sat.
         Closed Wed.

Specialise in framing and restoring Victorian watercolours and oil paintings.
PROVIDE Free Estimates. Free Collection/Delivery Service.
SPEAK TO Tom MacDonald.

OSBORNE ART & ANTIQUES
18C Osborne Road, Jesmond, Newcastle-upon-Tyne. **Tyne & Wear NE2 2AD**
TEL   091 281 6380
Specialise in restoring oil paintings, watercolours and conserving paper.
PROVIDE Home Inspections. Free Collection/Delivery Service.
SPEAK TO S. Jackman.
Member of FATG.

D.M. BEACH
52 High Street, Salisbury, **Wiltshire SP1 2PG**
TEL   0722 333801
OPEN   9–5.30 Mon–Sat.
Specialise in restoring oils, watercolours and prints.
PROVIDE Home Inspections. Free Estimates. Free Local Collection/Delivery Service.
SPEAK TO Anthony Beach.
SEE Books.

BOOTH'S ANTIQUE MAPS AND PRINTS
30 Edenvale Road, Westbury, **Wiltshire BA13 3NY**
TEL   0373 823271
FAX   0373 858185
OPEN   By Appointment.
Specialise in restoring antique prints.
PROVIDE Home Inspections. Chargeable Collection/Delivery Service.
SPEAK TO John Booth.
Mr. Booth is a FRSA.
SEE Books.

LANTERN GALLERY
Hazeland House, Kington St Michael,
Chippenham, **Wiltshire SN14 6JJ**
TEL   024 975 306
FAX   024 975 8896
OPEN   9–4 Mon–Fri or By
         Appointment.
Specialise in restoring prints,
watercolours, oil paintings and period
frames.
PROVIDE Home Inspections. Free
Estimates. Free Collection/Delivery
Service.
SPEAK TO Anne Campbell Macinnes.
Member of BADA, ABA and the Guild
of Master Craftsmen.
SEE Porcelain.

RESTORATIONS UNLIMITED
Pinkney Park, Malmesbury, **Wiltshire
SN16 0NX**
TEL   0666 840888
OPEN   9–12.30, 1.30–5 Mon–Fri; 9.30–
         12 Sat.
Specialise in restoring oil paintings and
watercolours.
PROVIDE Home Inspections. Free
Estimates. Free Collection/Delivery
Service.
SPEAK TO David Ellis.
SEE Furniture, Porcelain.

WINSTANLEY SALISBURY
BOOKBINDERS
213 Devizes Road, Salisbury, **Wiltshire
SP2 9LT**
TEL   0722 334998
OPEN   8.30–5.30 Mon–Fri.
Specialise in restoring prints and paper
conservation.
PROVIDE Free Estimates.
Collection/Delivery Service
SPEAK TO Alan Winstanley.
SEE Books.

FRANCIS W. DOWNING
The Studio, 19 Lancaster Park Road,
Harrogate, **North Yorkshire HG2 7SW**
TEL   0423 886962
OPEN   10–5 Mon–Fri or By
         Appointment.
Specialise in conserving and restoring oil
paintings.
PROVIDE Home Inspections. Free
Estimates. Free Collection/Delivery
Service.
SPEAK TO Francis Downing.
This workshop is included on the register
of conservators maintained by the
Conservation Unit of the Museums and
Galleries Commission.

W.C. GREENWOOD FINE ART
The Gallery, Oakdene Burneston,
Nr. Bedale, **North Yorkshire DL8 2JE**
TEL   0677 424830 and 423217
OPEN   By Appointment.
Specialise in restoring old frames.
PROVIDE Home Inspections. Chargeable
Collection/Delivery Service.
SPEAK TO William Greenwood.

KIRKGATE PICTURE GALLERY
18 Kirkgate, Thirsk, **North Yorkshire
YO7 1PQ**
TEL   0845 524085
OPEN   10–1, 2–5 Mon, Thur, Sat or By
         Appointment.
Specialise in restoring and conserving oil
paintings and framing.
PROVIDE Chargeable Estimates.
Collection/Delivery Service by
arrangement.
SPEAK TO Richard Bennett.
Member of ABPR.

GERRY TOMLINSON MEMORABILIA
Booth's Yard, Pudsey, **West Yorkshire**
TEL   0532 563653
OPEN   9.30–5 Mon–Sat.
Specialise in restoring sepia photographs.
PROVIDE Home Inspections. Free Collection/Delivery Service.
SPEAK TO Gerry Tomlinson.

PHYLLIS ARNOLD STUDIO GALLERY
24 Dufferin Avenue, Bangor, **Co. Down BT20 3AA**
TEL   0247 469899 or 853322 (answerphone)
OPEN   10–1.30 Wed, Fri; 11–5 Sat or By Appointment.
Specialise in restoring watercolours and portrait miniatures and conservation framing.
PROVIDE Free Estimates. Collection/Delivery Service by arrangement.
SPEAK TO Phyllis Arnold.
Member of the Royal Society of Miniature Painters.

JAMES A GORRY
20 Molesworth Street, Dublin 2, **Co. Dublin**
TEL   6795319
OPEN   10–6 Mon–Fri.
Specialise in restoring oil paintings and frames.
PROVIDE Home Inspections.
SPEAK TO James Gorry.

ROLAND HULME-BEAMAN
30 Leeson Park Avenue, Dublin 6, **Co. Dublin**
TEL   604850
OPEN   By Appointment.
Specialise in restoring easel paintings mainly Irish, European and American 18th–20th century.
PROVIDE Chargeable Home Inspections. Free/Chargeable Estimates.
SPEAK TO Roland Hulme-Beaman.

ALDER ARTS
57 Church Street, Inverness, **Highland IV1 1DR**
TEL   0463 243575
OPEN   9–5.30 Mon–Sat.
Specialise in cleaning and restoring 17th–19th century oil paintings and framing.
PROVIDE Home Inspections. Free/Chargeable Estimates. Free Collection/ Delivery Service.
SPEAK TO Ken Hardiman.

ORBOST GALLERY
Bolvean, Isle of Skye, **Highland IV55 8ZB**
TEL   047 022 207
OPEN   By Appointment.
Specialise in repairing and restoring oil paintings as well as ornate Victorian frames, and wood and marble finishes for interior restoration, framed presentation calligraphy and illumination.
PROVIDE Home Inspections. Free/Chargeable Collection/Delivery Service.
SPEAK TO Dr. David L. Roberts MA FSA (Scotland).

THURSO ANTIQUES
Drill Hall, 21 Sinclair Street, Thurso, **Highland**
TEL   0847 63291 or 05934 276
FAX   0847 62824
OPEN   10–5 Mon–Fri; 10–1 Sat.
Specialise in cleaning and restoring oil paintings and watercolours.

PROVIDE Free Estimates.
Collection/Delivery Service by
arrangement.
SPEAK TO G. Atkinson.
SEE Silver.

CELIA BLAIR
The Studio, Cramond Brig Farm,
Edinburgh, **Lothian EH4 6DY**
TEL   031 339 6502
OPEN   By Appointment.

Specialise in restoring easel paintings and
carrying out conservation surveys.

PROVIDE Home Inspections.
Free/Chargeable Estimates.
Free/Chargeable Collection/Delivery
Service.
SPEAK TO Celia Blair.

BOURNE FINE ART
4 Dundas Street, Edinburgh, **Lothian**
TEL   031 557 4050
FAX   031 557 8382
OPEN   10–6 Mon–Fri; 10–1 Sat.

Specialise in restoring paintings and
framing.

PROVIDE Home Inspections. Free
Estimates. Free/Chargeable
Collection/Delivery Service.
SPEAK TO Rosanne Munro.

CHRISTINE BULLICK
5 Bedford Terrace, Edinburgh, **Lothian
EH4 3DQ**
TEL   031 332 6948
OPEN   By Appointment.

Specialise in restoring early panel
painting, Elizabethan and Jacobean and
also contemporary painting.

PROVIDE Home Inspections.
Free/Chargeable Estimates.
SPEAK TO Christine Bullick.

Christine Bullick is a member of IIC,
UKIC and SSCR.

MALCOLM INNES GALLERY
67 George Street, Edinburgh, **Lothian
EH2 2JG**
TEL   031 226 4151
FAX   031 557 4709
OPEN   9.30–6 Mon–Fri.

Specialise in restoring oils, watercolours
and prints, especially Natural History,
Scottish and Sporting subjects. They also
have a framing department.

PROVIDE Home Inspections. Free
Estimates. Free/Chargeable
Collection/Delivery Service.
SPEAK TO Anthony Wood.

SEE Oil Paintings **London**

CLAIRE MEREDITH
Conservation Studio, Hopetoun House,
South Queensferry, **Lothian EH30 9SL**
TEL   031 331 2003
OPEN   By Appointment.

Specialise in restoring easel paintings and
will survey collections.

PROVIDE Home Inspections.
Free/Chargeable Estimates.
SPEAK TO Claire Meredith.

Claire Meredith is a member of SSCR,
UKIC, IIC and the Museums
Association.

PARKES & BORDONE
Unit 10, St Mary's Workshops,
Henderson Street, Leith, Edinburgh,
Lothian EH6 6DD
TEL   031 553 5111
FAX   031 553 5111
OPEN   9–5 Mon–Fri.

Specialise in conserving, cleaning and
restoring oil paintings, as well as some
frame repairs..

PROVIDE Home Inspections. Free
Estimates. Collection/Delivery Service
by arrangement.
SPEAK TO Jane Hutchison.

FIONA BUTTERFIELD
Overhall, Kikfield Bank, Lanark,
Strathclyde ML11 9TZ
TEL   0555 66291
OPEN   By Appointment.
Specialise in conserving paper, prints,
watercolours, drawings and screens.
PROVIDE Home Inspections.
Free/Chargeable Estimates.
SPEAK TO Fiona Butterfield.
Ms Butterfield is a member of SSCR.

DAPHNE FRASER
Glenbarry, 58 Victoria Road, Lenzie,
Glasgow, **Strathclyde G66 5AP**
TEL   041 776 1281
OPEN   By Appointment.
Specialise in restoring antique oil
paintings and ornate picture frames.
PROVIDE Free Estimates.
SPEAK TO Daphne Fraser.
SEE Collectors (Dolls; Toys), Furniture.

McIAN GALLERY
10 Argyll Square, Oban, **Strathclyde
PA34 4AZ**
TEL   0631 66755
OPEN   9–5.30 Mon–Sat.
Specialise in fine art restoration and
picture framing.
PROVIDE Chargeable Collection/Delivery
Service.
SPEAK TO Rory Campbell-Gibson.

JOHN MELROSE
74 Manse Road, Motherwell,
Strathclyde ML1 2PT
TEL   0698 64249
OPEN   By Appointment.
Specialise in restoring easel paintings.

PROVIDE Home Inspections.
Free/Chargeable Estimates. Chargeable
Collection/Delivery Service.
SPEAK TO John Melrose.
Mr.Melrose is a member of the ABPR
and the IIC. This workshop is included
on the register of conservators
maintained by the Conservation Unit of
the Museums and Galleries
Commission.

NEIL LIVINGSTONE
3 Old Hawkhill, Dundee, **Tayside
DD1 5EU**
TEL   0382 25517
OPEN   9–5 Mon–Fri.
Specialise in cleaning oil paintings and
framing.
PROVIDE Free Estimates. Chargeable
Collection/Delivery Service.
SPEAK TO Neil Livingstone.
SEE Collectors (Arms and Armour), Oil
Paintings, Silver.

MANOR HOUSE FINE ARTS
73 Pontcanna Street, Cardiff, **South
Glamorgan CF1 9HS**
TEL   0222 227787
OPEN   10.30–5.30 Tue, Thur, Fri, Sat or
        By Appointment.
Specialise in restoring and conserving oil
paintings, watercolours and prints. They
also offer a bespoke framing service.
PROVIDE Home Inspections. Free
Estimates at the Gallery. Chargeable
Collection/Delivery Service.
SPEAK TO Steven Denley-Hill.

Porcelain and Glass

Although glazed pottery or porcelain will not fade as a result of exposure to sunlight, it can be affected by several other factors that will make it look 'faded'. 'Onglaze' enamels may have faded, and in some extreme cases actually disappeared, because of the over-diligence of Victorian scullery-maids armed with abrasives and brushes. Some semi-matt glazes – popular in the mid-19th century because they had an attractive silk-like sheen rather than the usual glassy surface – have proved unstable after years of washing and have worn away, revealing the white porcelain beneath.

Even the more resilient types of glaze and enamels suffered when they were used on dessert services – the culprit was citric acid, found especially in oranges and lemons. During the early years of the present century, iridescent glazes used by William Howson Taylor on his Ruskin range of pottery and similar lustrous glazes advocated by William Moorcroft seem to have been particularly vulnerable to this type of glaze loss.

Gilding is always applied at the final stage of ceramic decoration and, because it is fired on to the pot at a comparatively low temperature, it is usually less stable than the rest of the glazing. Well-preserved gilding on 18th and 19th century pottery is always at a premium and, alas, is now the exception rather than the rule. French porcelain – the neo-classical and Empire styles in particular – favoured a soft gilt which was often applied unsparingly and very few pieces have survived in pristine condition.

Platinum and silver lustre-decorated Staffordshire pottery produced throughout the 19th century and in the first few decades of the 20th has also proved vulnerable to wear and tear – its surface is micro-thin and easily scratched.

Regrettably, none of the aforementioned effects can easily be made good, despite the improvement in ceramic restoration techniques and materials. But there are some simple, common-sense measures you can use to protect your porcelain and pottery from further damage.

The most serious modern-day enemy of gilding is the tape often used to secure covers to vases. When you take off the tape, you risk lifting the gold off the object at the same time. Japanese Satsuma pottery is another regular victim of the dreaded tape, and many a fine vase with wonderful miniature painting has had its subtle gilding removed in this way. The result is not only ugly, it leads to a marked decrease in the value of the vase. On no account should you use Sellotape or any similar product on the surface of pre-war Royal Doulton bone china figures. The onglaze colour enamels are relatively unstable and liable to flake, so again, the tape can lift off the enamel and drastically reduce the figure's value.

A word of warning to the owners of bone china figures fitted into wooden plinths, such as those retailed over the last 30 years by Wedgwood and Royal Worcester. I have had the unnerving experience of witnessing a figure from both of these esteemed potteries explode whilst it was resting on the shelves of my office. The Wedgwood example was without doubt the victim of an overtight base; the Royal Worcester is explained by their boffins as the result of faulty clay slip mix!

If an object is broken, the question arises whether to restore or simply repair. Repair means reassembling a broken object with no attempt to mask the damage, whereas restoration involves both reassembling and making the repair more or less invisible by overpainting. One of the main problems with restoration is that with the passage of time the overpainting tends to discolour, necessitating further treatment. As an auctioneer, I have to admit to a personal preference for the straightforward repair, largely because one can never be certain of the full extent of the damage when handling a restored object. Excessive restoration, incidentally, is often the kiss of death to an object's saleability, since the buyer cannot be sure of what he or she is buying.

Cleaning pottery and porcelain can give rise to a good many potential problems. Eighteenth century soft paste porcelain should be treated with great care, and it is prudent not to immerse any object in water warmer than room temperature. Contact with boiling water can be disastrous, causing anything from severe crazing to actual fractures. Fit rubber tap covers to your kitchen sink, as the vast majority of table china is chipped as a result of an unexpected collision with a wandering tap. For additional protection, wash pieces in a plastic bowl containing a section of immersible foam, plastic or rubber.

Stubborn stains may require localised treatment with cotton wool swabs soaked in hydrogen peroxide. Do not use ordinary domestic bleaches.

36

The floral-encrusted porcelains popular throughout the 19th century have proved a nightmare for generations of houseproud ladies and their maids. The more sensible placed them under glass domes, but most ran the risk of that deadly enemy to delicate china – the feather duster. Advances in technology have produced a more amenable solution in the form of the compressed air spray, and our photographer at Bonhams would certainly never be without one.

The display of pottery and porcelain is very much a matter of personal choice and often depends on whether you are buying as a collector or simply for interior decoration. As there is a plethora of tastefully illustrated books available on this subject, I will limit my comments to a simple plea. Do not use metal plate-hangers nor prop plates against wall racks secured by the odd nail. Both are a sure recipe for unsightly rim chips. Plastic-covered plate-hangers are relatively safe and available in a wide range of sizes, as are perspex plate-stands. But beware of overloading: too much weight will result in the back support snapping.

Unfortunately, despite the advances in the treatment of ceramics, glass can still prove difficult to repair and nigh on impossible to restore invisibly. Unsightly chips on the bases of Georgian wine glasses can be ground out and polished, but a deep chip can result in the base being ground away to a diameter less than that of the bowl – a state of affairs that should always set the alarm bells ringing.

The cleaning of glass follows the same principles as that of pottery and porcelain. Glass, however, is prone to its own particular problems, such as the cloudy bloom often seen within bowls and decanters. The only satisfactory treatment is to have the surface polished by an expert. Washing glass demands the same rubber-covered taps and plastic washing-up bowl advocated for ceramics. It is also useful to keep a hair-dryer handy for removing stubborn moisture in decanters.

Most of the problems and pitfalls discussed here can be avoided by simply using one's common sense and remembering that Josiah Wedgwood did not envisage his creamware being used in a microwave oven, nor did the glassmakers of Waterford design their wares with any thought of the hazards of man's best friend – the dishwasher.

Eric Knowles

IAN & DIANNE McCARTHY
Arcadian Cottage, 112 Station Road,
Clutton, **Avon BS18 4RA**
TEL   0761 53188
OPEN   By Appointment.
Specialise in restoring bronze and spelter
figures and table lamps.
PROVIDE Home Inspections. Free
Estimates. Chargeable
Collection/Delivery Service.
SPEAK TO Ian or Dianne McCarthy.
SEE Furniture, Silver.

HERITAGE RESTORATIONS
36B High Street, Great Missenden,
Buckinghamshire HP16 OAU
TEL   02406 5710
OPEN   10–5 Mon–Sat.
Specialise in restoring porcelain.
PROVIDE Free Estimates. Home
Inspections.
SPEAK TO John Wilshire.
SEE Furniture.

**SAFAVID CERAMIC
RESTORATIONS**
29 Blacksmiths Lane, Prestwood, Great
Missenden, **Buckinghamshire HP16 0AP**
TEL   02406 5231
OPEN   By Appointment.
Specialise in restoring ceramics,
particularly English blue & white
transfer wares.
PROVIDE Home Inspections. Free
Estimates.
SPEAK TO Bridget Syms.

MILLS ANTIQUES
1A St. Mary's Street, Ely,
Cambridgeshire CB7 4ER
TEL   0353 663114 or 664268
OPEN   10–1, 2–5 Mon–Sat; closed Tue.

Specialise in restoring china including
Meissen and Oriental. They also restore
terracottas.
PROVIDE Free Estimates.
SPEAK TO Mrs. Mills.

**MACLAREN CHAPPELL
(RESTORATIONS) LTD**
King Street, Bakewell, **Derbyshire
DE4 1DZ**
TEL   0629 812496
FAX   0629 814531
OPEN   9–6 Mon–Fri.
Specialise in restoring European and
Oriental porcelain in their own
workshops.
PROVIDE Home Inspections. Free
Estimates.Free Local
Collection/Delivery Service.
SPEAK TO W.N.Chappell.
SEE Furniture, Silver.

THE LANTERN SHOP
4 New Street, Sidmouth, **Devon
EX10 8AP**
TEL   0395 516320
OPEN   9.45–12.45, 2.15–4.45 Mon–Sat;
            closed Mon and Sat p.m.
Specialises in restoring antique items of
lighting and conversion to electricity.
PROVIDE Home Inspections. Free
Estimates. Chargeable
Collection/Delivery Service.
SPEAK TO Julia Creeke.

MRS.CATHERINE MATHEW
Kiwi Cottage, Maperton Road,
Charlton Horethorne, Sherborne, **Dorset
DT9 4NT**
TEL   096 322 595
OPEN   9–6 Mon–Fri or By
            Appointment.
Specialise in repairing ceramics and
glass.

PROVIDE Home Inspections. Free
Estimates. Free Collection/Delivery
Service.
SPEAK TO Catherine Mathew.
SEE Oil Paintings, Furniture.

QUARTER JACK ANTIQUES
Bridge Street, Sturminster Newton,
Dorset DT10 1BZ
TEL   0258 72558
OPEN   9–5.30 Mon–Sat.
Specialise in restoring glass including
grinding.
PROVIDE Home Inspections. Chargeable
Estimates. Chargeable
Collection/Delivery Service.
SPEAK TO Mr. A. J. Nelson.

CHARMAINE
P.O.BOX 255, Brentwood, **Essex
CM15 9AP**
TEL   0277 224224
OPEN   9–5 Mon–Fri.
Specialise in mechanically polishing the
inside of hollow glass vessels (decanters,
vases, glassware) to remove the etched
surface which causes the glass to look
white.
PROVIDE Free Estimates.
SPEAK TO Charmaine Cox.

MILLSIDE ANTIQUE
RESTORATION
Parndon Mill, Parndon Mill Lane,
Harlow, **Essex CM20 2HP**
TEL   0279 428148
FAX   0279 415075
OPEN   10–5 Mon–Fri.
Specialise in restoring Oriental and
European porcelain and coloured glass.
PROVIDE Home Inspections.
Free/Chargeable Estimates. Chargeable
Collection/Delivery Service.
SPEAK TO David Sparks or Angela
Wickliffe-Philp.

Also provide tuition courses in china and
porcelain restoration. Members of the
Guild of Master Craftsmen.
SEE Oil Paintings, Silver.

FRANCIS STEPHENS
Bush House, Church Road,
Corringham, Stanford-le-Hope,
Essex SS17 9AP
TEL   0375 673463
OPEN   By Appointment.
Specialise in restoring Staffordshire
figures 1775–1900 and advise on their
display.
PROVIDE Home Inspections. Free
Estimates. Free Collection/Delivery
Service.
SPEAK TO Francis Stephens.

KEITH BAWDEN
Mews Workshop, Montpellier Retreat,
Cheltenham, **Gloucestershire GL50 2XS**
TEL   0242 230320
OPEN   7–4.30 Mon–Fri.
Specialise in conserving and restoring all
aspects of porcelain.
PROVIDE Free Estimates. Home
Inspections. Local Collection/Delivery
Service.
SPEAK TO Keith Bawden.
SEE Silver, Furniture, Oil Paintings.

ATELIER FINE ART CASTINGS
LTD
Hulfords Lane, Nr. Hartley Wintney,
Hampshire RG27 8AG
TEL   025126 4388
OPEN   8.30–5 Mon–Fri.
Specialise in restoring bronze art work
and bronze casting.
PROVIDE Home Inspections. Free
Estimates. Chargeable
Collection/Delivery Service.
SPEAK TO Mrs. A. Wills.

JUST THE THING
High Street, Hartley Wintney,
Basingstoke, **Hampshire RG27 8NS**
TEL   025126 3393 and 2916
OPEN   9–5 Mon–Sat.
Specialise in china restoration.
SPEAK TO Sue Carpenter.
Members of LAPADA.

KATHARINE SILCOCK ANTIQUE
CHINA RESTORATION
Mercury Yacht Harbour, Satchell Lane,
Hamble, Southampton, **Hampshire
SO3 5HQ**
TEL   0703 455056
OPEN   9–6.30 Mon–Thur.
Specialise in restoring and repairing all
forms of china including Meissen, Bow,
Chelsea, Oriental, Belleek, Doulton and
Parian ware.
PROVIDE Estimates.
SPEAK TO Katharine Silcock
Also runs china restoration courses.

MARY ROSE WRANGHAM
Studio 304, Victory Business Centre,
Somers Road North, Portsmouth,
Hampshire PO1 1PJ
TEL   0705 829863
OPEN   10–5 Sun–Sat.
Specialise in restoring ceramics including
Oriental and Chinese style decorative
repairs in gold leaf.
PROVIDE Chargeable Home Inspections.
Chargeable Estimates. Chargeable
Collection/Delivery Service.
SPEAK TO Mary Rose Wrangham
Also provides studio ceramic repair
courses and has a 90 minute training
video.

THE ORIGINAL CHOICE
56 The Tything, Worcester, **Hereford and
Worcester WR1 1JT**
TEL   0905 613330
OPEN   10–6 Mon–Sat; 1–5.30 Sun.
Specialise in restoring fireplaces, stained
glass and tiles.
PROVIDE Home Inspections. Chargeable
Estimates. Chargeable
Collection/Delivery Service.
SPEAK TO Jake Ellis or Peter Thorington-
Jones.

PIPE ELM PORCELAIN
Pipe Elm, Leigh Sinton, Malvern,
Hereford and Worcester WR13 5EA
TEL   0886 32492
OPEN   By Appointment.
Specialise in restoring European and
Oriental pottery and porcelain including
antiquities.
PROVIDE Home Inspections. Free
Estimates. Free Collection/Delivery
Service.
SPEAK TO Fred or Maggie Covins.

BECKWITH & SON
St. Nicholas Hall, St. Andrew Street,
Hertford, **Hertfordshire SG14 1HZ**
TEL   0992 582079
OPEN   9–1, 2–5.30 Mon–Sat.
Specialise in restoring Oriental and
European porcelain.
PROVIDE Home Inspections. Chargeable
Estimates. Free Collection/Delivery
Service locally.
SPEAK TO G. Gray.
See Furniture, Oil Paintings.

WILLIAM H. STEVENS
8 Eton Avenue, East Barnet,
Hertfordshire EN4 8TU
TEL   081 449 7956
OPEN   9–5.30 Mon–Fri.

Specialise in restoring Japanese and Chinese pottery.

PROVIDE Home Inspections. Free Estimates. Free Collection/Delivery Service.

SPEAK TO John Robin or Daniel Stevens.

The fifth generation of a family firm founded in 1836.

SEE Silver.

BONCHURCH CONSERVATORY GLASS ART & DESIGN
Portland House, Bonchurch Village Road, Bonchurch, **Isle of Wight PO38 1RG**

TEL   0983 855608

OPEN   By Appointment.

Specialise in restoring medieval to modern stained glass.

PROVIDE Home Inspections. Free/Chargeable Estimates. Collection/Delivery Service by arrangement.

SPEAK TO Delian Fry or John Wheatley.

A. & S. ALLEN
40 Clarendon Way, Chislehurst, **Kent BR7 6RF**

TEL   0689 826345

OPEN   9–5 Mon–Fri.

Specialise in restoring ceramics, European and Oriental porcelain and pottery, enamels and clock dials.

PROVIDE Free Estimates. Collection/Delivery Service by arrangement.

SPEAK TO Adrian Allen.

AUDREY BURFORD
North West **Kent** (full address witheld by request).

TEL   081 467 9757

OPEN   9–5 Mon–Fri.

Specialise in restoring European ceramics, principally earthenware, tinglaze and ironstone pieces.

PROVIDE Free Estimates. Collection/Delivery Service by arrangement.

SPEAK TO Audrey Burford.

SARGEANT RESTORATIONS
21 The Green, Westerham, **Kent TN16 1AX**

TEL   0959–62130

OPEN   8.30–5.30 Mon–Sat.

Specialise in restoration, cleaning and wiring of chandeliers , lustres, candelabra and general light fittings.

PROVIDE Home Inspections. Free Estimates. Chargeable Collection/Delivery Service.

SPEAK TO Ann, David or Denys Sargeant.

C. W. ALLISON & SONS
Hillview, Bilsborrow Lane, Bilsborrow, Preston, **Lancashire PR3 ORN**

TEL   0995 40344

OPEN   10–5 Mon–Fri.

Specialise in restoring pottery and porcelain.

PROVIDE Home Inspections. Free Estimates. Chargeable Collection/Delivery Service.

SPEAK TO Richard Allison.

SEE Furniture, Oil Paintings.

BROTHERIDGE CHANDELIERS
3 Maytree Walk, Woodley Park, Skelmersdale, **Lancashire WN8 6UP**

TEL   0695 26276

FAX   0695 35634

OPEN   By Appointment.

Specialise in conserving and restoring glass chandeliers.

PROVIDE Home Inspections. Free Estimates. Chargeable Collection/Delivery Service.

SPEAK TO Terry Brotheridge.

E. & C. ROYALL
10 Waterfall Way, Medbourne, Nr.
Market Harborough, **Leicestershire
LE15 8EE**
TEL   0858 83744
OPEN   8.30–5 Mon–Fri.
Specialise in restoring European
bronzes, as well as Oriental ivories,
bronzes and woodcarvings.
PROVIDE Home Inspections. Free
Estimates. Chargeable
Collection/Delivery Service.
SPEAK TO C. Royall.
SEE Furniture.

WILLIAM DAWSON
Brentwood, Wragby Road, Sudbrooke,
Lincoln, **Lincolnshire LN2 2QU**
TEL   0522 750006
OPEN   By Appointment.
Specialise in repairing and restoring
ceramics, particularly Oriental and
English porcelain, as well as 19th/20th
century decorative pottery and figures.
PROVIDE Home Inspections. Free
Estimates. Chargeable
Collection/Delivery Service.
SPEAK TO William Dawson.

KATE BADEN FULLER
90 Greenwood Road, **London E8 1NE**
TEL   071 249 0858
OPEN   By Appointment.
Specialise in construction, restoration
and repair of stained glass. Ms Fuller
will also restore other types of glass, e.g.
glass set in bronze or brass, but does not
do decorative objects.
PROVIDE Home Inspections. Refundable
Estimates. Chargeable
Collection/Delivery Service.
SPEAK TO Kate Fuller.

DAVID TURNER
4 Atlas Mews, Ramsgate Street, **London
E8 2NA**
TEL   071 249 2379
OPEN   10–6 Mon–Fri.
Specialise in restoring glass light fittings
and lamp conversions.
PROVIDE Home Inspections. Free
Estimates. Free Collection/Delivery
Service.
SEE Furniture, Silver.

RUPERT HARRIS
Studio 5, 1 Fawe Street, **London E14 6PD**
TEL   071 987 6231 or 071 515 2020
FAX   071 987 7994
OPEN   9–6 Mon–Fri.
Specialise in restoring fine sculpture.
PROVIDE Home Inspections. Chargeable
Estimates. Collection/Delivery Service
by arrangement.
SPEAK TO Rupert Harris
Member of UKIC and IIC. This
workshop is included on the register of
conservators maintained by the
Conservation Unit of the Museums and
Galleries Commission.
SEE Silver.

THE CONSERVATION STUDIO
Unit 17, Pennybank Chambers, 33–35
St. Johns Square, **London EC1M 4DS**
TEL   071 251 6853
OPEN   9.30–5 Mon–Fri.
Specialise in restoring ceramics and glass
including pieces for chandeliers.
PROVIDE Home Inspections (large items
only). Refundable Estimates.
Chargeable Collection/Delivery Service.
SPEAK TO Sandra Davison.
SEE Furniture, Silver.

CERAMIC RESTORATIONS
7 Alwyne Villas, **London N1 2HG**
TEL　　071 359 5240
OPEN　　By Appointment Only.

Specialise in all types of pottery and porcelain restoration especially decorative items.

PROVIDE Home Inspections. Free/Chargeable Estimates. Collection/Delivery Service by arrangement.

SPEAK TO John Parker.

Members of the UKIC. This workshop is included on the register of conservators maintained by the Conservation Unit of the Museums and Galleries Commission.

PETER CHAPMAN ANTIQUES
Incorporating CHAPMAN
RESTORATIONS
10 Theberton Street, **London N1 0QX**
TEL　　071 226 5565
FAX　　081 348 4846
OPEN　　9.30–6 Mon–Sat.

Specialise in repairing bronze and other metalwork, stained glass and leaded lights.

PROVIDE Home Inspections. Refundable Estimates. Chargeable Collection/Delivery Service.

SPEAK TO Peter Chapman or Tony Holohan.

SEE Furniture, Oil Paintings, Silver.

ROCHEFORT ANTIQUES LTD
32–34 The Green, **London N21 1AX**
TEL　　081 886 4779 or 081 363 0910
OPEN　　10–6 Mon–Tues, Thur, Sat.

Specialise in restoring porcelain.

PROVIDE Home Inspections. Free Estimates. Chargeable Collection/Delivery Service.

SPEAK TO L. W. Stevens-Wilson.

SEE Furniture, Silver.

CHINA REPAIRERS
64 Charles Lane, **London NW8 7SB**
TEL　　071 722 8407
OPEN　　9.30–5.30 Mon–Thur; 9.30–4.30 Fri.

Specialise in conservation and restoration of all antique and modern ceramics. They use invisible and museum techniques with the modelling of missing parts being a speciality. Glass repairs are also undertaken.

PROVIDE Free Estimates.

SPEAK TO Virginia Baron.

Provide courses and individual tuition in restoration. Member of the Guild of Master Craftsmen.

WELLINGTON GALLERY
1 St. John's Wood High Street, **London NW8 7NG**
TEL　　071 586 2620
OPEN　　10–5.30 Mon–Sat.

Specialise in restoring glass and European and Oriental porcelain.

PROVIDE Home Inspections. Free Estimates. Chargeable Collection/Delivery Service.

SPEAK TO Mrs. Maureen Barclay or Mr. K. J. Barclay.

Member of LAPADA.

SEE Silver, Oil Paintings, Furniture.

VOITEK
Conservation of Works of Art, 9
Whitehorse Mews, Westminster Bridge
Road, **London SE1 7QD**
TEL　　071 928 6094
FAX　　071 928 6094
OPEN　　10.30–5 Mon–Fri.

Specialise in conservation of sculpture in marble, stone, terracotta.

PROVIDE Home Inspections with advice on condition, display, damage assessments and conservation strategy subject to fee. Chargeable Collection/Delivery Service.
SPEAK TO Wojtek Sobczynski.

R WILKINSON & SON
5 Catford Hill, **London SE6 4NU**
TEL   081 314 1080
FAX   081 690 1524
OPEN   9–5 Mon–Fri.

Specialise in restoring glass chandeliers, decanters, glasses and stoppers. Will also make glass shades to match existing ones.
PROVIDE Home Inspections. Free Estimates. Chargeable Collection/Delivery Service.
SPEAK TO Peter Prickett, Jane Milnes or David Wilkinson.
SEE Silver.

ASHTON–BOSTOCK (CHINA REPAIRS)
21 Charlwood Street, **London SW1V 2EA**
TEL   071 828 3656
OPEN   9.30–1, 2–5.30 Tue–Thur.

Specialise in restoring fine porcelain.
PROVIDE Refundable Estimates.
SPEAK TO David Ashton–Bostock.

GRANVILLE & BURBRIDGE
111 Kingsmead Road, **London SW2 3HZ**
TEL   081 674 1969
OPEN   9–6 Mon–Sat.

Specialise in conserving and restoring sculpture, wall-paintings and decorative arts including polychrome, wood, stone, marble, terracotta, alabaster and plaster.
PROVIDE Home Inspections. Free Estimates in the London area. Chargeable Collection/Delivery Service.

SPEAK TO John Burbidge.
Will also do condition surveys and historical research and provision and/or recommendations for maintenance, display facilities, packing and transport.

W. G. T. BURNE (ANTIQUE GLASS) LTD.
11 Elystan Street, **London SW3 3NT**
TEL   071 589 6074
FAX   081 944 1977
OPEN   9–5 Mon–Sat; closed Thur and Sat afternoons.

Specialise in restoring English and Irish 18th and 19th century glass including chandeliers, candelabra, lustres, wall-lights, decanters, tableware and collectors' pieces. Also remove chips from glasses and arrange for glass linings.
PROVIDE Home Inspections. Free Estimates. Free Collection/Delivery Service.
SPEAK TO Andrew Burne.

IMOGEN PAINE LIMTED
15A Kings Road, **London SW3 4RP**
TEL   071 223 4648
FAX   071 223 7113
OPEN   9–5 Mon–Fri.

Specialise in restoring sculpture in bronze, marble, terracotta, plaster, stone, especially 19th century works.
PROVIDE Home Inspections. Free Estimates. Chargeable Collection/Delivery Service.
SPEAK TO Imogen Paine.

JOHN HEAP
No.1 The Polygon, **London SW4**
TEL   071 627 4498
OPEN   By Appointment.

Specialise in restoring terracotta figures, remodelling sculpture.
PROVIDE Home Inspections. Free Estimates. Free Collection/Delivery Service.
SPEAK TO John Heap.
SEE Furniture, Silver.

SCULPTURE RESTORATIONS
1 Michael Road, Kings Road, **London SW6 2ER**
TEL   071 736 7292
OPEN   8–4.30 Mon–Fri.
Specialise in restoring, repairing and conserving all works under the general classification of sculpture i.e. bronze, other metals, wood, ivory, stone, marble, also including works which are painted or gilded.
PROVIDE Home Inspections. Free Estimates. Chargeable Collection/Delivery Service.
SPEAK TO John Doubleday or Michael Gaskin.

CHRISTOPHER WRAY'S LIGHTING EMPORIUM
600 Kings Road, **London SW6 2DX**
TEL   071 736 8434
FAX   071 731 3507
OPEN   9.30–6 Mon–Sat.
Specialise in restoring original Victorian and Edwardian light fittings.
PROVIDE Free Estimates. Chargeable Collection/Delivery Service.
SPEAK TO Christopher Wray.
SEE Silver.

WHITEWAY & WALDRON LTD
305 Munster Road, **London SW6 6BJ**
TEL   071 381 3195
OPEN   10–6 Mon–Fri; 11–4 Sat.
Specialise in restoring stained glass.
PROVIDE Free Estimates. Free Local Collection/Delivery Service.
SPEAK TO Graham Kirkland.

H. W. POULTER & SON
279 Fulham Road, **London SW10 9PZ**
TEL   071 352 7268
FAX   071 351 0984
OPEN   9–5 Mon–Fri;10–1 Sat.
Specialise in restoring antique marble and sculpture.

PROVIDE Home Inspections Refundable Estimates. Chargeable Collection/Delivery Service.
SPEAK TO Douglas Poulter.
Have a workshop at 1A Adelaide Grove, off Uxbridge Road, London W12, TEL 081 749 4557; OPEN 7.30–5.30 Mon–Fri.

PETER & FRANCES BINNINGTON
65 St Johns Hill, **London SW11**
TEL   071 223 9192
FAX   071 924 1668
OPEN   8.30–5.30 Mon–Fri.
Specialise in restoring Verre Eglomisé (gilt glass). They also make copies to commission including table tops and wall panels.
PROVIDE Home Inspections. Free Estimates. Chargeable Collection/Delivery Service.
SPEAK TO Joanne Neal.
SEE Furniture.

THORNHILL GALLERIES LTD
78 Deodar Road, **London SW15 2NJ**
TEL   081 874 5669 or 2101
FAX   081 877 0313
Specialise in restoring English and French period marble and stone chimney-pieces, period statuary and garden ornaments.
PROVIDE Home Inspections. Free Estimates. Free/Chargeable Collection/Delivery Service.
SPEAK TO Mr. G. Wakefield or Mrs. V. Haigh.
Established in 1880.
SEE Furniture.

PLOWDEN & SMITH LTD
190 St. Ann's Hill, **London SW18 2RT**
TEL   081 874 4005
FAX   081 874 7248
OPEN   9–5.30 Mon–Fri.

Specialise in restoring and conserving bronze, stone, marble, ceramics, glass, ivory.

PROVIDE Home Inspections. Free Estimates. Chargeable Collection/Delivery Service.
SPEAK TO Bob Butler.

They also advise on conservation strategy, environmental control and micro–climates for collections, as well as installing, mounting and displaying temporary and permanent exhibitions.
SEE Oil Paintings, Furniture, Silver.

BLOOMFIELD CERAMIC
RESTORATIONS LTD
4th Floor, 58 Davies Street, **London W1Y 1LB**
TEL   071 580 5761
FAX   071 636 1625
OPEN   By Appointment.

Specialise in restoring antique European and Oriental ceramics and bronzes.
PROVIDE Free Estimates.
SPEAK TO Steven P. Bloomfield.
SEE Silver.

W. SITCH & CO. LTD
48 Berwick Street, **London W1V 4JD**
TEL   071 437 3776
OPEN   8.30–5.30 Mon–Fri; 9–10 Sat.

Specialise in restoring late 19th century lighting.
PROVIDE Home Inspections. Free Estimates. Free/Chargeable Collection/Delivery Service.
SPEAK TO Ron Sitch.

N. DAVIGHI
117 Shepherds Bush Road, **London W6**
TEL   071 603 5357
OPEN   9–5 Mon–Sat.

Specialise in gilding, polishing and repairing lighting, especially crystal and ormolu chandeliers.
PROVIDE Home Inspections. Free Estimates. Chargeable Collection/Delivery Dervice.
SPEAK TO Mr. N. Davighi

ANTHONY BELTON
14 Holland Street, **London W8 4LT**
TEL   071 937 1012
OPEN   10–1 Mon–Fri;10–4.30 Sat.

Specialise in restoring English and Continental pottery.
PROVIDE Home Inspections.
SPEAK TO Anthony Belton.
SEE Oil Paintings.

BRETT MANLEY
Studio 1D, Kensington Church Walk, **London W8 4NB**
TEL   071 937 7583
OPEN   11–5 Mon–Fri.

Specialise in restoring ceramics.
PROVIDE Free Estimates (minimum quote £18.00 per item).
SPEAK TO Brett Manley.

Run a two-week beginners' course in ceramic restoration three times a year.

ROSEMARY COOK RESTORATION
78, Stanlake Road, **London W12 7HJ**
TEL   081 749 7977
OPEN   By Appointment.

Specialise in restoring statuary including polychrome surfaces.
PROVIDE Home Inspections. Free Estimates. Free Collection/Delivery Service in London.
SPEAK TO Rosemary Cook.
SEE Furniture, Silver.

THE GLASSHOUSE
65 Long Acre, **London WC2E 9JH**
TEL   071 836 9785
FAX   071 240 7508
OPEN   10–6 Mon–Fri; 11–5 Sat.

Specialise in restoring both antique and contemporary glass, including making liners, shades and pieces for chandeliers.
PROVIDE Home Inspections.
SPEAK TO Claudia Lake.

JOHN HUBBARD ANTIQUES
224–226 Court Oak Road, Harborne, Birmingham, **West Midlands B32 2EG**
TEL   021 426 1694
FAX   021 428 1214
OPEN   9–6 Mon–Sat.

Specialise in restoring lighting.
PROVIDE Home Inspections. Refundable Estimates. Collection/Delivery Service.
SPEAK TO John Hubbard or David Taplin.
SEE Furniture, Oil Paintings, Silver.

WILLIAM ALLCHIN
22–24 St. Benedicts Street, Norwich, **Norfolk NR2 4AQ**
TEL   0603 660046
FAX   0603 660046
OPEN   10.30–5 Mon–Sat.

Specialise in restoring period lighting including glass chandeliers and wall brackets.
PROVIDE Home Inspections. Free Estimates.
SPEAK TO William Allchin.
SEE Silver.

JASPER ANTIQUES
11A Hall Road, Snettisham, King's Lynn, **Norfolk PE31 7LU**
TEL   0485 541485 (Home 0485 540604)
OPEN   10.30–1 Mon,Wed,Fri; 10.30–1, 2–4 Sat.

Specialise in repairing ceramics and gilt mirrors.

PROVIDE Home Inspections. Free Estimates. Free Collection/Delivery Service.
SPEAK TO Mrs. A. Norris.
SEE Furniture, Silver.

MARIANNE MORRISH
South Cottage Studio, Union Lane, Wortham Ling, Diss, **Norfolk IP22 ISP**
TEL   0379 643831
OPEN   10–4 Mon–Fri.

Specialise in restoring 18th century porcelain and early Staffordshire.
PROVIDE Home Inspections. Free Estimates. Chargeable Collection/Delivery Service.
SPEAK TO Marianne Morrish.

Ms. Morrish is a member of the Guild of Master Craftsmen.
SEE Silver.

SUSAN NOEL
The Studio, Roundways, Holt, **Norfolk NR25 6BN**
TEL   0263 711362
OPEN   10–4 Tue, Wed, Thur, or By Appointment.

Specialise in restoring ceramic figures, bowls and vases both European and Oriental.
PROVIDE Free Estimates. Free Collection/Delivery Service.
SPEAK TO Susan Noel.

RICHARD SCOTT
30 High Street, Holt, **Norfolk NR21 0QT**
TEL   0263 712479
OPEN   11–5 Mon–Wed; 10–5 Fri–Sat.

Specialise in undertaking some repairs and restoration of porcelain and pottery.
PROVIDE Free Estimates.
SPEAK TO Richard Scott.

GIUDICI–MARTIN
The Old Chapel, Newtown Street,
Woodford, Kettering,
Northamptonshire NN14 4HW
TEL   0536 743787
FAX   0536 745900
OPEN   By Appointment.

Specialise in conservation, restoration
and reproduction of all types of stone
sculpture both internal and external;
chimney-pieces, garden statuary,
architectural detail.
PROVIDE Home Inspections. Refundable
Estimates. Chargeable
Collection/Delivery Service.
SPEAK TO Paul Giudici.

For conservation purposes they will
provide a detailed condition report with
recommendation, specification and
estimates.

FLORENCE CONSERVATION & RESTORATION
102 Nottingham Road, Long Eaton,
Nottingham, **Nottinghamshire
NG10 2BZ**
TEL   0602 733625
OPEN   8–5 Mon–Fri; 9–12 Sat.

Specialise in repairing ceramics, bronzes
and marbles.
PROVIDE Home Inspections. Refundable
Estimates. Chargeable
Collection/Delivery Service.
SPEAK TO Ron Florence.
SEE Oil Paintings, Furniture.

F. C. MANSER & SON LTD
53–54 Wyle Cop, Shrewsbury,
Shropshire SY1 1XJ
TEL   0743 351120
FAX   0743 271047
OPEN   9–5.30 Mon–Wed, Fri; 9–1
       Thur; 9–5 Sat.

Specialise in restoration of glass; chipped
glass repaired, decanter stoppers,
mirrors, light fittings, porcelain repairs,
specialists in Tunbridge ware.

PROVIDE Home Inspections. Free
Estimates. Chargeable
Collection/Delivery Service.
SPEAK TO Paul Manser.
LAPADA and Guild of Master
Craftsmen.
SEE Furniture, Silver.

THE ANTIQUE RESTORATION STUDIO
The Old Post Office, Haughton,
Staffordshire ST18 9JH
TEL   0785 780424
FAX   0785 780157
OPEN   9–5 Mon–Fri.

Specialise in restoring antique and
modern ceramics.
PROVIDE Home Inspections. Free
Estimates. Free Collection/Delivery
Service.
SPEAK TO D. P. Albright.
SEE Furniture, Oil Paintings, Textiles.

COURTLANDS RESTORATION
Courtlands, Park Road, Banstead,
Surrey SM7 3EF
TEL   0737 352429
OPEN   8–7 Mon–Sat.

Specialise in replacement glass and
mirror plates.
PROVIDE Home Inspections. Free
Estimates. Free Collection/Delivery
Service.
SPEAK TO David Sayer.
SEE Furniture.

NORMAN FLYNN RESTORATIONS
37 Lind Road, Sutton, **Surrey SM1 4PP**
TEL   081 661 9505
OPEN   7.45–3.30 Mon–Fri.

Specialise in restoring antique and
modern porcelain and pottery. Also
specialise in lamp conversions.

PROVIDE Home Inspections. Free
Estimates. Free Collection/Delivery
Service each week to London.
SPEAK TO Norman Flynn.
Member of the Guild of Master
Craftsmen.
SEE Silver.

SAGE ANTIQUES & INTERIORS
High Street, Ripley, **Surrey GU23 6BB**
TEL   0483 224396
FAX   0483 211996
OPEN   9.30–5.30 Mon–Sat.
Specialise in restoring English and
Oriental ceramics.
PROVIDE Free Estimates. Free
Collection/Delivery Service.
SPEAK TO Howard or Chrissie Sage.
Members of LAPADA and the Guild of
Master Craftsmen.
SEE Furniture, Oil Paintings.

R. SAUNDERS
71 Queens Road, Weybridge, **Surrey
KT13 9UQ**
TEL   0932 842601
OPEN   9.15–5 Mon–Sat; closed Wed.
Specialise in restoring English porcelain.
PROVIDE Home Inspections. Free
Estimates. Free Collection/Delivery
Service.
SPEAK TO J. B. Tonkinson.
SEE Silver, Furniture, Oil Paintings.

SIMPSON DAY RESTORATION
Studio 13, Acorn House, Cherry
Orchard Road, Croydon, **Surrey
CR0 6BA**
TEL   081 681 8339
OPEN   9.30–6 Mon–Fri.
Specialise in restoring fine porcelain and
pottery.

PROVIDE Free Estimates.
SPEAK TO Sarah Simpson or Sarah Day.
SEE Silver.

DOREEN BROWN
1 Dunstan Terrace, Cockmount Lane,
Wadhurst, **East Sussex TN5 6UF**
TEL   089288 3432
OPEN   By Appointment.
Specialise in restoring European and
Oriental porcelain and pottery and
antique ceramic figures. Missing pieces
are replaced, previous outdated repairs
removed.
PROVIDE Local Home Inspections. Free
Estimates. Free Local
Collection/Delivery Service.
SPEAK TO Doreen Brown.
Ms Brown is West Dean trained.

DAVID CRAIG
Toll Cottage, Station Road, Durgates,
Wadhurst, **East Sussex TN5 6RS**
TEL   089 288 2188
OPEN   9–5.30 Mon–Fri.
Specialise in restoring antique porcelain
and pottery.
PROVIDE Chargeable Estimates.
Chargeable Collection/Delivery Service.
SPEAK TO David Sutcliffe.
SEE Silver.

**GOLDEN FISH GILDING &
RESTORATION**
94 Gloucester Road, Brighton, **East
Sussex BN1 4AP**
TEL   0273 691164
FAX   0273 691164
OPEN   9–5 Mon–Fri.
Specialise in Eglomisé panels.
PROVIDE Home Inspections. Free
Estimates. Free Collection/Delivery
Service.
SPEAK TO Marianne Hatchwell.
Also teaches gilding techniques.
SEE Furniture, Oil Paintings.

HAZEL WELDON
Flat 1, 11 Holland Road, Hove, **East Sussex BN3 1JF**
TEL   0273 726281
OPEN   By Appointment.

Specialise in restoring porcelain and pottery figures particularly European. Will also restore plaster figures.
PROVIDE Free Estimates.
SPEAK TO Hazel Weldon.

CAROL BANKS
September Cottage, 88 Victoria Road, Shoreham-by-Sea, **West Sussex BN4 5WS**
TEL   0273 461647 after 5pm.
OPEN   By Appointment.

Specialise in restoring European and Oriental porcelain, Staffordshire figures and Majolica ware. Blackamoor/Nubian figures and spelter figures are also undertaken.
PROVIDE Local Home Inspections. Free Estimates.
SPEAK TO Carol Banks.

SEE Furniture.

DAVID FILEMAN ANTIQUES
Squirrels, Bayards, Steyning, **West Sussex BN44 3AA**
TEL   0903 813229
OPEN   By Appointment.

Specialise in restoring and repairing 18th and 19th century glass chandeliers and candelabra. This includes cleaning and repinning
PROVIDE Home Inspections. Free Estimates. Chargeable Collection/Delivery Service.
SPEAK TO David Fileman.

GARNER & CO.
Stable Cottage, Steyning Road, Wiston, **West Sussex BN44 3DD**
TEL   0903 814565
OPEN   By Appointment (Tel Mon–Fri 9–5.30)

Specialise in the conservation and repair of lead and bronze sculpture and glass chandeliers.
PROVIDE Home Inspections. Estimates.
SPEAK TO Sid Garner.

SEE Furniture, Silver.

WEST DEAN COLLEGE
West Dean, Chichester, **West Sussex PO18 00Z**
TEL   0243 63 301
FAX   0243 63 342
OPEN   9–5 Mon–Fri.

Specialise in training conservators and restorers in the field of antique porcelain and will also undertake restoration.
PROVIDE Local Home Inspections. Free Estimates.
SPEAK TO Peter Sarginson.

SEE Books, Furniture, Silver.

DELOMOSNE & SON LTD
Court Close, North Wraxall, Chippenham, **Wiltshire SN14 7AD**
TEL   0225 891505
FAX   0225 891907
OPEN   9.30–5.30 Mon–Sat.

Specialise in restoring English period glass light fittings.
PROVIDE Home Inspections. Free Estimates. Collection/Delivery Service available.
SPEAK TO Martin Mortimer or Timothy Osborne.

LANTERN GALLERY
Hazeland House, Kington St. Michael,
Chippenham, **Wiltshire SN14 6JJ**
TEL   024 975 306
FAX   024 975 8896
OPEN   9–4 Mon–Fri or by
         appointment.
Specialise in supplying eglomisé glass.
PROVIDE Home Inspections. Free
Estimates. Free Collection/Delivery
service.
SPEAK TO Anne Campbell Macinnes.
SEE Oil Paintings.

ROD NAYLOR
208 Devizes Road, Hilperton,
Trowbridge, **Wiltshire BA14 7QP**
TEL   0225 754497
OPEN   By Appointment.
Specialise in supplying hand blown glass
caddy bowls.
PROVIDE Home Inspections. Free
Estimates. Free Local
Collection/Delivery Service.
SPEAK TO Rod Naylor.
SEE Display, Furniture.

RESTORATIONS UNLIMITED
Pinkney Park, Malmesbury, **Wiltshire
SN16 0NX**
TEL   0666 840888
OPEN   9–12.30, 1.30–5 Mon–Fri; 9.30–
         12 Sat.
Specialise in restoring European and
Oriental ceramics.
PROVIDE Home Inspections. Free
Estimates. Free Collection/Delivery
Service.
SPEAK TO David Ellis
SEE Furniture, Oil Paintings.

JANE WINCH CHINA REPAIRS
Westport Granary, Malmesbury,
Wiltshire SN16 OAL
TEL   0666 822119
OPEN   10–5 Mon–Fri.
Specialise in restoring and repairing
decorative ceramics, antique and
modern.
PROVIDE Home Inspections. Free
Estimates.
SPEAK TO Jane Winch or Pat Paterson.

NIDD HOUSE ANTIQUES
Nidd House, Bogs Lane, Harrogate,
North Yorkshire HG1 4DY
TEL   0423 884739
OPEN   9–5 Mon–Fri or By
         Appointment.
Specialise in repairing statues up to 24
inches high.
PROVIDE Home Inspections. Free Local
Estimates. Chargeable
Collection/Delivery Service.
SPEAK TO Mr. D. Preston.
Members of the Guild of Master
Craftsmen, UKIC. This workshop is
included on the register of conservators
maintained by the Conservation Unit of
the Museums and Galleries
Commission.
SEE Collectors (Scientific Instruments),
Furniture, Silver.

DUNLUCE ANTIQUES
33 Ballytober Road, Bushmills, **Co.
Antrim BT57 8UU**
TEL   02657 31140
OPEN   10–6 Mon–Thur; 2–6 Sat.
Specialise in restoring European and
Oriental porcelain.
PROVIDE Home Inspections. Free
Estimates. Chargeable
Collection/Delivery Service.
SPEAK TO Clare Ross.
Clare Ross is West Dean trained.

DESIREE SHORT
38 North Great George Street, Dublin 1,
Co. Dublin
TEL   722285
OPEN   9.30–5 Mon–Fri or By
        Appointment Sat, Sun.
Specialise in restoring porcelain, jade,
stone, plastic, ivory.
PROVIDE Local Home Inspections. Free
Estimates.
SPEAK TO Desirée Short.

ST. JAMES'S GALLERY LTD
18–20 Le Bordage, St. Peter Port,
Guernsey, Channel Islands
TEL   0481 720070
OPEN   9–5.30 Mon–Sat or By
        Appointment.
Specialise in some porcelain restoration.
PROVIDE Home Inspections. Chargeable
Estimates. Collection/Delivery Service
by arrangement.
SPEAK TO Mr. or Mrs. Whittam.
SEE Furniture.

BENITA MILLER
30 Wester Links, Fortrose, **Highland
IV10 8RZ**
TEL   0381 20479
OPEN   By Appointment.
Specialise in restoring European and
Oriental ceramics.
PROVIDE Home Inspections.
Free/Chargeable Estimates. Chargeable
Collection/Delivery Service.
SPEAK TO Benita Miller.
Member of SSCR.

BEAVER GLASS RESTORATION
23 Hatton Place, Edinburgh, **Lothian
EH9 1UB**
TEL   031 667 8996
OPEN   9–5 Mon–Fri.

Specialise in restoring glass including
grinding and polishing. Able to clean
non-leaded glass decanters.
PROVIDE Free Estimates.
SPEAK TO Marilyn or Derek Beaver.
Members of SSCR.

ELLEN BREHENY
Conservation Studio, Hopetoun House,
South Queensferry, **Lothian EH30 9SL**
TEL   031 331 2003
OPEN   By Appointment.
Specialise in restoring all ceramics and
vessel glass.
PROVIDE Home Inspections.
Free/Chargeable Estimates.
Free/Chargeable Collection/Delivery
Service.
SPEAK TO Ellen Breheny.
Member of SSCR and UKIC.

**HOUNDWOOD ANTIQUES
RESTORATION**
7 West Preston Street, Edinburgh,
Lothian EH8 9PX
TEL   031 667 3253
OPEN   By Appointment.
Specialise in restoring antique ceramics.
PROVIDE Home Inspections. Free
Estimates. Chargeable
Collection/Delivery Service.
SPEAK TO Mr. A. Gourlay.
SEE Furniture, Silver.

ROSS–SMITH STAINED GLASS
Ashlea, Mossend, Gorebridge, **Lothian
EH23 4NL**
TEL   0875 20242
FAX   0875 20242
OPEN   8.30–5.30 Mon–Fri.
Specialise in restoring and conserving
leaded, stained and acid etched stained
glass.

PROVIDE Home Inspections. Refundable Estimates. Chargeable Collection/Delivery Service.
SPEAK TO Patrick Ross–Smith

CATHERINE RITCHIE
72 Novar Drive, Glasgow, **Strathclyde G12 9TZ**
TEL   041 339 0331
OPEN   By Appointment.
Specialise in restoring European and Oriental ceramics.
PROVIDE Free Estimates.
SPEAK TO Catherine Ritchie.

THE WEE GLASS WORKS in YER GRANNY'S ATTIC
176 Main Street, Prestwick, **Strathclyde KA9 1PQ**
TEL   0292 76312
OPEN   10–6 Mon–Sat.

Specialise in stained glass commission work and restoration.
PROVIDE Home Inspections. Free Estimates. Free/Chargeable Collection/Delivery Service.
SPEAK TO Barry Dickson or Joan Twelves-Dickson
Member of the Guild of Master Craftsmen.

IRENA ANTIQUES
111 Broad Street, Barry, **South Glamorgan CF6 8SX**
TEL   0446 747626 or 732517
OPEN   10–4 Mon–Fri.
Specialise in restoring European and Oriental porcelain.
PROVIDE Free Estimates. Free Collection/Delivery Service.
SPEAK TO Irena Halabuda.
SEE Furniture.

Furniture, Clocks and Watches, Barometers, Mirrors

A consideration of the care and restoration of antique furniture raises a number of questions: How far is it wise to go with restoration? How much is it advisable to do oneself without involving professional help? How should a suitable restorer be chosen? To answer any of these, one needs first an idea of the value and merits of the furniture in question, for which expert advice may have to be sought. Besides quality and authenticity, a good deal of the value of a piece of furniture depends upon its condition and the degree of restoration it has received in the past. Many pieces may just not warrant a great deal of money spent on them, except for sentimental reasons, but others will and there is no excuse for allowing shoddy work on a fine object. Proper handling and care of furniture will minimise the need for restoration, rather like looking after a car between periodic servicing to keep it in good running order and avoid a major breakdown.

Unlike modern ply and fibre boards, natural wood absorbs moisture and lets moisture out depending on the environment it is in. This makes it expand and contract across the grain (and only minutely along the grain). If it cannot move adequately, whether because of restrictions in the construction of a piece of furniture, or if it is transferred too quickly between cold and hot or wet and dry surroundings, or if it is left to dry out without attention for a long period, it is likely to crack, distort, joints loosen, and veneer and mouldings lift and become detached.

The ideal relative humidity in which to keep furniture is about 50% at 68° F. This makes for the best museum conditions but is not always easy to maintain in the home. Likewise, with ultra violet radiation from sunlight which is often excluded in museums, a certain amount can mellow the colour of furniture beautifully, but too much will dry it out, perish the surface polish and can lead to unattractive uneven fading. A compromise has to be reached: for example, some pieces of furniture can be turned round periodically to even the fading process and curtains might be kept drawn when a room is not in use for long periods. Local areas of low humidity can arise near radiators. These can be compensated for to an extent with bowls of water or humidifiers but valuable furniture should never be kept near a source of heat. Potted plants, bowls of flowers and leaving doors open to circulate the air can also help to redress the balance.

There are a number of simple things which are so often forgotten in the handling of furniture which put unnecessary strains on it. These include tilting back on the legs of chairs which quickly weakens the joints, picking up chairs by the arms rather than by the seat rails, opening drawers using one handle instead of two and dragging tables across the floor instead of carrying them. Besides keeping a regular eye on furniture when it is dusted, it is advisable to give a thorough check over at least once a year. A duster can so easily catch the edge of a veneer or brass inlay and help it to loosen. This may be unavoidable but it is important to keep safely any pieces that might fall off. Fixing them back again is both infinitely preferable and easier than having to match in new ones. A periodic check should include an inspection for lifting, stringing, mouldings or veneer (which will sound hollow if lightly tapped), loose joints and for woodworm. Make sure cabinets are securely fixed on to walls and that screws in door hinges are tight: the weight when they are open can lead to their sagging and difficulty in closing them. If locks, hinges or door bolts are stiff, a little lubricating oil will help. Castor wheels can put unnecessary stress on legs if they get jammed up, often with threads, which stop them rotating.

Turning now to the question of how much restoration should be done to a piece of furniture, a structural problem such as a broken leg should clearly be seen to as soon as possible so that as clean and strong a job can be done as may be. If a piece of furniture is to be fit for daily use, it is no good having half a job done. For example, if one loose joint is tightened on a chair, additional strain will be put on it if others are slightly loose. On gilded or painted furniture joints must be particularly tight or cracks will soon appear on the surface. However, if a part needs to be replaced, such as a seat rail because of serious woodworm damage, it is often possible to retain part of the old rail, using new wood of the same type to take the strain. Missing veneer or mouldings should be carefully matched with wood of the same character and colour, but only after the cause of the loss has been investigated. This often means shrinkage or bowing of the wood on which it is laid. Sometimes quite superficial damage can reveal something much more serious beneath which must be sorted out first. Moving parts such as drawers will in time cause wear and necessitate the replacement of the runners beneath, while shrinkage of the carcase might make drawers stiff to open. Shaving off of wood should always be done on the carcase rather than on the linings of the drawer. Before embarking on expensive work due to movement, twisting or warping, it is worth transferring the piece of furniture in question to a different, perhaps cooler, environment which might help to rectify the problem.

The matter of surface treatment is a rather more vexed one. Some people are troubled by old marks and blemishes. Recent stains and ring marks and some more unsightly older ones can often be improved upon or even eradicated by a skilled restorer without destroying an old surface, but to 'refinish' a piece can lead to a flat, lifeless and uniform surface which barely looks old, and the value of the piece can be diminished accordingly. There is a school of thought, notably in France, that furniture should be cleaned and restored to its original colourful appearance. However, it should be remembered that much sophisticated French furniture relies for its interest on marquetry and ormolu mounts, while the typically more restrained character of British work lays stress on the colour, figure and beauty of the wood itself. The lustrous depth of a good patina is caused by a gradual build up of wax polish, grease from handling, dust, smoke and marks of general wear and tear, combined with the oxidisation of the wood and the mellowing of the colour in sunlight which can bring out a whole range of different shades. If patina like this remains, and so often it does not, it should be treated with the utmost care. Once ruined, it cannot be regained except by a further long ageing process.

A number of conflicting theories exist about traditional finishes, but generally speaking, a form of varnish was used to protect and enhance the aesthetic appeal of furniture. Broadly, this was based on linseed and other oils in the 17th century, resin and spirit in the 18th and shellac in the 19th. Stain to colour the wood was applied either before or in the varnish itself. After the first quarter of the last century French polishing became increasingly popular and a large proportion of earlier pieces were 'modernised' with this part gloss finish. The only essential difference was one of technique, the shellac being applied with a pad lubricated with linseed oil. Compared to a wax polished surface, a French polished one has much less resistance to water marks, burns and scratches, and the glossing agents and oils that were additionally employed by the end of the century have often crazed over leaving a perished surface which will not shine, however much waxing is done on top of it. Bleached out white grain filler is also often in evidence. French polish has no place on pre-19th century furniture, but any change in finish should be handled sensitively to avoid stripping back any further than is necessary. Modern synthetic finishes, such as poly-urethane, seal the surface so completely that moisture cannot pass through it. It should never be used on pre-plywood furniture.

A certain amount of antique furniture was wax finished when it was made and until the 19th century this was always done with natural waxes. Sine then polishes have often included a variety of oil products which tend to float on the surface without drying and leave a gooey residue. Fluid preparations and creams are a potential hazard, particularly to marquetry work, as they can penetrate joints and loosen veneer, while silicon-based polishes and other modern spray polishes seal the surface of the wood and build up a dull stickiness which can be difficult to remove. There really is no alternative to a traditional simple polish of yellow beeswax and turpentine. This takes a while to harden but in time can be fully burnished. Up to 50% of Carnauba wax can be added which will make a harder wax with a higher shine. There are numerous commercial waxes on the market and it is vital to check the contents before purchase.

On a dry surface wax can be applied generously and rubbed well in with a circular motion to build up a durable surface, but it should be remembered that once a surface is sealed, wax will not soak into the wood and it is the surface not the wood that is being polished. It is therefore important not to overwax but to use it sparingly with a good deal of rubbing. On most pieces that do not receive heavy abrasion, waxing once a year with an occasional good burnishing should suffice. A show brush and soft toothbrush are useful assets in cleaning or waxing mouldings and carved areas, while dining table tops, which suffer some of the heaviest use and can develop a sticky or greasy surface, can often be improved with periodical energetic brushing along the grain of the wood. Leather panels and seat coverings need to be keep well fed with soft leather dressing to avoid drying out and deterioration. Early leather is a rare survival and should always be retained if possible.

Since it is mildly abrasive, wax polish will gently clean dirt from surfaces as it polishes. There are also a number of commerical cleaners and revivers available which generally contain oils and stains and can pose problems such as penetrating the wood and causing blotches where the surface has rubbed thin. Traditional home-made recipes which include such things as linseed oil, white spirit and methylated spirits should be used sparingly to avoid sticky deposits which will attract more dirt. Recent knocks and scratches which go through the surface into the wood can be effectively disguised as old ones, provided they have not already been polished over using scratch cover polish or brown shoe polish. On heat or water marks it is worth trying a little linseed oil on a finger tip and plenty of friction, leaving a good time before polishing. Most commercial products for such problems are too drastic and should be avoided. If unsightly marks persist, a professional should be consulted. Small cracks and damage can be filled with commercial hard wax sticks which come in a range of colours, but these will not prevent further movement of the wood and larger areas of damage will require expert patching in and disguising. Some cracks which are not structural or so aesthetically important might just be covered up, such as those in drawer bottoms with lining paper, or in backboards with sticky paper to keep dust out of the carcase.

The secret of a good gluing job is to clean the surface to be fixed together thoroughly and then use glue sparingly and make a really close fit using clamps or other means of pressure. There is a wide range of adhesives available, but the only one that can be safely recommended is traditional animal or Scotch glue, which has to be heated in a double boiler. Unlike almost all others this is water based and is fairly easily reversible if required. Over a long period it does dry out and lose its adhesion, which is why when one joint becomes loose others may not be far behind and should be checked over. Rather than risk the loss of loose veneer and mouldings it is wise to fix them back as soon as possible (a piece of masking tape can be useful to hold them in place), but most other gluing jobs are best seen to by professionals.

If treatment for furniture beetle (woodworm) is necessary, it is wise to glue joints up first if possible since proprietary fluids can affect adhesion. Some people become over-alarmed at the presence of worm holes. Usually in antique furniture they are relics of the past as the beetle much prefers moist soft wood to old dry wood, but softer timbers such as beech and walnut can sometimes be reinfested. Loose sawdust may be a tell-tale sign, although it may still fall out of old channels if the piece of furniture is moved around. The best time for treatment is the Spring when larvae are hatching near the surface before they burrow their way out and fly away around May or June. A useful test is to fill all visible holes with wax after treatment, which will not only be an aesthetic improvement but also any holes which appear thereafter will show there is further activity. Non-structural parts that are badly weakened with internal channels may be professionally consolidated with resin solution, but others may need to be replaced.

One of the most common places where this can prove necessary is on beech seat rails of chairs. The widespread habit of using a black undercloth is both unnecessary and inhibits regular inspection of the rails. In order to do a thorough job to rails and joints one must expect to have to go to the added expense of having the seat stripped out and reupholstered. The way that this is done can have a considerable effect on the chair aesthetically. Traditional horsehair stuffing and tacks should be used, rather than foam rubber and a staple gun. This will keep its shape much longer and be kinder to the seat rails. Basically, hard square edges and tufting are authentic for 18th century pieces and more rounded shapes with springs and buttoning for much of the 19th. Horsehair can be kept and reused where possible and on the rare

58

occasions where the upholstery turns out to be original (which one can tell from the lack of previous tack holes in the rails), the old webbing might be retained by stretching new over it and it might be possible to put back the old covering after a clean. Cane and rushed seats should be replaced if it is necessary with materials of the right gauge and quality which can be stained to match in.

A word should be included about brass mounts. Most English handles and mounts, except sometimes on the very finest pieces, were not fire-gilded as were most French ones, but gilt lacquered. If it has not been cleaned off, this lacquer tends to darken with time, sometimes to the extent that the brass colour is lost completely. To overclean handles can harm the overall mellowed effect of a piece of furniture, but a judicious cleaning of highlights can create a good balance. Ormolu (gilded bronze or brass) can often be successfully cleaned with soapy water to which a dash of ammonia can be added. Great care should be taken not to get any cleaning fluids on to wooden surfaces. If one or more handles are missing from an original or old set, a good restorer can have replacements cast for you or will repair damaged ones. This is greatly preferable to putting on a new set, particularly of cheap modern reproductions.

A good deal of antique furniture, besides the more obvious mirrors and picture frames, started life with surface decoration, whether lacquered, grained, painted or gilded. Much painting on furniture has been lost though wear, refinishing and not least in more recent years in the stripper's tank. Thankfully, the 'pine tide' seems to be turning and remaining grained surfaces are being kept and restored for their own sakes. Generally graining was done on a cheaper wood to resemble a more expensive one. Worn painted decoration often needs a very talented restorer to blend in new work without overpainting the original.

Lacquering and gilding are both done on a prepared gesso ground. When the wood, generally softwood, beneath shrinks, this ground does not, with resultant cracking, lifting and eventual loss. It is therefore rare to find examples without heavy restoration or, more often than not, complete over-painting or regilding at a later date. The survival of picture frames is thankfully better than furniture which has had more physical use. Sometimes it is possible with careful stripping to recover enough original beneath later gilding or the application of gold paint or paste, to restore it without having to clean it off completely and start again. Dry stripping is time-consuming and therefore expensive, but the possible result cannot be matched in any other way.

Most 18th century gilding was water gilding, the gold leaf being floated on to a surface dampened with size (animal glue and water). As this dries, the gold is drawn on and can be burnished to a shine. The leaf is very thin and where it is distressed, areas of ground colour varying from red to aubergine according to the period, will show through. As with copper on Sheffield plate, this can be most attractive, provided there is not too much of it. Water gilding should only be dusted in cleaning, any fluid or cream is likely to find its way round the inert gold and destabilise the leaf.

Oil gilding is even easier to rub off. This was used on inferior work, and particularly in the 19th century. It involves less skill, the gold being applied with oil, and it will not burnish, leaving a flat matt finish. The ground colour beneath is generally yellow. A majority of 19th century frame decoration will be found to be not carved wood but composition, made in a wooden mould and applied to a wooden frame. This mixture of materials encourages uneven shrinkage and loss which is not found to the same extent on carved wood ones. However, matching sections can be cast from existing ones and, as with water gilding, a sensitive restorer can tone them in and distress them almost imperceptibly.

The fragility of mirror plates means that more often than not they have had to be replaced at some time or other. The presence of an original 18th century one without a doubt enhances the value of a mirror. If the silvering is too damaged for practical use, it is unwise to attempt to have it resilvered, which is often not very successful anyway, but better to have a new mirror plate made, which can be a little dulled down if required, and to keep the original so that it can be put back again at a later date.

There are no short cuts to cleaning the movement of a clock or watch. A thorough professional job has to be done every so often, including dismantling, attending to worn parts and lubricating the right areas. To repair one part only is, as was the case with chairs, likely to put additional strain elsewhere. The cleaning of moving parts is generally done with a brush and chalk. It is important not to abrade the surfaces and to make sure that your chosen restorer does not clean clocks electronically, at least unless they are very inferior examples. As with furniture, the more original parts that can be retained the better, but sometimes the extent of wear does necessitate replacement. Once cleaned and rebrushed as necessary, the pivots (and not the pinions) should be oiled. Too much oil can attract dirt and encourage abrasion which is likely to renew your problems.

Once it is properly set up again, the clock should work satisfactorily for a considerable time, although it should ideally be checked over by a specialist's eye every few years. Bracket and longcase clocks should be placed on a perfectly level surface and if a longcase clock is to stand on carpet, it is wise to secure it to a wall by screwing through the backboards to prevent any possible movement which can conspire to upset the beat and stop it. Ensure also that the weights are rehung the correct way round.

The cleaning of movements need not extend to the faces or cases of clocks, as unfortunately seems to be a temptation to some clock restorers. Here we are back in the realms of aesthetics rather than function. One-piece dials, unless painted or enamelled, were always silvered to show up the hands, although it is not uncommon to find them brass today where the silvering has worn and has been rubbed away. Apart from a few very early examples, this applies also to the register plates of barometers. It is a matter of how authentic one wants to be as to whether they are resilvered. If done, the surface can be slightly mellowed with gentle abrasion. Surface discoloration can often be improved by merely relacquering, for example on chapter (numeral) rings on clock faces. Mercury barometers, when transported, can develop air bubbles in their tubes which need to be sorted out professionally. Apart from a check over if the accuracy is in question, barometers should need little other restoration. The treatment of clock and barometer cases requires as sensitive handling as any other pieces of furniture. Finding a beautifully patinated example is pretty rare.

Good restoration is time-consuming and is unlikely to be cheap, but it is worth remembering that often a lot of time has to be spent on undoing previous poor restoration, for example joints glued with irreversible adhesives or wooden dowels or nails driven in to hold mortice and tenon joints tight when they begin to loosen, and very little can be done once a fine surface is ruined. The wide range of topics covered in this introduction illustrates the variety of specialities that there are, and there can be few restorers who are skilled at everything. It is well worth finding out what a restorer enjoys working at most, as this is likely to be what he is best at. A good restorer needs, besides the right skills and experience, a stock of old materials and sufficient knowledge of woods to use the right ones in repairs, a working knowledge of the development of furniture to be able to make authentic suggestions, an understanding of the importance of retaining old surfaces, and a general interest in conserving the past.

Before any work commences it is important for the client and restorer to understand and agree exactly what is to be done. Conservation (to arrest deterioration) should be the ideal, but careful compromise with authentic restoration (to return a piece to its original condition) is generally the most sensible option. Apart from necessary structural work, a general rule should be to under- rather than over-restore. Antique furniture in the home should be enjoyed, and if it is sensibly used with respect and periodically checked over by a sensitive specialist restorer, there is no reason why it should not last into the next generation of ownership, and beyond.

Christopher Claxton Stevens

T. H. DEWEY
The Cottage, Kelston, Bath, **Avon
BA1 9AF**
TEL   0225 447944
OPEN   8–5 Mon–Fri or by
          appointment.
Specialise in restoring antique period
furniture including metalwork, but will
repair a kitchen chair if requested.
PROVIDE Home Inspections. Free
Estimates locally. Free
Collection/Delivery Service locally.
SPEAK TO Tim Dewey.

FRANK DUX ANTIQUES
33 Belvedere, Bath, **Avon BA1 5HR**
TEL   0225 312367
OPEN   10–6 Mon–Sat.
Specialise in restoring antique furniture,
all cabinet work and polishing.
PROVIDE Home Inspections. Refundable
Estimates. Free Collection/Delivery
Service on small items.
SPEAK TO Frank Dux
Member of the UKIC.

JOHN AND CAROL HAWLEY
'The Orchard', Clevedon Lane, Clapton
Wick, Clevedon, **Avon BS21 7AG**
TEL   0275 852052
OPEN   By Appointment.
Specialise in repairing and restoring all
types of antique clocks. Do not
undertake watches.
PROVIDE Home Inspections. Free
Estimates unless travel involved. Free
Collection/Delivery Service.
SPEAK TO John or Carol Hawley.
They are CMBHI and MBWCG.

IAN & DIANNE McCARTHY
Arcadian Cottage, 112 Station Road,
Clutton, **Avon BS18 4RA**
TEL   0761 53188
OPEN   By Appointment.
Specialise in restoring period upholstery.
PROVIDE Home Inspections. Free
Estimates. Chargeable
Collection/Delivery Service.
SPEAK TO Ian or Dianne McCarthy.
SEE Silver, Porcelain.

PENNARD HOUSE ANTIQUES
3/4 Piccadilly, London Road, Bath, **Avon
BA1 6PL**
TEL   0225 313791
FAX   0225 448196
OPEN   9.30–5.30 Mon–Sat.
Specialise in restoring English and
French country furniture. Also
undertake upholstery work, rushing and
caning.
PROVIDE Home Inspections. Free
Estimates. Free Collection/Delivery
Service.
SPEAK TO Martin Dearden.
SEE Porcelain.

ANTHONY REED
94–96 Walcot Street, Bath, **Avon
BA1 5BG**
TEL   0225–461969 or 0272 333595
OPEN   9–6 Mon–Sat.
Specialise in cleaning, restoring and
gilding frames.
PROVIDE Home Inspections. Chargeable
Estimates. Chargeable Local
Collection/Delivery Service.
SPEAK TO Anthony Reed.
Member of the IIC.
SEE Oil Paintings.

D. M. E. RESTORATIONS LTD
11 Church Street, Ampthill, **Bedfordshire MK45 2PL**
TEL   0525 405819
OPEN   8–5.30 Mon–Fri; 8–1 Sat or by appointment.

Specialise in restoring English furniture including polishing and gilding.
PROVIDE Home Inspections. Free Estimates. Collection/Delivery Service by arrangement.
SPEAK TO Duncan Everitt.

RICHARD HAGEN
The Stables, Wakes End Farm, Eversholt, **Bedfordshire MK17 9EA**
TEL   0525 28505
OPEN   By Arrangement.

Specialise in conserving and restoring antique furniture and woodwork sympathetically.
PROVIDE Home Inspections by arrangement. Free Estimates.
SPEAK TO Richard Hagen.

THOMAS HUDSON
The Barn, 117 High Street, Odell, **Bedfordshire MK43 7AS**
TEL   0234 721133
OPEN   8–6 Mon–Fri; 8–12 Sat.

Specialise in restoring antique furniture and old woodwork sympathetically. Can also make chairs to match existing sets.
PROVIDE Home Inspections. Chargeable Estimates.
SPEAK TO Thomas Hudson.

Please ring to discuss your requirements or to make an appointment to visit the workshop.

J. MOORE RESTORATIONS
College Farmhouse Workshops, Chawston, **Bedfordshire MK44 3BH**
TEL   0480 214165
OPEN   8.30–5.30 Mon–Fri.

Specialise in restoring Georgian and fine antique furniture.
PROVIDE Home Inspections. Free/Refundable Estimates. Free Collection/Delivery Service locally.
SPEAK TO Mr. J. Moore.

Mr. Moore has over 20 years experience and holds a COSIRA Course Certificate.

SIMON PALLISTER
33 Albion Road, Luton, **Bedfordshire LU2 0DS**
TEL   0582 452292
OPEN   8.30–6 Mon–Fri.

Specialise in restoring antique English and Continental furniture.
PROVIDE Home Inspections. Free Estimates. Free Collection/Delivery Service.
SPEAK TO Simon Pallister.

Member of BAFRA.

WATERLOO HOUSE ANTIQUES
Unit 2/3, College Farm, High Street, Pulloxmill, **Bedfordshire MK45 5HP**
TEL   0525 717786
OPEN   10.30–4 Mon–Fri; 10.30–12 Sat. Closed Tue.

Specialise in restoring and re–upholstering Victorian and Edwardian furniture by traditional methods. Recaning service also available.
PROVIDE Home Inspections. Free Estimates within 15-mile radius. Free Collection/Delivery Service.
SPEAK TO Mr. R. J. Jennings.

ALPHA ANTIQUE RESTORATIONS
High Street, Compton, **Berkshire
RG16 ONL**
TEL   0635 578245
OPEN   7–4 Mon–Fri.

Specialise in fine furniture restoration, both English and Continental, veneering, inlaying, specialised copy chair making.
PROVIDE Home Inspections. Free/Chargeable Estimates. Chargeable Collection/Delivery Service.
SPEAK TO Graham Childs.
Member of BAFRA.

**ASHLEY ANTIQUES AND
FURNITURE**
129 High Street, Hungerford, **Berkshire
RG17 0DL**
TEL   0488 682771
OPEN   10–1, 2–5 Mon–Fri; 11–1, 2–5 Sat.

Specialise in restoring English and Continental furniture and making furniture to order. Can also repair clocks.
PROVIDE Home Inspections. Free Estimates. Free Local Collection/Delivery Service.
SPEAK TO Robert Duff.

THE CLOCK WORKSHOP
17 Prospect Street, Caversham, Reading, **Berkshire RG4 8JB**
TEL   0734–470741
FAX   0734–474194
OPEN   9.30–5.30 Mon–Fri; 10–1 Sat.

Specialise in restoring antique clocks including grande–sonnerie striking, pull quarter repeating and chronometers. They also restore barometers.
PROVIDE Home Inspections. Free Estimates. Collection/Delivery Service by arrangement.
SPEAK TO John Yealland FBHI.

HAMILTON HAVERS
58 Conisboro Avenue, Caversham Heights, Reading, **Berkshire RG4 7JE**
TEL   0734 473379
OPEN   Daily By Appointment.

Specialise in restoring Boulle, marquetry, ivory, tortoiseshell, mother-of-pearl, brass, lapis lazuli and malachite on furniture and clock-cases. and objets d'art.
PROVIDE Free/Chargeable Estimates.
SPEAK TO Hamilton Havers.
Mr Havers has worked for the National Trust.
SEE Silver.

BEN NORRIS
Knowl Hill Farm, Knowl Hill, Kingsclere, Newbury, **Berkshire
RG15 8WY**
TEL   0635 297950
FAX   0635 299851
OPEN   8.30–5.30 Mon–Fri.

Specialise in restoring antique furniture pre–1830, gilding and supplying and restoring brass furniture fittings.
PROVIDE Home Inspections. Free/Refundable Estimates. Free Local Collection/Delivery Service and to London.
SPEAK TO Ben Norris.
Member of BAFRA.

S. J. BIRT & SON
21 Windmill Street, Brill, Aylesbury, **Buckinghamshire HP18 9TG**
TEL   0844–237440
OPEN   By Appointment.

Specialise in restoring clocks, barometers and tower clocks.
PROVIDE Home Inspections. Free Estimates. Free Collection/Delivery Service.
SPEAK TO Mr. S. J. Birt.
SEE Collectors (Mechanical Music).

BROWNS OF WEST WYCOMBE
Church Lane, West Wycombe,
Buckinghamshire HP14 3AH

TEL   0494 524537

FAX   0494 439548

OPEN   8–6 Mon–Fri; 8–12 Sat.

Specialise in restoring antique furniture.
Are also chair-makers and will make
chairs to match existing sets.

PROVIDE Home Inspections.
Free/Refundable Estimates. Free
Collection/Delivery Service.

SPEAK TO D. A. Hines.

CHESS ANTIQUES
85 Broad Street, Chesham,
Buckinghamshire HP5 3EF

TEL   0494 783043

FAX   0494 791302

OPEN   8–5 Mon–Sat.

Specialise in restoring clocks, French
polishing and cabinet work. Upholstery
is also undertaken.

PROVIDE Home Inspections. Chargeable
Estimates. Chargeable
Collection/Delivery Service.

SPEAK TO M. Wilder.

SEE Oil Paintings.

CONY CRAFTS
Half Acre Workshops, Watchet Lane,
Nr. Great Missenden, **Buckinghamshire
HP16 ODR**

TEL   02406 5668

OPEN   9–5.30 Mon–Fri. (Answering
service after these hours.)

Specialise in sympathetically restoring
antique and modern furniture including
traditional upholstery work, wood–
carving, chair-rushing, chair-caning, and
French polishing. Pieces can be made to
individual commission.

PROVIDE Home Inspections. Free
Estimates. Collection/Delivery Service.

SPEAK TO Mr. Bowlem.

Member of the Guild of Master
Craftsmen.

HERITAGE RESTORATIONS
36B High Street, Great Missenden,
Buckinghamshire HP16 OAU

TEL   02406 5710

OPEN   10–5 Mon–Sat.

Specialise in restoring furniture, clocks
and watches, caning and rushing and
upholstery.

PROVIDE Free Estimates. Home
Inspections.

SPEAK TO John Wilshire.

SEE Porcelain.

ALAN MARTIN
Farthing Cottage, Clickers Yard,
Yardley Road, Olney, **Buckinghamshire
MK46 5DX**

TEL   0234 712446

OPEN   9–5 Mon–Sat; Sun By
Appointment.

Specialise in repairing antique clocks and
pocket watches.

PROVIDE Home Inspections.
Free/Chargeable Estimates. Free
Collection/Delivery Service.

SPEAK TO Alan Martin.

Mr Martin is a MBHI and a member of
the Clock & Watchmakers' Guild.

WYCOMBE CANE AND RUSH WORKS
Victoria Street, High Wycombe,
Buckinghamshire HP11 2LU

TEL   0494 442429

OPEN   9–5 Mon–Fri.

Specialise in all types of canework
including spider and fan work patterns
and blind or secret cane. Also carry out
rush seating.

PROVIDE Local Home Inspections.
Refundable Estimates.

SPEAK TO Peter Gilbert.

Established in 1880. Visitors are always
welcome to come and see work being
carried out.

PERIOD FURNITURE SHOWROOMS
49 London End, Beaconsfield,
Buckinghamshire HP9 2HW
TEL   0494 674112
OPEN   9–5 Mon–Sat.

Specialise in restoring English furniture including cabinetmaking, chair making, polishing and upholstery.
PROVIDE Home Inspections. Free Estimates. Free Collection/Delivery Service.
SPEAK TO R. E. W. Hearne.

TINGEWICK ANTIQUES CENTRE
Main Street, Tingewick,
Buckinghamshire MK18 4PB
TEL   0280 847922
OPEN   10.30–5 Mon–Sat; 11–5 Sun.

Specialise in restoring metalware on furniture and clocks.
PROVIDE Home Inspections. Free Estimates. Collection/Delivery Service by arrangement.
SPEAK TO Rosemarie or Barry Smith

GRAHAM BARNES
14 St. Mary's Street, Ely, **Cambridgeshire CB7 4ES**
TEL   0353 665218
OPEN   By Appointment.

Specialise in restoring pre–1830 fine furniture, marquetry and brass inlay.
PROVIDE Free Estimates.
SPEAK TO Graham Barnes.
Member of BAFRA.

CLADGILD LTD
Vine House, Reach, Cambridge,
Cambridgeshire CB5 0JD
TEL   0638 741989
FAX   0638 743239
OPEN   By Appointment.

Specialise in restoring wood products including antique furniture and panelling. Also offer an upholstery service. Replicas can be made to order.
PROVIDE Home Inspections. Free Collection/Delivery Service.
SPEAK TO Jo Ann Dudley.

Members of the Association of Master Upholsterers and the Guild of Master Craftsmen.

DODDINGTON HOUSE ANTIQUES
2 Benwick Road, Doddington, Nr. March, **Cambridgeshire PE15 0TG**
TEL   0354 740755
OPEN   10–6 Mon–Sat.

Specialise in restoring painted furniture, lacquer work, clock–cases, barometers, cane and rush work.
PROVIDE Refundable Estimates. Free Collection/Delivery Service.
SPEAK TO Brian or Lynette Frankland.

EUROOM INTERNATIONAL (UK) LTD
Vine House, Reach, **Cambridgeshire CB5 0JD**
TEL   0638 741989
FAX   0638 743239
OPEN   By Appointment.

Specialise in restoring antique and modern furniture, including French polishing, marquetry, carving, upholstery, re-leathering, gold tooling, resilvering, caning and rushing. Also restore barometers and clocks.
PROVIDE Home Inspections. Free Estimates. Free Collection/Delivery Service.
SPEAK TO Mr. A. Dudley.

Members of the Guild of Master Craftsmen and the Association of Master Upholsterers.
SEE Collectors (Dolls, Toys).

FRANK GOODINGHAM
Studio 3, Hope Street Yard, Hope Street, Cambridge, **Cambridgeshire CB1 3NA**
TEL   0223 410702
OPEN   10–6 Mon–Fri.

Specialise in restoring 18th and 19th century gilded work including composition or carved overmantles and pier glass frames.

PROVIDE Home Inspections. Refundable Estimates. Collection/Delivery by arrangement.

SPEAK TO Frank Goodingham.

SEE Oil Paintings.

PETER JOHN
38 St Mary's Street, Eyresbury, St. Neots, **Cambridgeshire PE19 2TA**
TEL   0480 216297
OPEN   9–5 Mon–Sat.

Specialise in restoring antique English and French clocks.

PROVIDE Home Inspections. Free Estimates. Chargeable Collection/Delivery Service.

SPEAK TO Kym or Peter John.

SEE Silver.

KENDAL FURNITURE RESTORATIONS
2 Clifton Road, Huntingdon, **Cambridgeshire PE18 7EJ**
TEL   0480 411811
FAX   0480 411811
OPEN   8–5 Mon–Fri.

Specialise in repairing, polishing and upholstering antique furniture as well as cane and rush seating, desk leather lining, manufacturing individually hand-made furniture.

PROVIDE Home Inspections. Free Collection/Delivery Service.

SPEAK TO Terence Brazier.

A. ALLEN ANTIQUE RESTORERS
Buxton Rd, Newtown, Newmills, Via Stockport, **Cheshire SK12 3JS**
TEL   0663 745274
OPEN   8–5 Mon–Fri; 9–12 Sat.

Specialise in restoring antique furniture including 17th and 18th century oak and walnut pieces. Also restore Boulle work, inlay, gilding, upholstery and metalwork. Clocks and furniture can be designed or copied.

PROVIDE Home Inspections. Free/Chargeable Estimates. Collection/Delivery Service.

SPEAK TO Tony Allen.

SEE Oil Paintings, Silver.

ARROWSMITH ANTIQUES AND RESTORATIONS
Unit 1A, Bridge Street Mill, Macclesfield, **Cheshire**
TEL   0625 611880
OPEN   8.30–5.30 Mon–Sat.

Specialise in restoring 18th and 19th century furniture.

PROVIDE Home Inspections. Free Estimates. Free Collection/Delivery Service.

SPEAK TO Paul Arrowsmith.

PETER D. BOSSON
10B Swan St, Wilmslow, **Cheshire SK9 1HE**
TEL   0625 525250 and 527857
OPEN   10–12.45, 2.15–5 Tue–Sat.

Specialise in restoring barographs, barometers, clocks.

PROVIDE Home Inspections. Free Estimates. Free Collection/Delivery Service within 50 miles.

SPEAK TO Peter Bosson.

SEE Collectors (Scientific Instruments).

COPPELIA ANTIQUES
Holford Lodge, Plumley Moor Rd,
Plumley, **Cheshire WA16 9RS**
TEL   0565 722197
OPEN   By Appointment.

Specialise in restoring longcase and other
clocks, mahogany, oak and walnut
antique furniture.
PROVIDE Home Inspections and
Estimates by arrangement. Chargeable
Collection/Delivery Service.
SPEAK TO K. R. Clements

STEWART EVANS
Church View, Church Street, Malpas,
Cheshire SY14 8PD
TEL   0948 860974 or 860214
OPEN   By Appointment.

Specialise in restoring antique furniture.
He also makes hand-made fine quality
reproduction furniture using old timber.
PROVIDE Home Inspections.
Free/Chargeable Estimates. Chargeable
Collection/Delivery Service.
SPEAK TO Stewart Evans.
Established in 1953.

JOHN HETHERINGTON
FURNITURE
Unit 2, First Floor, Albion Mill,
Hollingworth, Via Hyde, **Cheshire
SK14 8LS**
TEL   0457 765781
OPEN   8.30–5.30 Mon–Fri.

Specialise in restoring oak and walnut
country furniture.
PROVIDE Home Inspections. Free
Estimates. Chargeable
Collection/Delivery Service.
SPEAK TO John Hetherington.

MILL FARM ANTIQUES
50 Market St, Disley, Stockport,
Cheshire SK12 2DT
TEL   0663 764045
OPEN   9–6 Mon–Sat.

Specialise in restoring antique clocks and
barometers.
PROVIDE Home Inspections. Free
Estimates. Free Collection/Delivery
Service.
SPEAK TO F. E. Berry.
SEE Collectors (Mechanical Music).

THE OLD BAKERY
21–23 Lower Fold, Marple Bridge, Via
Stockport, **Cheshire SK6 5DU**
TEL   061 427 4699
OPEN   9–6 Mon–Fri.

Specialise in antique furniture
restoration and the supply of feet,
rockers, mouldings etc. No upholstery
work carried out
SPEAK TO Geoffrey Douglas.

DEREK RAYMENT ANTIQUES
Orchard House, Barton Road, Barton,
Nr. Farndon, **Cheshire SY14 7HT**
TEL   0829 270 429
OPEN   By Appointment.

Specialise in repairing and restoring
antique barometers.
PROVIDE Home Inspections. Free
Estimates.
SPEAK TO Derek or Tina Rayment.
Member of BADA.

ANN & DEREK MASON
11 Redmire Road, Grangefield,
Stockton-on-Tees, **Cleveland TS18 4JR**
TEL   0642 614583
OPEN   9–7 Mon–Fri.

Specialise in restoring antique furniture.

PROVIDE Free estimates.
SPEAK TO Derek Mason
Will do on-site work within a 30-mile radius of Stockton.

FELIKS B. SADOWSKI
10 Chapel Street, Penzance, **Cornwall TR18 4AJ**
TEL   0736 63124
OPEN   10–5 Mon–Sat.

Specialise in restoring antique furniture including Boulle work and marquetry.
PROVIDE Home Inspections. Free Estimates. Chargeable Collection/Delivery Service.
SPEAK TO Feliks Sadowski.

A family business which spans three generations back to the beginning of the century.

ST. AUSTELL ANTIQUES CENTRE
(formerly The Furniture Store)
37/39 Truro Road, St. Austell, **Cornwall PL25 5JE**
TEL   0726 63178 or 0288 81548
OPEN   10–5 Mon–Sat or By
        Appointment.

Specialise in furniture restoration.
PROVIDE Home Inspections. Free Estimates. Free Local Collection/Delivery Service.
SPEAK TO Roger Nosworthy.
SEE Silver.

PETER STANTON
The Old Pottery, Chapel Hill, Truro, **Cornwall TR1 3BN**
TEL   0872 70262
OPEN   9–5 Mon–Fri.

Specialise in restoring 17th and 18th century furniture and upholstery.
PROVIDE Home Inspections. Free Estimates. Chargeable Collection/Delivery Service.
SPEAK TO Peter Stanton.

TUDOR ROSE DEVELOPMENTS
Court Cottage, Higher Porthpean, St. Austell, **Cornwall PL26 6AY**
TEL   0726 75653
OPEN   9–4 Mon–Fri.

Specialise in restoring English and some Continental furniture.
PROVIDE Home Inspections. Chargeable Estimates. Chargeable Collection/Delivery Service.
SPEAK TO Christopher Pascoe.

Also give restoration tuition.

PETER HALL & SON
Danes Road, Staveley, Kendal, **Cumbria LA8 9PL**
TEL   0539 821633
FAX   0539 821905
OPEN   9–5 Mon–Fri.

Specialise in restoring antique furniture, structural and inlay repair, repolishing, gilding, carving, marquetry, metalwork and traditional re-upholstery.
PROVIDE Home Inspections. Free Estimates. Chargeable Collection/Delivery Service.
SPEAK TO Jeremy Hall.

JOSEPH JAMES ANTIQUES
Corney Square, Penrith, **Cumbria CA11 7PX**
TEL   0768 62065
OPEN   9–12, 1.30–5.30 Mon–Sat; closed
        Wed.

Specialise in repairing antique furniture, French polishing and re-upholstering.
PROVIDE Home Inspections. Free Estimates. Free Local Collection/Delivery Service.
SPEAK TO Gordon Walker.

Also have soft furnishings workrooms.

THE OLD MAN ANTIQUES
Coniston, **Cumbria LA21 8DU**
TEL   05394 41389
OPEN   2–4 daily from Easter to 5th
       November. Phone calls advised
       during winter months.
Specialise in repairing and restoring
wheel (mercury) barometers.
SPEAK TO Ron or Yvonne Williams.

SHIRE ANTIQUES
The Post House, High Newton, Newton-
in-Carmel, Nr. Grange-Over-Sands,
Cumbria LA11 6JQ
TEL   05395 31431
OPEN   9.30–5 Mon, Wed–Sat; 10–4
       Sun; closed Tues.
Specialise in restoring 16th–18th century
furniture.
PROVIDE Home Inspections. Free
Estimates. Free Local
Collection/Delivery Service.
SPEAK TO Brian or Jean Shire.
It is best to telephone first.

R. UDALL
Merlin Cragg, Howgill, Sedbergh,
Cumbria LA10 5HU
TEL   05396 20719
OPEN   10–5 daily.
Specialise in restoring period furniture.
PROVIDE Free Estimates. Chargeable
Collection/Delivery Service.
SPEAK TO Mr. R. Udall.

CANE AND RUSH SEATING
50 Ashbourne Road, **Derbyshire
DE3 3AD**
TEL   0332 44363
OPEN   10–4 Mon–Fri.
Specialise in replacing cane and rush in
chairs, settees, bedheads. All patterns of
cane can be reproduced including single
set, double set, sunset patterns, blind

holes. Chairs which have been
upholstered because nobody could be
found to re-cane or rush them may be
restored to their original appearance.
PROVIDE Home Inspections, Free
Estimates.
SPEAK TO Joan Gilbert.

DERBYSHIRE CLOCKS
104 High Street West, Glossop,
Derbyshire SK13 8BB
TEL   0457 862677
OPEN   1–5 Mon–Sat, closed Tues; Sun
       1–4.30.
Specialise in restoring antique clocks and
barometers.
PROVIDE Home Inspections. Refundable
Estimates. Free Collection/Delivery
Service.
SPEAK TO Terence Peter Lees.

D. W. & J. E. FODDY
Derby Antique Centre, 11 Friargate,
Derby, **Derbyshire DE1 1BU**
TEL   0332 385002
OPEN   10–5.30 Mon–Sat.
Specialise in restoring antique furniture
and clock cases.
PROVIDE Home Inspections. Chargeable
Estimates. Free Collection/Delivery.
SPEAK TO Mr. Foddy.

MACLAREN CHAPPELL (RESTORATIONS) LTD
King Street, Bakewell, **Derbyshire
DE4 1DZ**
TEL   0629 812496
FAX   0629 814531
OPEN   9–6 Mon–Fri.
Specialise in restoring antique and other
furniture and bracket, longcase and
carriage clocks.
PROVIDE Home Inspections. Free
Estimates. Free Local
Collection/Delivery Service.

SPEAK TO W. N. Chappell.
Members of the Guild of Master
Craftsmen.
SEE Silver, Porcelain.

MELBOURNE HALL FURNITURE RESTORERS
The Old Saw Mill, Melbourne Hall Craft
Centre, Melbourne Hall, **Derbyshire
DE7 1EN**
TEL　　0332 864131
OPEN　　9–5 Mon–Fri; 10–5 Sat and 1.30–
　　　　5 Sun but phone first.
Specialise in furniture repairs including
hand polishing.
PROVIDE Home Inspections.
Free/Refundable Estimates.
Collection/Delivery Service.
SPEAK TO Neil Collumbell.

C. REYNOLDS
The Spindles, Tonge, Melbourne,
Derbyshire DE7 1BD
TEL　　0332 862609 and 0836 752602
OPEN　　By Appointment.
Specialise in restoring verge movement
watches 1780–1880.
PROVIDE Home Inspections. Chargeable
Estimates.
SPEAK TO Mr. T. Reynolds.

NIGEL F. THOMPSON
Antiques Warehouse, 25 Lightwood Rd,
Buxton, **Derbyshire**
TEL　　0298 871932
OPEN　　10–5 Mon–Sat.
Specialise in restoring brass and brass
and iron bedsteads and some furniture,
mainly Victorian mahogany and
Georgian oak, also re-upholstery,
re-caning and rushing.

PROVIDE Home Inspections.
Discretionary Estimates. Chargeable
Collection/Delivery Service.
SPEAK TO Nigel Thompson.

WATER LANE ANTIQUES
Water Lane, Bakewell, **Derbyshire
DE4 1EU**
TEL　　062981 4161
OPEN　　9.30–5 Mon–Sat.
Specialise in the restoration of antique
furniture.
PROVIDE Home Inspections. Free
Estimates. Free Collection/Delivery
Service
SPEAK TO Michael Pembery.

D. J. BENT
Stonecourt, Membland, Newton
Ferrers, Plymouth, **Devon PL8 1HP**
TEL　　0752 872 831
OPEN　　By Appointment.
Specialise in restoring antique English
and Continental furniture, particularly
oak, walnut and mahogany.
PROVIDE Home Inspections. Free
Estimates. Chargeable
Collection/Delivery Service.
SPEAK TO Mr. D. J. Bent.

Mr. Bent teaches furniture restoration
and is a member of BAFRA and UKIC.
This workshop is included on the register
of conservators maintained by the
Conservation Unit of the Museums and
Galleries Commission.

BRITANNIA RESTORATIONS
Old Britannia House, Castle Street,
Combe Martin, Nr. Ilfracombe, **Devon
EX34 0JF**
TEL　　0271 882887
OPEN　　9–5.30 Mon–Sat or By
　　　　Appointment.
Specialise in restoring traditional
Windsor chairs, farmhouse furnishings,
non–caustic strip and polish service,
brass and ironware.

PROVIDE Home Inspections. Free
Estimates. Chargeable
Collection/Delivery Service.
SPEAK TO Stephen Lloyd Malsom.
Member of Guild of Master Craftsmen.

RODERICK BUTLER
Marwood House, Honiton, **Devon
EX14 8PY**
TEL   0404 42169
OPEN   9.30–5.30 Mon–Sat.
Specialise in restoring antique furniture
and works of art.
PROVIDE Home Inspections. Free
Estimates. Chargeable
Collection/Delivery Service.
SPEAK TO Roderick Butler.

CLIVE & LESLEY COBB
Newhouse Farm, Bratton Fleming,
Barnstaple, **Devon EX31 4RT**
TEL   0598 710465
OPEN   9–5.30 Sun–Sat.
Specialise in restoring lacquer work,
chinoiserie, painted clock dials and
decorative painted artefacts. Also create
individual decorative items to
customers' requirements.
PROVIDE Home Inspections. Free
Estimates. Chargeable
Collection/Delivery Service.
SPEAK TO Clive or Lesley Cobb.

J. COLLINS & SON
63 High St, Bideford, **Devon EX39 2AN**
TEL   0237 473103
OPEN   9.30–5 Mon–Sat; closed Wed.
Specialise in restoring antique furniture.
PROVIDE Home Inspections. Free
Estimates. Free Local
Collection/Delivery Service.
SPEAK TO Mr. J. C. Biggs.
Established 1953.

LOVE'S FURNITURE
RESTORATIONS
The Workshop, South Street,
Axminster, **Devon EX13 5AD**
TEL   0297 35059
OPEN   8.30–5 Mon–Sat. Closed Wed.
Specialise in restoring and repairing
antique and grand furniture, French
polishing, rushing, caning and
re-upholstery.
PROVIDE Home Inspections. Free
Estimates. Chargeable
Collection/Delivery Service.
SPEAK TO Jamie Love.
Member of the Guild of Master
Craftsmen; the family has been trading
in Axminster since 1873.

MERTON ANTIQUES
Quicksilver Barn, Merton,
Okehampton, **Devon EX20 3DS**
TEL   08053 443
OPEN   8–5 Mon–Sat.
Specialise in restoring antique
barometers and furniture.
PROVIDE Home Inspections by
arrangement. Free Estimates.
Chargeable Collection/Delivery Service.
SPEAK TO Philip Collins.
This workshop is included on the register
of conservators maintained by the
Conservation Unit of the Museums and
Galleries Commission.

PETER MOORE
The Workshop, 56 Sherwell Lane,
Torquay, **Devon TQ2 6BE**
TEL   0803 605334
OPEN   8.30–5 Mon–Sat.
Specialise in restoring antique and solid
timber furniture.
PROVIDE Home Inspections. Free
Estimates. Chargeable
Collection/Delivery Service.
SPEAK TO Peter Moore.
Member of Guild of Master Craftsmen
and Guild of Woodworkers.

LAURIE PENMAN
Castle Workshop, 61 High St, Totnes,
Devon TQ9 5PB
TEL   0803 866344
OPEN   7am–10pm Mon–Sat; Sun
           telephone first.

Specialise in repairing and restoring clocks.

PROVIDE Home Inspections. Free Estimates.

SPEAK TO Laurie Penman.

Also provide workshop tuition and a correspondence course.

PETTICOMBE MANOR ANTIQUES
Petticombe Manor, Monkleigh,
Bideford, **Devon EX39 5JR**
TEL   0237 475605
OPEN   9–6 Sun–Sat.

Specialise in restoring antique furniture including cabinet work, French polishing and upholstery.

PROVIDE Home Inspections by arrangement. Free Estimates. Chargeable Collection/Delivery Service.

SPEAK TO Mr. O. Wilson.

TEMPUS FUGIT
16c Fore Street, Shaldon, Teignmouth,
Devon TQ14 0DE
TEL   0626 872752
OPEN   10–1, 2–5 Mon–Sat.

Specialise in repairing barometers, watches and clocks.

PROVIDE Home Inspections. Free Estimates. Usually Free Collection/Delivery Service.

SPEAK TO Roger Walkley.

Established 1982.

TONY VERNON
15 Follett Road, Topsham, **Devon**
EX3 0JP
TEL   0392 874635
OPEN   9–6 Mon–Fri.

Specialise in restoring and conserving antique English and Continental furniture. Do marquetry inlay, Boulle work, gilding, re-veneering and French polishing.

PROVIDE Home Inspections. Refundable Estimates. Chargeable Collection/Delivery Service.

SPEAK TO Tony Vernon.

LAURENCE G. WOOTTON
2 Church Street, South Brent, **Devon**
TQ10 9AB
TEL   0364 72553
OPEN   By Appointment (telephone
           between 9.30am–12.30pm).

Specialise in repairing clocks and watches.

PROVIDE Home Inspections.

SPEAK TO Laurence Wootton.

MICHAEL BARRINGTON
The Old Rectory, Warmwell,
Dorchester, **Dorset DT2 8HQ**
TEL   0305 852104
OPEN   8.30–5.30 or By Appointment.

Specialise in restoring antique furniture and associated metalwork, gilding, painting, marquetry, longcase clock cases, organ casework and pipe gilding.

PROVIDE Free Estimates Locally. Free/Chargeable Collection/Delivery Service.

SPEAK TO Michael Barrington.

Member of BAFRA.

SEE Collectors (Musical Instruments, Toys).

BLACKWOODS
805 Christchurch Road, Boscombe,
Bournemouth, **Dorset BH7 6AP**
TEL   0202 395467
OPEN   9–5 Mon–Fri.

Specialise in restoring antique English
furniture including marquetry, inlay,
carving, turning and gilding, also
upholstery and all types of polishing.
PROVIDE Home Inspections.
Free/Refundable Estimates. Free
Collection/Delivery Service.
SPEAK TO Richard Owen.

Members of BAFRA.

RICHARD BOLTON
Ash Tree Cottage, Whitecross,
Netherbury, Bridport, **Dorset DT6 5NH**
TEL   030 888 474
OPEN   8.30–6 Mon–Fri.

Specialise in restoring antique furniture.
PROVIDE Home Inspections. Free
Estimates. Free Collection/Delivery
Service.
SPEAK TO Richard Bolton.

Member of BAFRA.

PETER BRAZIER
Nash Court Farmhouse, Marnhull,
Sturminster Newton, **Dorset DT10 1JZ**
TEL   0258 820255
OPEN   8.30–5.30 Mon–Fri or By
       Appointment.

Specialise in all aspects of furniture
restoration and finishing excluding
gilding. Also runs a non-ferrous foundry
where missing mounts can be cast using
the lost wax method.
PROVIDE Home Inspections. Free
Estimates. Free Local
Collection/Delivery Service.
SPEAK TO Peter Brazier.

Mr. Brazier is West Dean qualified and
a member of BAFRA.

D. J. JEWELLERY
166–168 Ashley Road, Parkstone, Poole,
Dorset BH14 9BY
TEL   0202 745148
OPEN   9.30–5 Mon–Sat.

Specialise in repairing antique clocks.
PROVIDE Home Inspections. Free
Estimates. Chargeable
Collection/Delivery Service.
SPEAK TO Dennis O Sullivan.
SEE Silver.

GOOD HOPE ANTIQUES
2 Hogshill Street, Beaminster, **Dorset
DT8 3AE**
TEL   0308 862119
OPEN   9.30–5 Mon–Sat; closed Wed.

Specialise in restoring barometers and
clocks, especially longcase, bracket and
English wall clocks.
PROVIDE Chargeable Estimates.
Chargeable Collection/Delivery Service.
SPEAK TO David Beney.

MRS. CATHERINE MATHEW
Kiwi Cottage, Maperton Road,
Charlton Horethorne, Sherborne, **Dorset
DT9 4NT**
TEL   096 322 595
OPEN   9–6 Mon–Fri or By
       Appointment.

Specialise in repairing furniture,
cleaning, regilding, cane seating.
PROVIDE Home Inspections. Free
Estimates. Free Collection/Delivery
Service.
SPEAK TO Catherine Mathew.
SEE Porcelain, Oil Paintings.

G. A. MATTHEWS
The Cottage Workshop, 174
Christchurch Road, Parley Cross,
Wimborne, **Dorset BH22 8SS**
TEL   0202 572665
OPEN   9–5 Mon–Fri.

Specialise in restoring antique furniture, all types of finishing and both modern and antique cabinet-making.
PROVIDE Home Inspections. Free Estimates. Chargeable Collection/Delivery Service.
SPEAK TO G. A. Matthews

PROVIDE Home Inspections. Free Estimates. Chargeable Collection/Delivery Service
SPEAK TO Maurice Yarham
Craft Member of British Horological Institute.
SEE Collectors (Mechanical Music).

OLD BARN ANTIQUES CO.
Flamberts, Trent, Sherborne, **Dorset DT9 4SS**
TEL   0935 850648
OPEN   By Appointment.
Specialise in restoring and repairing 18th and 19th century furniture including upholstery. Individual items made to order.
PROVIDE Home Inspections. Free Estimates. Free/Chargeable Collection/Delivery Service.
SPEAK TO Geoffrey Mott.

THE COLLECTOR
Douglas House, 23–25 The Bank, Barnard Castle, **Durham DL12 8PH**
TEL   0833 37783
OPEN   10–5 or By Appointment.
Specialise in restoring clocks, early oak and period furniture including metalwork.
PROVIDE Home Inspections. Refundable Estimates. Chargeable Collection/Delivery Service.
SPEAK TO Robert Jordan or Paul Hunter.
Also provide a full design service.

TOLPUDDLE ANTIQUE RESTORERS
The Stables, Tolpuddle, Dorchester, **Dorset DT2 7HF**
TEL   0305 848739
OPEN   9–6 Mon–Fri; 12–5 Sat.
Specialise in restoring antique furniture, clocks and barometers.
PROVIDE Home Inspections. Free Estimates. Free Collection/Delivery Service.
BAFRA.

MAURICE YARHAM
Holly Cottage, Birdsmoorgate, Paynes Downe, Nr. Bridport, **Dorset DT6 5PL**
TEL   02977 377
OPEN   7–7 Mon–Fri.
Specialise in repairing, restoring and conserving antique clocks, particularly bracket and longcase clocks. He will also repair turret (stable) clocks.

CLIVE BEARDALL
104B High Street, Maldon, **Essex CM9 7ET**
TEL   0621 857890
FAX   0621 857565
OPEN   8–6 Mon–Fri; 8–1 Sat.
Specialise in restoring period furniture including marquetry, carving, gilding, leather desk lining, traditional hand French polishing and wax finishing. Does rush and cane seating.
PROVIDE Home Inspections. Free/Chargeable Estimates. Free/Chargeable Collection/Delivery Service.
SPEAK TO Clive Beardall.
Member of BAFRA and UKIC. This workshop is included on the register of conservators maintained by the Conservation Unit of the Museums and Galleries Commission.

S. BOND & SON
14/15 North Hill, Colchester, **Essex**
CO1 1DZ
TEL   0206 572925
OPEN   9–5 Mon–Sat.
Specialise in restoring antique and
Victorian furniture.
PROVIDE Home Inspections. Free
Estimates. Free Local
Collection/Delivery Service..
SPEAK TO Robert Bond
This family firm has been established 140
years and is run by the fifth generation.
SEE Oil Paintings.

DAVID JEAN & JOHN ANTIQUES
587 London Road, Westcliff, **Essex**
SS0 9PQ
TEL   0702 339106
FAX   0268 560563
OPEN   10–5 Mon–Sat; closed Wed.
Specialise in restoring Victorian and
Edwardian furniture. Also undertake
clock and watch repairs.
PROVIDE Home Inspections. Refundable
Estimates. Free Collection/Delivery
Service.
SPEAK TO David Howard.

A. DUNN & SON
The White House, 8 Wharf Road,
Chelmsford, **Essex CM3 4XL**
TEL   0245 354452
FAX   0245 494991
OPEN   7–5 Mon–Fri; Sat a.m. telephone
         first.
Specialise in restoring antique furniture
of all periods especially marquetry and
Boulle. Will also make new panels.
PROVIDE Home Inspections. Free Local
Estimates. Collection/Delivery Service
available.
SPEAK TO Bob Dunn.

The third generation firm was started in
1896. They made the marquetry panels
for the VSOE Orient Express and liners
including the *Queen Mary* and *Queen
Elizabeth.*

FORGE STUDIO WORKSHOPS
Stour Street, Manningtree, **Essex**
CO11 1BE
TEL   0206 396222
OPEN   8.30–5 Mon–Fri; 9–12 Sat.
Specialise in restoring fine antique
furniture, bespoke cabinet-making,
chair matching, church and heraldic
carving.
PROVIDE Home Inspections.
Free/Chargeable Estimates. Chargeable
Collection/Delivery Service.
SPEAK TO Dick Patterson.
Member of BAFRA.

TERRY HILLIARD
The Barn, Master Johns, Thoby Lane,
Mountnessing, Brentwood, **Essex**
CM15 0JY
TEL   0277 354717
OPEN   By Appointment.
Specialise in restoring gilded furniture,
mirror frames and carving and gilding.
PROVIDE Home Inspections. Free
Estimates. Free Collection/Delivery
Service.
SPEAK TO Terry Hilliard.
Member of the Guild of Master
Craftsmen.
SEE Oil Paintings.

LITTLEBURY ANTIQUES
58–60 Fairycroft Road, Saffron Walden,
Essex CB10 1LZ
TEL   0799 27961
FAX   0799 27961
OPEN   8.30–5.15 Mon–Fri; Sat By
         Appointment.
Specialise in restoring furniture, clocks
and barometers of all periods.

PROVIDE Home Inspections. Free
Estimates. Free/Chargeable
Collection/Delivery Service..
SPEAK TO N. H. D'Oyly.

GREVILLE MARCHANT
Coach House (Courtyard), Market
Place, Abridge, **Essex RM4 1UA**
TEL   0992 812996
FAX   0992 814300
OPEN   8.30–6 Mon to Fri; 10–5.30 Sun.
Specialise in restoring all types of
furniture, especially chairs. Copies made
to match existing pieces; also
architectural joinery.
PROVIDE Home Inspections. Free
Estimates. Free Collection/Delivery
Service.
SPEAK TO Greville Marchant.
Mr. Marchant holds a Licentiateship to
the City & Guilds.

MILLERS ANTIQUES KELVEDON
46 High Street, Kelvedon, Colchester,
Essex CO5 9AG
TEL   0376 570098
FAX   0376 572186
OPEN   9–5.30 Mon–Fri; 10–4 Sat.
Specialise in restoring antique furniture,
French polishing, carving and gilding.
Also do desk and table top re-lining,
upholstery and bespoke furniture
making.
PROVIDE Home Inspections. Free
Estimates. Chargeable
Collection/Delivery Service.
SPEAK TO Mr. M. J. Woolford.

ANTONY PALMER ANTIQUES
169 St. Mary's Lane, Upminster, **Essex**
TEL   04022 26620
OPEN   9.30–5.30 Tues–Sat.
Specialise in repairing and restoring
Victorian furniture and clocks.

PROVIDE Home Inspections. Free
Estimates. Free/Chargeable
Collection/Delivery Service.
SPEAK TO Antony Palmer.

SMALLCOMBE CLOCKS
Gee House, Globe Industrial Estate,
Rectory Road, Grays, **Essex RM17 6ST**
TEL   0375 379980
FAX   0375 390286
OPEN   8.30–5 Mon–Fri.
Specialise in repairing and restoring
longcase clocks.
PROVIDE Home Inspections. Free
Estimates. Free /Chargeable
Collection/Delivery Service.
SPEAK TO Brett Smallcombe or Tony
Holland.

TURPINS ANTIQUES
4 Stoney Lane, Thaxted, **Essex**
TEL   0371 830495 or 0860 883302
OPEN   10–5 Mon–Sat.
Specialise in restoring 18th century
English furniture.
PROVIDE Home Inspections. Free
Estimates. Chargeable
Collection/Delivery Service.
SPEAK TO John Braund.

WEDMID & SIMPSON LTD
232–234 High Street, Epping, **Essex**
CM16 7PW
TEL   0378 560309
FAX   0378 73027
OPEN   10–5.30 Sun–Sat.
Specialise in restoring furniture and
French polishing.
PROVIDE Home Inspections. Free
Estimates. Free Collection/Delivery
Service.
SPEAK TO Mr. Levan.

KEITH BAWDEN
Mews Workshop, Montpellier Retreat,
Cheltenham, **Gloucestershire GL50 2XG**
TEL   0242 230320
OPEN   7–4.30 Mon–Fri.

Specialise in conserving and restoring
antique furniture, upholstery and
clocks.

PROVIDE Free Estimates. Home
Inspections. Local Collection/Delivery
Service.

SPEAK TO Keith Bawden

SEE Oil Paintings, Porcelain, Silver.

C. A. COOK ANTIQUE FURNITURE
RESTORATION
Gloucester Antique Centre, 1 Severn
Road, Gloucester, **Gloucestershire
GL1 2LE**
TEL   0452 529716
FAX   0452 307161
OPEN   9.30–5 Mon–Sat; 12–5 Sun.

Specialise in restoring Georgian and
Regency furniture as well as marquetry.

PROVIDE Home Inspections. Free
Estimates. Free Collection/Delivery
Service.

SPEAK TO C. A. Cook.

WILLIAM COOK CABINET
MAKER
Primrose Cottage, 11 Northfield Road,
Tetbury, **Gloucestershire GL8 8HD**
TEL   0666 502877
OPEN   9–5 Mon–Fri.

Specialise in restoring clockcases
including gilding.

PROVIDE Free Estimates.

SPEAK TO William or Ruth Cook.

FORUM ANTIQUES
20 West Way, Cirencester,
Gloucestershire GL7 1JA
TEL   0285 658406
OPEN   9–5.30 Mon–Sat.

Specialise in restoring 17th century oak
furniture.

PROVIDE Home Inspections. Free
Estimates. Free Collection/Delivery
Service.

SPEAK TO Weston Mitchell.

G. M. S. RESTORATIONS
The Workshops (rear of Bell Passage
Antiques), High Street, Wickwar,
Gloucestershire GL12 8NP
TEL   0454 294251
FAX   0454 294251
OPEN   8–5 Mon–Fri.

Specialise in restoring furniture,
polishing, carving, gilding and
traditional upholstery.

PROVIDE Home Inspections. Refundable
Estimates. Chargeable
Collection/Delivery Service.

SPEAK TO Mr. G. M. St.George-Stacey.

Members of LAPADA, Association of
Master Upholsterers, Guild of Master
Craftsmen, Guild of Woodcarvers,
Guild of Antique Dealers and Restorers.

SEE Oil Paintings.

MRS. JANET GIBBS
The Hope, Ampney St.Peter,
Cirencester, **Gloucestershire GL7 5SH**
TEL   0285 851227
OPEN   By Appointment.

Specialise in chair caning and rushing.

PROVIDE Home Inspections. Free
Estimates.

SPEAK TO Janet Gibbs.

ALAN HESSEL
The Old Town Workshop, St George's
Close, Moreton in Marsh,
Gloucestershire GL56 0LP
TEL 0608 50026
OPEN 8–5 Mon–Fri or By
Appointment.
Specialise in restoring 17th–early 19th
century English furniture, including
marquetry, parquetry and oyster work
with an emphasis on patina retention.
PROVIDE Home Inspections. Free
Estimates. Free/Chargeable
Collection/Delivery Service.
SPEAK TO Alan Hessel.
Member of BAFRA and UKIC.

DONALD HUNTER
The Old School Room, Shipton Oliffe,
Cheltenham, **Gloucestershire GL54 4JQ**
TEL 0242 820755
OPEN 8–6 Mon–Fri.
Specialise in carving, gilding and painted
finishes to mirror frames, lacquer work
and antique furniture.
PROVIDE Home Inspections.
Free/Chargeable Estimates.
Collection/Delivery Service by
arrangement.
SPEAK TO Donald Hunter.
Member of BAFRA.

ANDREW LELLIOTT
6 Tetbury Hill, Avening, Tetbury,
Gloucestershire GL8 8LT
TEL 045 383 5783
OPEN By Appointment.
Specialise in restoring 18th century
English furniture including walnut,
mahogany, satinwood and clock cases.
PROVIDE Home Inspections. Free
Estimates. Free Collection/Delivery
Service.
SPEAK TO Andrew Lelliott.

Member of BAFRA. This workshop is
included on the register of conservators
maintained by the Conservation Unit of
the Museums and Galleries
Commission.

A. J. PONSFORD ANTIQUES
51–53 Dollar Street, Cirencester,
Gloucestershire GL7 2AS
TEL 0285 652355
OPEN 8.30–5.30 Mon–Fri.
Specialise in restoring antique furniture
and upholstery.
PROVIDE Home Inspections. Free
Estimates. Free Collection/Delivery
Service.
SPEAK TO A. J. Ponsford.
SEE Oil Paintings.

ANGUS STEWART
Bourton Industrial Park, Bourton-on-
the-Water, Nr. Cheltenham,
Gloucestershire GL54 2HQ
TEL 0451 21611
OPEN 8–5.30 Mon–Fri.
Specialise in restoring English and
Continental furniture, lacquer work,
carving, painted finishes, water gilding,
veneering, marquetry.
PROVIDE Home Inspections. Free
Estimates. Free Collection/Delivery
Service.
SPEAK TO Angus Stewart.
Member of BAFRA.

UEDELHOVEN AND CAMPION
Post Office, Gretton, Cheltenham,
Gloucestershire GL54 5EP
TEL 0242 602306
OPEN 9–5.30 Mon–Fri; Sat a.m.
Specialise in restoring furniture
including Boulle work, brass inlays,
turning. Also make up a chair to match
a set or another piece of furniture.

79

PROVIDE Home Inspections. Free
Estimates. Free/Chargeable
Collection/Delivery Service.
SPEAK TO Mr. Uedelhoven or Mr.
Campion.

GUY BAGSHAW
Plain Farm, Old Dairy, Tisted, Alton,
Hampshire GU34 3RT
TEL   0420 58362
OPEN   8–6 Mon–Fri or By
       Appointment.
Specialise in 18th and early 19th century
English furniture copy pieces.
PROVIDE Home Inspections.
Free/Chargeable Estimates. Free Local
Collection/Delivery Service.
SPEAK TO Guy Bagshaw.
Member of BAFRA. This workshop is
included on the register of conservators
maintained by the Conservation Unit of
the Museums and Galleries
Commission.

BRYAN CLISBY ANTIQUE
CLOCKS
Andwells Antiques, The Row, Hartley
Wintney, **Hampshire RG27 8NY**
TEL   025126 2305
OPEN   9–5.30 Mon–Fri; 9.30–5.30 Sat.
Specialise in restoring antique clocks and
barometers.
PROVIDE Home Inspections. Free
Estimates. Chargeable
Collection/Delivery Service.
SPEAK TO Bryan Clisby.

DYER AND FOLLETT LTD
Coward Road, Alverstoke, Gosport,
Hampshire PO12 2LD
TEL   0705 582204
OPEN   9–12.45, 2.15–5.30 Mon–Fri;
       9.15–12.45, 2.15–5 Sat.
Specialise in restoring of antique English
and Continental furniture, French
polishing, upholstery.

PROVIDE Local Home Inspections.
Refundable Estimates, Free Local
Collection/Delivery Service.
SPEAK TO Mr. E. A. Dyer.

EVANS & EVANS
40 West Street, Alresford, **Hampshire
SO24 9AU**
TEL   0962 732170
OPEN   9–1, 2–5 Fri–Sat; Mon–Thur By
       Appointment.
Specialise in restoring good English and
French clocks.
PROVIDE Home Inspections. Refundable
Estimates. Free Collection/Delivery
Service.
SPEAK TO David or Noel Evans.

A. FLEMING (SOUTHSEA) LTD
The Clock Tower, Castle Road,
Southsea, **Hampshire PO5 3DE**
TEL   0705 822934
OPEN   8.30–5 Mon–Fri; 8.30–1 Sat.
Specialise in a full restoration service for
antique furniture, as well as upholstery.
PROVIDE Home Inspections. Free
Estimates. Free Collection/Delivery
Service.
SPEAK TO A. Fleming.
This family firm was founded in 1908
and is now run by the third generation.

JOHN MICHAEL FOY
'Hilkrest', 10 Little Park Avenue,
Bedhampton, Havant, **Hampshire
PO9 3QY**
TEL   0705 474439
OPEN   9–6 Mon–Fri.
Specialise in extensive, sympathetic
restoration of most antique house
clocks, particularly English bracket and
longcase clocks. Services include wheel
and pinion cutting, dial resilvering, hand
manufacture. Also work on barometers.

PROVIDE Home Inspections. Free
Estimates. Free/Chargeable
Collection/Delivery Service.
SPEAK TO John Michael Foy.

Mr. Foy is a CMBHI, holds a West Dean
Diploma, and is a member of the Guild
of Master Craftsmen and the A.H.S.

GAYLORDS ANTIQUES
75 West Street, Titchfield, Fareham,
Hampshire PO14 4DG
TEL   0329 43402
OPEN   10–4 Mon–Sat.

Specialise in restoring antique furniture,
French polishing and upholstery.
PROVIDE Home Inspections. Free
Estimates. Free Collection/Delivery
Service.
SPEAK TO Mr. Hebbard.

DAVID C. E. LEWRY
'Wychelms', 66 Gorran Avenue,
Rowner, Gosport, **Hampshire
PO13 0NF**
TEL   0329 286901
OPEN   By Appointment.

Specialise in conserving and restoring
17th and 18th century furniture.

PROVIDE Home Inspections. Refundable
Estimates. Free/ Chargeable
Collection/Delivery Service.
SPEAK TO David Lewry.

Mr. Lewry is West Dean trained and is
the current Chairman of BAFRA.

**GERALD MARSH ANTIQUE
CLOCKS LTD.**
32A The Square, Winchester, **Hampshire
SO23 9EX**
TEL   0962 844443
OPEN   9.30–5 Mon–Sat.

Specialise in restoring antique English
and French clocks, watches and
barometers.

PROVIDE Home Inspections. Free
Estimates. Free Collection/Delivery
Service.
SPEAK TO Gerald Marsh.

Member of Worshipful Company of
Clockmakers, Craftsman of British
Horological Institute, Member of
NAWCC (USA) and BADA.
SEE **Oxfordshire** (opens January 1992).

A. W. PORTER
High St, Hartley Wintney, Nr.
Basingstoke, **Hampshire RG27 8NY**
TEL   025 126 2676
FAX   025 126 2064
OPEN   9–5.30 Mon–Fri; 9.30–5 Sat.

Specialise in restoring antique clocks,
watches and barometers.

PROVIDE Home Inspections. Free
Estimates. Chargeable
Collection/Delivery Service.
SPEAK TO Mr. Porter.

Established 1844.
SEE Silver.

**HUMPHREY SLADDEN FINE
FURNITURE RESTORATION**
Yard House, South Harting, Petersfield,
Hampshire GU31 5NS
TEL   0730 825339
OPEN   8–4.30 Mon–Fri; 8–12 Sat.

Specialise in restoring 18th and early
19th century English furniture, cabinetwork, veneering, polishing, turning.

PROVIDE Home Inspections by
arrangement. Free/Chargeable
Estimates.
SPEAK TO H. P. Sladden or John Birkett.

Mr. Sladden is currently a tutor at West
Dean.
Although the postal address is
Hampshire, Harting is actually in West
Sussex.

MR. D. J. SMITH
34 Silchester Road, Pamber Heath, Nr.
Basingstoke, **Hampshire RG26 6EF**
TEL   0734 700595
OPEN   8–6 Mon–Sat or By
            Appointment.

Specialise in restoration and
reproduction of fine 18th century carved
and giltwood furniture. Fine carving in
wood and oil or water gilding and
distressing.
PROVIDE Local Home Inspections. Free
Estimates. Free Local
Collection/Delivery Service.
SPEAK TO Douglas Smith.

THE TANKERDALE WORKSHOP
Tankerdale Farm, Steep Marsh,
Petersfield, **Hampshire GU32 2BH**
TEL   0730 893839
FAX   0730 894523
OPEN   8–6 Mon–Fri.

Specialise in conserving and restoring
furniture including carving, gilding,
lacquer work, japanning and
cabinetmaking.
PROVIDE Home Inspections. Refundable
Estimates. Chargeable
Collection/Delivery Service.
SPEAK TO John Hartley.

BEARWOOD MODELS
20 Westminster Road, Malvern Wells,
Hereford & Worcester WR14 4EF
TEL   0684 568977
OPEN   By Appointment.

Specialise in repairing and restoring old
clocks.
PROVIDE Free Estimates.
SPEAK TO R. W. Chester-Lamb.
SEE Collectors (Toys).

I. & J. L. BROWN LTD
58 Commercial Road, Hereford,
Hereford & Worcester HR1 2BP
TEL   0432 58895
FAX   0432 275338
OPEN   9–5.30 Mon–Sat.

Specialise in restoring English country
and French provincial furniture. Also
undertake chair rush work.
PROVIDE Free/Chargeable Estimates.
Free/Chargeable Collection/Delivery
Service.
SPEAK TO Ian Brown.
SEE **London SW6**.

HANSEN CHARD ANTIQUES
126 High Street, Pershore, **Hereford &
Worcester WR10 1EA**
TEL   0386 553423
OPEN   10–5 Tues, Wed, Fri, Sat or By
            Appointment.

Specialise in restoring clocks and
barometers.
PROVIDE Home Inspections. Free
Estimates. Free Local
Collection/Delivery Service.
SPEAK TO P. W. Ridler.
Member of BHI.

JENNINGS & JENNINGS
30 Bridge Street, Leominster, **Hereford
& Worcester HR6 9JQ**
TEL   05448 586
OPEN   By Appointment.

Specialise in conserving and restoring
gilded items including furniture and
mirror frames.
PROVIDE Home Inspections. Free
Estimates. Free/Chargeable
Collection/Delivery Service.
SPEAK TO Sabina Jennings.
SEE Oil Paintings.

H. W. KEIL LTD
Tudor House, Broadway, **Hereford &
Worcester WR12 7DP**
TEL   0386 852408
OPEN   9.15–12.45, 2.15–5.30 Mon–Sat.
       Closed Thur p.m.
Specialise in restoring 17th, 18th and
sometimes 20th century furniture mainly
in oak and mahogany.
PROVIDE Refundable Estimates. Free
Local Collection/Delivery Service.
SPEAK TO P. J. W. Keil.

KIMBER AND SON
6 Lower Howsell Road, Malvern Link,
Hereford & Worcester WR14 1EF
TEL   0684 574339
OPEN   8.30–1, 2–5 Mon–Fri; 9–12.30
       Sat.
Specialise in restoring fine 18th and 19th
century furniture.
PROVIDE Home Inspections. Free
Estimates. Free Collection/Delivery
Service.
SPEAK TO Mr. E. M. Kimber.

MALVERN STUDIOS
56 Cowleigh Road, Malvern, **Hereford
& Worcester WR14 1QD**
TEL   0684 574913
OPEN   9–5 Mon–Thur. 9–4.45 Fri, Sat.
Specialise in restoring antique furniture,
hand polishing, Boulle and gilt work.
PROVIDE Home Inspections. Refundable
Estimates. Chargeable
Collection/Delivery Service.
SPEAK TO Mr. L. M. Hall.
Members of BAFRA and UKIC. This
workshop is included on the register of
conservators maintained by the
Conservation Unit of the Museums and
Galleries Commission.

MERIDIEN ANTIQUES
41 Upper Tything, Worcester, **Hereford
and Worcester WR1 1JT**
TEL   0905 29014
OPEN   9–5.30 Mon–Sat.
Specialise in restoring antique furniture,
particularly dining tables and desks.
Also do traditional French polishing and
upholstery work.
PROVIDE Home Inspections. Free
Estimates. Free Collection/Delivery
Service.
SPEAK TO Robert Hubbard.

NEIL POSTONS RESTORATIONS
29 South Street, Leominster, **Hereford &
Worcester HR6 8JQ**
TEL   0568 616677
OPEN   8.30–5.30 Mon–Fri.
Specialise in restoring period furniture,
carving, tooling, carcase work, French
polishing, re-leathering desk tops,
PROVIDE Home Inspections. Free Local
Estimates. Chargeable
Collection/Delivery Service.
SPEAK TO Neil Postons.

WOODLAND FINE ART
16 The Square, Alvechurch, **Hereford &
Worcester B48 7LA**
TEL   021 445 5886
OPEN   10–6 Mon–Sat.
Specialise in restoring furniture.
PROVIDE Home Inspections. Free
Estimates. Free Collection/Delivery
Service.
SPEAK TO C. J. Haynes.
SEE Oil Paintings.

BECKWITH & SON
St. Nicholas Hall, St. Andrew Street,
Hertford, **Hertfordshire SG14 1HZ**
TEL   0992 582079
OPEN   9–1, 2–5.30 Mon–Sat.

Specialise in restoring antique English furniture, cabinet-making and polishing. They also restore English and French clocks.

PROVIDE Home Inspections. Chargeable Estimates. Free Local Collection/

Delivery Service.
SPEAK TO G. Gray.
SEE Oil Paintings, Porcelain.

CENTRE OF RESTORATION AND ARTS
11–15 Victoria Street, St. Albans, **Hertfordshire AL1 3JJ**
TEL   0727 51555
FAX   0727 811508
OPEN   8.30–5.30 Mon–Fri.

Specialise in chair caning.

PROVIDE Local Home Inspections. Free/Chargeable Estimates. Chargeable Collection/Delivery Service.
SPEAK TO Paul Roe.

THE CLOCK SHOP
161 Victoria Street, St. Albans, **Hertfordshire AL1 3TA**
TEL   0727 56633
OPEN   10.30–6.30 Mon–Fri; 10.30–4 Sat. Closed Thur.

Specialise in restoring antique and modern clocks, watches and barometers.

PROVIDE Free Estimates. Chargeable Collection/Delivery Service.
SPEAK TO Mr. P. E. Setterfield.

COUNTRY CLOCKS
3 Pendley Bridge Cottages, Tring Station, Tring, **Hertfordshire HP23 5QU**
TEL   044282 5090
OPEN   By Appointment.

Specialise in restoring antique clocks including movements, dials and cases. No watch repairs.

PROVIDE Home Inspections. Free Estimates. Free Local Collection/Delivery Service.
SPEAK TO Terence Cartmell.

FARRELLY ANTIQUE RESTORATION
The Long Barn, 50 High Street, Tring, **Hertfordshire HP23 5AG**
TEL   0442 891905
OPEN   9–4 Mon–Fri.

Specialise in restoring cabinets and chairs, carving, gilding, upholstery, polishing.

PROVIDE Home Inspections. Free Estimates. Chargeable Collection/Delivery Service.
SPEAK TO Paul Farrelly.

W. B. GATWARD & SON LTD
20 Market Place, Hitchin, **Hertfordshire SG5 1DU**
TEL   0462 434273
OPEN   9.15–5.15 Mon–Sat, closed Wed.

Specialise in repairing and restoring antique clocks and watches.

PROVIDE Home Inspections locally. Free Estimates. Chargeable Collection/Delivery Service. Speak to Miss Gatward or Mr. Hunter.
SEE Silver.

HOWARD ANTIQUE CLOCKS
33 Whitehorse Street, Baldock, **Hertfordshire SG7 6QF**
TEL   0462 892385
OPEN   9.30–5 Tues–Sat.

Specialise in restoring and repairing antique clocks.

PROVIDE Home Inspections. Free Estimates. Free Local Collection/Delivery Service.
SPEAK TO Mr. D. Howard.

Mr. Howard is a CMBHI.

CHARLES PERRY RESTORATIONS LTD
Praewood Farm, Hemel Hempstead Road, St Albans, **Hertfordshire AL3 6AA**
TEL   0727 53487
FAX   0727 46668
OPEN   Mon–Fri 8.30–6; By Appointment Sat.
Specialise in furniture restoration and allied trades including gilding, carving, polishing, marquetry, lacquerwork, clocks, marble, traditional upholstery, caning and rushing and expert advice and reports to clients intending to purchase at auction.
PROVIDE Home Inspections. Free Estimates. Chargeable Collection/Delivery Service.
SPEAK TO John Carr.

PHILLIPS OF HITCHIN
The Manor House, Hitchin, **Hertfordshire SG5 1JW**
TEL   0462 432067
FAX   0462 459405
OPEN   9–5.30 Mon–Sat.
Specialise in restoring English and Continental furniture.
PROVIDE Home Inspections. Free/Chargeable Estimates. Chargeable Collection/Delivery Service.
SPEAK TO Jerome Phillips.
SEE Display.

GRAHAM PORTER
Graham Porter Antiques, 31 Whitehorse Street, Baldock, **Hertfordshire SG7 6QF**
TEL   0462 895351
FAX   0462 892711
OPEN   9.30–5 Mon–Sat; 11–4 Sun.
Specialise in restoring antique furniture, especially country pieces and period pine.
PROVIDE Home Inspections. Collection/Delivery Service.
SPEAK TO Graham Porter.

ST. OUEN ANTIQUES LTD
Vintage Corner, Old Cambridge Road, Puckeridge, **Hertfordshire SG11 1SA**
TEL   0920 821336
FAX   0920 822877
OPEN   10–5 Mon–Sat.
Specialise in restoring 18th and 19th century English, Continental and gilded furniture, 19th century paintings.
PROVIDE Home Inspections. Refundable Estimates. Chargeable Collection/Delivery Service.
SPEAK TO Tim or John Blake.
SEE Oil Paintings.

TRACY'S FRENCH POLISHING CONTRACTORS
4 Station Mews, Station Close, Potters Bar, **Hertfordshire AL9 7RL**
TEL   0707 52144
FAX   0707 45153
OPEN   8–5 Mon–Fri.
Specialise in all aspects of original hand-rubbed French polishing and wood-finishing.
PROVIDE Home Inspections. Free Estimates. Free Collection/Delivery Service.
SPEAK TO Susan Tracy.
They prefer to carry out their work in situ.

VICTOR WHINES
29 River Close, Waltham Cross, **Hertfordshire EN8 7QR**
TEL   0992 712246
OPEN   9–5.30 Mon–Fri.
Specialise in restoring antique painted furniture and Chinese lacquer. Also do graining, marbling and gilding.

PROVIDE Home Inspections. Free
Estimates.
SPEAK TO Victor Whines.

WREN-OVATIONS
8 Hemel Hempstead Road, Redbourn,
Hertfordshire AL3 7NL
TEL   0923 260666
OPEN   8–6 Mon–Fri.

Specialise in restoring antique and
modern furniture, French polishing and
spray finishes.

PROVIDE Home Inspections. Free
Estimates. Free Local Collection/
Delivery Service.
SPEAK TO Barbara Murphy or David
Withers.

---

55 ANTIQUES
55–57 Spring Bank, Hull, **North
Humberside HU3 1AG**
TEL   0482 224510
OPEN   9–6 Mon–Sat.

Specialise in restoring antique furniture,
garden furniture and papier mâché.

PROVIDE Home Inspections. Estimates.
Collection/Delivery Service by
arrangement.
SPEAK TO Gerald Etherington.

If shop is closed the owner can be
contacted at No. 57.

OLD ROPERY ANTIQUES
East Street, Kilham, Nr. Driffield, **North
Humberside YO25 0ST**
TEL   026282 233
OPEN   9.30–5 Mon–Sat.

Specialise in restoring antique clocks and
furniture.

PROVIDE Home Inspections. Chargeable
Estimates. Chargeable
Collection/Delivery Service.
SPEAK TO John Butterfield.

SEE Collectors (Scientific Instruments).

ADRIAN J. BLACK
36A Freeman Street, Grimsby, **South
Humberside DN32 7AG**
TEL   0472 824823 and 355668
OPEN   By Appointment.

Specialise in restoring English antique
furniture and cabinet-making.

PROVIDE Home Inspections. Free
Estimates. Chargeable
Collection/Delivery Service.
SPEAK TO Adrian Black.

ROBIN FOWLER (PERIOD
CLOCKS)
The Manor House, Great Coates,
Grimsby, **South Humberside DN37 9NW**
TEL   0472 883264
OPEN   By Appointment.

Specialise in restoring antique clocks and
barometers. He also supplies and
restores all types of turret clocks.

PROVIDE Home Inspections. Free
Estimates. Free Collection/Delivery
Service.
SPEAK TO Robin Fowler.

Work guaranteed 5 years in case of
spring-driven movements and 10 years
for weight-driven movements.

ANTIQUE RESTORATIONS
The Old Wheelwright's Shop, Brasted
Forge, Brasted, Westerham, **Kent
TN16 1JL**
TEL   0959 563863
FAX   0959 561262
OPEN   9–5 Mon–Fri; 10–1 Sat.

Specialise in restoring 18th century
furniture, longcase and bracket clocks,
brass castings.

PROVIDE Refundable Estimates. Free
Collection/Delivery Service.
SPEAK TO Raymond Konyn.

Member of BAFRA.

ROBERT COLEMAN
The Oasthouse, Three Chimneys,
Biddenden, **Kent TN27 8LW**
TEL   0580 291520
OPEN   By Appointment.

Specialise in restoring mahogany and
walnut English furniture.

PROVIDE Home Inspections. Free
Estimates. Free Collection/Delivery
Service.
SPEAK TO Robert Coleman.
Member of BAFRA and the Guild of
Master Craftsmen.

FORGE ANTIQUES & RESTORATION
Rye Road, Sandhurst, Hawkhurst, **Kent
TN18 5JG**
TEL   0580 850308 and 850665
OPEN   9–5 daily.

Specialise in repairing and polishing
furniture, wood turning, carving,
veneering.

PROVIDE Home Inspections. Free
Estimates. Chargeable
Collection/Delivery Service.
SPEAK TO James Nesfield.

GILTWOOD RESTORATION
71 Bower Mount Road, Maidstone, **Kent
ME16 8AS**
TEL   0622 752273
OPEN   9–6 Mon–Fri.

Specialise in restoring fine gilded
furniture, frames and architectural
ornament, water-gilded or oil-gilded.

PROVIDE Home Inspections. Free
Estimates. Free Collection/Delivery
Service.
SPEAK TO Martin Body.

ANTHONY HARRINGTON
Squerryes Court Workshops, Squerryes
Court, Westerham, **Kent TN16 ISJ**
TEL   0959 64936
FAX   0959 64936
OPEN   9–5 Mon–Fri.

Specialise in restoring antique wood
carving and gilding.

PROVIDE Home Inspections. Free
Estimates. Free Collection/Delivery
Service.
SPEAK TO Anthony Harrington.

RICKY HOLDSTOCK
Hillside Cottage, The Forstal, Hernhill,
Faversham, **Kent ME13 9JQ**
TEL   0227 751204
FAX   0227 751204
OPEN   9–5 Mon–Fri.

Specialise in replacing chair seats and
panels in cane, rush and Danish cord.

PROVIDE Home Inspections. Free
Estimates. Free/Chargeable Delivery
Service.
SPEAK TO Ricky Holdstock.

LANGOLD ANTIQUES
Oxon Hoath, Tonbridge, **Kent**
TEL   0737 810577
OPEN   9–5 Mon,Thur–Fri.

Specialise in restoring furniture.

PROVIDE Free Collection/Delivery
Service.
SPEAK TO Mr. Bayne-Powell.

TIMOTHY LONG RESTORATION
26 High Street, Seal, Nr. Sevenoaks,
Kent TN15 OAP
TEL   0732 62606
OPEN   By Appointment.

Specialise in restoring 18th and 19th
century English and Continental
furniture.

PROVIDE Home Inspections. Free Local

Estimates. Free Local
Collection/Delivery Service.
SPEAK TO Tim Long.

Member of BAFRA. This workshop is
included on the register of conservators
maintained by the Conservation Unit of
the Museums and Galleries
Commission.

MANDARIN GALLERY
32 London Road, Riverhead,
Sevenoaks, **Kent TN13 2DE**
TEL   0732 457399
OPEN   9.30–5 Mon–Sat; closed Wed.

Specialise in restoring 18th–19th century
Chinese hardwood furniture.
PROVIDE Free Estimates. Free
Collection/Delivery Service.
SPEAK TO Joseph Liu.

R. M. RESTORATIONS
Chaddesden Barn, Morants Court
Road, Dunton Green, **Kent TN13 2TR**
TEL   0732 741604
OPEN   7.30–5.30 Mon–Sat.

Specialise in restoring English furniture
from 1700 to 1830.
PROVIDE Home Inspections. Free
Estimates. Chargeable
Collection/Delivery Service.
SPEAK TO Richard Marson.
Member of BAFRA.

J. T. RUTHERFORD & SON
55 Sandgate High Street, Folkestone,
Kent CT20 3AH
TEL   0303 49515
OPEN   8.30–6 Mon–Sat or By
         Appointment.

Specialise in restoring period furniture.
PROVIDE Home Inspections. Refundable
Estimates. Free/Chargeable
Collection/Delivery Service.
SPEAK TO John Rutherford.

R. G. SCOTT
Furniture Mart, Bath Place and Grotto
Hill, Margate, **Kent CT9 2BU**
TEL   0843 220653
FAX   0843 227207
OPEN   9.30–1, 2–5 Mon–Sat; closed
         Wed.

Specialise in restoring furniture,
veneering, cabinet work, marquetry.
PROVIDE Home Inspections. Free
Estimates. Free Local
Collection/Delivery Service.
SPEAK TO Ron Scott.

C. W. ALLISON & SONS
Hillview, Bilsborrow Lane, Bilsborrow,
Preston, **Lancashire PR3 ORN**
TEL   0995 40344
OPEN   10–5 Mon–Fri.

Specialise in restoring furniture.
PROVIDE Home Inspections. Free
Estimates. Chargeable
Collection/Delivery Service.
SPEAK TO Richard Allison.
SEE Porcelain, Oil Paintings.

DROP DIAL ANTIQUES
Last Drop Village, Hospital Road,
Bolton, **Lancashire**
TEL   0204 57186
OPEN   12–5 Daily.

Specialise in restoring antique clocks
including dials and movements although
casework is limited. Restoring mercury
but not aneroid barometers.
PROVIDE Free Estimates.
SPEAK TO Mr. or Mrs. I. Roberts.

ALAN GRICE ANTIQUES
106 Aughton Street, Ormskirk,
Lancashire L39 3BS
TEL   0695 572007
OPEN   10–6 Mon–Sat.

Specialise in restoring English and
Continental antique furniture.

PROVIDE Home Inspections.
Free/Chargeable Estimates. Chargeable
Collection/Delivery Service.
SPEAK TO Alan Grice.

HARROP FOLD CLOCKS
Harrop Fold, Bolton-by-Bowland, Nr.
Clitheroe, **Lancashire BB7 4PJ**
TEL   02007 665
OPEN   By Appointment.

Specialises in restoring antique longcase
clocks.

PROVIDES Home Inspections. Free
Estimates. Free Collection/Delivery
Service.
SPEAK TO Mr. F. Robinson

BARBARA WILDMAN
9 Woodside Terrace, Nelson, **Lancashire
BB9 7TB**
TEL   0282 699679
OPEN   By Appointment.

Specialises in restoring gilt frames, gesso
work and gold leaf.

PROVIDES Home Inspections. Free
Estimates. Chargeable
Collection/Delivery Service.
SPEAK TO Barbara Wildman.
SEE Oil Paintings.

ROBERT BINGLEY ANTIQUES
Church Street, Wing, Oakham,
Leicestershire LE15 8RS
TEL   057 285 725 or 314
OPEN   9–5 Mon–Sat; 11–4 Sun.

Specialise in restoring antique furniture
including walnut, oak, mahogany and
rosewood.

PROVIDE Home Inspections. Free
Estimates. Free Collection/ Delivery
Service.
SPEAK TO Robert Bingley.

N. BRYAN-PEACH ANTIQUES
28 Far Street, Wymeswold,
Loughborough, **Leicestershire
LE12 6TZ**
TEL   0509 880425
OPEN   9–6 Mon–Sat.

Specialise in restoring clocks and
barometers; resilvering, dial repair.
PROVIDE Home Inspections.
SPEAK TO Mr. N. Bryan-Peach.

CHARLES ANTIQUES
3 Market Place, Whitwick, **Leicestershire
LE6 4AE**
TEL   0530 36932
OPEN   10–5 Tues, Thur-Sat.

Specialise in repairing and restoring
clocks.

PROVIDE Home Inspections. Free
Estimates. Chargeable
Collection/Delivery Service.
SPEAK TO N. Haydon.

JOHN GARNER
51–53 High Street East, Uppingham,
Leicestershire LE15 9PY.
TEL   0572 823607
FAX   0572 821654
OPEN   9–5.30 Mon–Sat; Sun By
              Appointment.

Specialise in restoring antique furniture
mainly 18th and 19th century.

PROVIDE Home Inspections. Free
Collection/Delivery Service.
SPEAK TO John or Wendy Garner.
SEE Oil Paintings.

ALEXANDER A. JESSOP
142A London Road, Leicester,
Leicestershire. LE2 1EB
TEL   0533 544836
OPEN   9–5 Mon–Fri; 9–12.30 Sat.

Specialise in restoring antique furniture,
including French polishing, wood–

carving, wood-turning and leather-lining.

PROVIDE Home Inspections. Free Estimates. Free Collection/Delivery Service.

SPEAK TO Alexander Jessop.

E. & C. ROYALL
10 Waterfall Way, Medbourne, Nr.
Market Harborough, **Leicestershire.**
LE15 8EE
TEL   0858 83744
OPEN   8.30–5 Mon–Fri.

Specialise in restoring antique English, Continental and Oriental furniture including lacquer, Boulle and inlay work, carving, veneering, French polishing and mouldings.

PROVIDE Home Inspections. Free Estimates. Chargeable Collection/Delivery Service.

SPEAK TO C. Royall.

SEE Porcelain.

TATTERSALL'S
14 Orange Street, 2 Bear Yard, Orange Street, Uppingham, **Leicestershire**
LE15 9SQ
TEL   0572 821171
OPEN   9–5 Mon–Sat; closed Thur.

Specialise in restoring of upholstered furniture and mirrors. Specialist restorers of rush and cane furniture.

PROVIDE Home Inspections. Free Estimates. Chargeable Collection/Delivery Service.

SPEAK TO Janice Tattersall.

SEE Carpets.

BURGHLEY FINE ART CONSERVATION
Burghley House, Stamford, **Lincolnshire**
PE9 3JY
TEL   0780 62155
OPEN   By Appointment.

Specialise in conserving and restoring painted furniture, European lacquer, mirror frames and gilding.

PROVIDE Home Inspections. Free Estimates. Chargeable Collection/Delivery Service.

SPEAK TO Michael Cowell.

Any work undertaken is fully documented.

SEE Oil Paintings.

E. CZAJKOWSKI & SON
96 Tor-O-Moor Road, Woodhall Spa,
Lincolnshire LN10 6SB
TEL   0526 52895
OPEN   9–5 Mon–Fri.

Specialise in restoring antique furniture, clocks and barometers including marquetry, lacquerwork, carving, gilding and upholstery. Also copy furniture.

PROVIDE Home Inspections. Free Estimates. Free Local Collection/Delivery Service.

SPEAK TO Mr. M. J. Czajkowski.

Member of COSIRA and West Dean trained.

JAMES DOAK
84 Keddington Road, Louth,
Lincolnshire LN11 OBA
TEL   0507 609135
OPEN   By Appointment.

Specialise in restoring 18th century English country chairs.

PROVIDE Home Inspections. Free Estimates. Free Collection/Delivery Service.

SPEAK TO James Doak.

Member of BAFRA.

GRANTHAM CLOCKS
30 Lodge Way, Grantham, **Lincolnshire NG31 8DD**
TEL   0476 61784
OPEN   By Appointment.
Specialise in repairing and restoring all types of antique clocks.
PROVIDE Home Inspections. Free Estimates. Free Collection/Delivery Service.
SPEAK TO Roy Conder.
Member of BHI.

RODDY McVITTIE
24 Bow Bridge House, 19–21 Payne Road, **London E3**
TEL   081 981 4083
OPEN   8–6 Mon–Fri.
Specialise in restoring and conserving 17th, 18th and 19th century furniture, clocks and barometers, both English and Continental.
PROVIDE Home Inspections. Free Estimates. Free Collection/Delivery Service.
SPEAK TO Roddy McVittie.

ELMER-MENAGE
78A Cecilia Road, **London E8 2ET**
TEL   071 923 1338
OPEN   9–6 Mon–Fri.
Specialise in restoring 18th–19th century rosewood furniture. Will also undertake marquetry restoration including Boulle.
PROVIDE Refundable Home Inspections. Chargeable Collection/Delivery Service.
SPEAK TO Chris Elmer.

DAVID TURNER
4 Atlas Mews, Ramsgate Street, **London E8 2NA**
TEL   071 249 2379
OPEN   10–6 Mon–Fri.
Specialise in restoring small pieces of furniture and leather screens.

PROVIDE Home Inspections. Free Estimates. Free Collection/Delivery Service.
SEE Porcelain, Silver.

CANE AND RUSH SEATING
47 Spratt Hall Road, **London E11 2RP**
TEL   081 530 7052
OPEN   By Appointment.
Specialise in restoring cane and rush seating of antique and modern furniture.
PROVIDE Home Inspections. Estimates. Free/Chargeable Collection/Delivery Service.
SPEAK TO Jane Swan.
Also at rear of 2 Voluntary Place, **London E11 2RQ**

YOUNG'S FRENCH POLISHING
572–574 Commercial Road, **London E14 7JD**
TEL   071 537 4917 and 790 4691
FAX   071 265 9476
OPEN   8.30–6 Mon–Sat. Closed Thur.
Specialise in polishing, renovating, repairing, French polishing-door-barring and glazing. Leather-lining tables and desk–tops, upholstery repairs and coverings.
PROVIDE Home Inspections. Free Estimates. Chargeable Collection/Delivery Service.
SPEAK TO Mr. S. R. Young.

O. COMITTI & SON LTD.
656 Forest Road, **London E17 3ED**
TEL   081 509 0011
FAX   081 521 3320
OPEN   9–5 Mon–Fri.
Specialise in repairing and restoring mercury and aneroid barometers and clocks including case work.

PROVIDE Free Estimates.
SPEAK TO Simon Barker.
Established 1850.

ALBION CLOCKS
4 Grove End, Grove Hill, **London
E18 2LE**
TEL   081 530 5570 and 0860 487830
OPEN   7.30–7 Mon–Sat.

Specialise in restoring fine antique
clocks, fine furniture, lacquer work,
water-gilding and oil-gilding.
PROVIDE Home Inspections. Free
Estimates. Free Collection/Delivery
Service.
SPEAK TO C. D. Bent.
Mr.Bent is a CMBHI.

THE CONSERVATION STUDIO
Unit 17, Pennybank Chambers, 33–35
St. Johns Square, **London EC1M 4DS**
TEL   071 251 6853
OPEN   9.30–5 Mon–Fri.

Specialise in restoring enamel watch
dials.
PROVIDE Home Inspections (large items
only). Refundable Estimates.
Chargeable Collection/Delivery Service.
SPEAK TO Sandra Davison.
SEE Silver, Porcelain.

PETER CHAPMAN ANTIQUES
Incorporating CHAPMAN
RESTORATIONS
10 Theberton Street, **London N1 0QX**
TEL   071 226 5565
FAX   081 348 4846
OPEN   9.30–6 Mon–Sat.

Specialise in restoring period furniture,
cabinet-making, French polishing and
wax finishing, upholstery and repairing
gesso and composition frames.
Specialise in Arts and Crafts, Gothic
Revival and Aesthetic Movement
furniture.

PROVIDE Home Inspections. Refundable
Estimates. Chargeable
Collection/Delivery Service.
SPEAK TO Peter Chapman or Tony
Holohan.
Members of LAPADA.
SEE Oil Paintings, Porcelain, Silver.

MATTHEW CRAWFORD
FURNITURE RESTORATION
Basement, 74–77 White Lion Street,
London N1 1QP
TEL   071 278 7146
OPEN   9–5 Mon–Fri.

Specialise in restoring 16th–early 20th
century English furniture including
inlay, recarving, leather, cane and
upholstery. Can also copy existing
pieces.
PROVIDE Home Inspections. Free
Estimates. Free Collection/Delivery
Service.
SPEAK TO Matthew Crawford.

JULIAN KELLY
26A Gopsall Street, **London N1**
TEL   071 739 2949
FAX   071 739 2949
OPEN   9–5 Mon–Fri.

Specialise in restoring antique furniture,
wood–carving and can make chairs to
match existing sets.
PROVIDE Free Estimates.
SPEAK TO Julian Kelly.

RICHARD G. PHILLIPS
(RESTORATIONS) LTD
3 Ardleigh Road, **London N1 4HS**
TEL   071 923 0921 or 0922
FAX   071 923 3668
OPEN   8–5 Mon–Fri.

Specialise in restoring antique furniture.

PROVIDE Home Inspections. Refundable Estimates. Chargeable Collection/Delivery Service.
SPEAK TO Richard Phillips.

RILEY ANTIQUES
Mall Antique Arcade, 359 Upper Street, **London N1 0PD**
TEL   071 226 0939 and 354 1719
OPEN   10–4 Wed; 10–5 Sat.
Specialise in restoring Victorian and Edwardian furniture.
PROVIDE Home Inspections. Chargeable Estimates. Free Collection/Delivery Service.
SPEAK TO George Riley.
SEE **London N5**

BARBARA SEBTI
34–36 Cross Street, **London N1 2BQ**
TEL   071 226 3374
FAX   071 226 3374
OPEN   9.30–6 Mon–Sat; Sun By Appointment.
Specialise in carving and gilding decorative furniture but will take on all furniture restoration.
PROVIDE Home Inspections. Refundable Estimates. Chargeable Collection/Delivery Service.
SPEAK TO Barbara Sebti.

NORTH LONDON CLOCK SHOP LTD
72 Highbury Park, **London N5 2XE**
TEL   071 226 1609
OPEN   9–6 Mon–Fri.
Specialise in repairing and restoring all types of antique clocks and barometers.
PROVIDE Home Inspections. Free Estimates.
SPEAK TO Derek Tomlin.
Mr Tomlin is a CMBHI.

RILEY ANTIQUES
233 Blackstock Road, **London N5**
TEL   071–354–1719 and 226 0939
OPEN   10–4 Mon–Fri.
Specialise in restoring Victorian and Edwardian furniture.
PROVIDE Home Inspections. Free/Chargeable Collection/Delivery Service.
SPEAK TO George Riley.
SEE **London N1**

ALEXANDER LEY & SON
13 Brecknock Rd, **London N7 0BL**
TEL   071 267 3645
FAX   071 267 4462
OPEN   8–6 Mon–Fri.
Specialise in restoring antique frames, gilt furniture and mirrors. Also reproduction carving and gilding.
PROVIDE Home Inspections. Free Estimates. Free Collection/Delivery Service.
SPEAK TO Alexander or Anthony Ley.
SEE Oil Paintings.

B. S. H. RESTORERS LTD
7a Tynemouth Terrace, Tynemouth Road, **London N15 4AP**
TEL   081 808 7965
OPEN   7–3.30 Mon–Fri.
Specialise in restoring antique English and Continental furniture.
PROVIDE Home Inspections. Free/Chargeable Estimates. Free Collection/Delivery Service.
SPEAK TO Barry Howells.

CLIFFORD J. TRACY
6–40 Durnford Street, **London N15 5NQ**
TEL   081 800 4773 or 4774
FAX   081 800 4351
OPEN   7.30–5 Mon–Thur; 7.30–4 Fri.
Specialise in restoring furniture

including carving, marquetry, Boulle, leather-lining and re-upholstery. Also restore clock cases and movements.

PROVIDE Home Inspections. Free Estimates. Free Collection/Delivery Service.

SPEAK TO Clifford Tracey.

Members of BAFRA and the UKIC. Will do minor repairs on site.

W. PAIRPOINT & SONS LTD
10 Shacklewell Road, **London N16 7TA**
TEL 071 254 6362
FAX 071 254 7175
OPEN 8.30–5.30 Mon–Fri.

Specialise in regilding carriage clocks.

PROVIDE Free Estimates. Free Collection/Delivery Service in the London area.

SPEAK TO Eric Soulard.

SEE Silver.

THE COLLECTORS WORKSHOP
Heathrow House, Factory Lane, **London N17 9BY**
TEL 081 808 1920
OPEN 8–5 Mon–Fri; Sat By Appointment.

Specialise in restoring fine English and Continental furniture.

PROVIDE Home Inspections. Free Estimates. Free Collection/Delivery Service.

SPEAK TO Barrie Branwan.

Member of the Guild of Master Craftsmen.

A. J. BRETT & CO. LTD
Blenheim Works, 168c Marlborough Rd, **London N19 4NP**
TEL 071 272 8462
FAX 071 272 5102
OPEN 7–4.30 Mon–Fri.

Specialise in restoring antique furniture

including upholstery, metalwork, gilding and decorating, French polishing, table–lining.

PROVIDE Home Inspections. Free Estimates. Free Collection/Delivery Service.

SPEAK TO Emma Whiteley.

Members of the Guild of Master Craftsmen. Successfully restored the furniture damaged in the fire at Hampton Court.

MAX E. OTT LTD
1A Southcote Road, **London N19 5BJ**
TEL 071 607 1384
FAX 071 607 3506
OPEN 6.30–8.30 Mon–Fri.

Specialise in restoring antique furniture of all periods. Also copy period furniture.

PROVIDE Home Inspections. Free Estimates. Free Collection/Delivery Service.

SPEAK TO Max Ott.

ROCHEFORT ANTIQUES LTD
32–34 The Green, **London N21 1AX**
TEL 081 886 4779 or 363 0910
OPEN 10–6 Mon–Tues, Thur, Sat.

Specialise in restoring furniture.

PROVIDE Home Inspections. Free Estimates. Chargeable Collection/Delivery Service.

SPEAK TO L.W.Stevens-Wilson.

SEE Porcelain, Silver.

K. RESTORATIONS
2A Ferdinand Place, **London NW1 8EE**
TEL 071 482 402
FAX 071 267 6712
OPEN 8–6 Mon–Fri.

Specialise in restoring all antique furniture including French polishing and renovation of leather upholstery and the supply of desk leathers.

PROVIDE Home Inspections. Free
Estimates. Chargeable
Collection/Delivery Service.
SPEAK TO David Peston.
Member of the Guild of Antique Dealers
and Restorers.

THE MORLEY UPHOLSTERY
WORKS LTD
82–86 Troutbeck, Albany St, **London
NW1 4EJ**
TEL   071 387 3846 and 388 0651
OPEN   8–4.30 Mon–Fri.

Specialise in renovating antique and
modern upholstery.

PROVIDE Home Inspections. Chargeable
Estimates. Free Collection/Delivery
Service.
SPEAK TO Mr. E. G. Vidler.

MURGA CANDLER LTD
57 Bayham Place, **London NW1 0ET**
TEL   071 387 7830
OPEN   8–5 Mon–Fri.

Specialise in leather-lining of desk and
table-tops, loose leathers, upholstery in
suede and leather.

PROVIDE Free Estimates.
SPEAK TO John Murga.

A. SPIGARD
236 Camden High Street, **London
NW1 8QS**
TEL   071 485 4095
OPEN   9–6 Mon–Sat.

Specialise in restoring antique furniture.

PROVIDE Refundable Estimates.
Chargeable Collection/Delivery Service.
SPEAK TO A. Spigard.

JOHN SZAKALY
2 Chartley Avenue, **London NW2 7RA**
TEL   081 450 5882
OPEN   9–6 Mon–Fri.

Specialise in restoration of antique
furniture and polishing.

PROVIDE Home Inspections. Free
Estimates. Free Collection/Delivery
Service.
SPEAK TO John Szakaly.

ANTIQUE LEATHERS
4 Park End, South Hill Park, **London
NW3 2SE**
TEL   071 435 8582
FAX   071 435 7799
OPEN   8–5 Mon–Fri.

Specialise in restoring leather work of all
kinds, upholstery, bellows, desk–tops
with gold tooling, screens,
backgammons.

PROVIDE Free Estimates.
Free/Chargeable Collection/Delivery
Service.
SPEAK TO Jackie Crisp or Roy Holliday.

J. CRISP
48 Roderick Road, **London NW3 2NL**
TEL   081 340 0668
FAX   071 485 8566
OPEN   10–6 Mon–Fri.

Specialise in restoring antique and
modern and office furniture, leather
work, staining, polishing, reviving
bookshelf leather, loose leathers.

PROVIDE Home Inspections. Refundable
Estimates. Free/Chargeable
Collection/Delivery Service.
SPEAK TO Mr. J. Crisp.

PARKHILL RESTORATIONS
11 Park End, South Hill Park, **London NW3 2ST**
TEL   071 794 5624
OPEN   10–6 Mon–Fri or By
       Appointment.
Specialise in restoring antique furniture, carving, gilding, rushing, caning, upholstering. Also small bracket and longcase clocks.
PROVIDE Home Inspections. Free Estimates. Chargeable Collection/Delivery Service.
SPEAK TO Peter Colgin.

RODERIC COWING
Unit 12, Liddell Road, **London NW6 2EW**
TEL   071 328 6025
OPEN   10–6 Mon–Fri.
Specialise in upholstery restoration.
PROVIDE Home Inspections. Chargeable/Refundable Estimates. Chargeable Collection/Delivery Service.
SPEAK TO Roderic Cowing.

JOHN CHAMBERS
4 Nugent Terrace, **London NW8 9QB**
TEL   071 289 1393
OPEN   9–5 Mon–Fri.
Specialise in restoring and repairing English 17th and 18th century oak, walnut and mahogany furniture.
PROVIDE Home Inspections. Free Estimates in Central London only. Chargeable Collection/Delivery Service.
SPEAK TO John Chambers.

WELLINGTON GALLERY
1 St. John's Wood High Street, **London NW8 7NG**
TEL   071 586 2620
OPEN   10–5.30 Mon–Sat.
Specialise in restoring furniture.
PROVIDE Home Inspections. Free Estimates. Chargeable Collection/Delivery Service.
SPEAK TO Mrs. Maureen Barclay or Mr. K. J. Barclay.
Member of LAPADA.
SEE Oil Paintings, Porcelain, Silver.

B. C. METALCRAFTS
69 Tewkesbury Gardens, **London NW9 0QU**
TEL   081 204 2446
OPEN   By Appointment.
Specialise in restoring and repairing French clocks and clock sets.
SPEAK TO F. Burnell or M. A. Burnell.
Member of LAPADA.
SEE Silver.

ADAMS & SHERIDAN
7 Ashbourne Parade, Finchley Road, **London NW11 0AD**
TEL   081 455 6970
OPEN   9–5.30 Mon–Sat.
Specialise in repairing antique and modern furniture, French polishing and re-covering.
PROVIDE Home Inspections. Free/Refundable Estimates. Collection/Delivery Service.
SPEAK TO Mrs Healy.
Members of the Association of Master Upholsterers.

JEREMY CZERKAS
103 Wentworth Road, **London NW11 0RH**
TEL   081 458 5140
OPEN   By Appointment.
Specialise in restoring antique furniture, including traditional upholstery and caning.

PROVIDE Home Inspections. Free
Estimates. Free/Chargeable
Collection/Delivery Service.
SPEAK TO Jeremy Czerkas.

PHOENIX ANTIQUE FURNITURE RESTORATION LIMITED
96 Webber Street, **London SE1 0QN**
TEL   071 928 3624
OPEN   8–6

Specialise in restoring and conserving
furniture, including cabinet-making,
polishing, upholstery, metalwork, desk
lining. Specialist chair doctors and can
make furniture to order.
PROVIDE Home Inspections. Free
Estimates. Chargeable
Collection/Delivery Service.
SPEAK TO David Battle.

CRAWLEY STUDIOS
Unit 17, Carew Street, **London SE5 9DF**
TEL   071 733 1276
FAX   071 733 1014
OPEN   9–6.15 Mon–Fri.

Specialise in restoring painted furniture,
lacquer, gilding, papier mâché and
polishing.
PROVIDE Home Inspections. Free
Estimates. Chargeable
Collection/Delivery Service.
SPEAK TO Marie Louise Crawley.
Member of BAFRA and UKIC.
SEE Silver.

PARAGON FURNITURE
Unit 2C, Ashleigh Commercial Estate,
Westmoor Street, **London SE7 8NQ**
TEL   081 305 2332
OPEN   8–5 Mon–Fri.

Specialise in restoring antique furniture
and conversions.
PROVIDE Home Inspections. Free
Estimates. Free Collection/Delivery
Service.
SPEAK TO G. Matthews or I. Watson.

R. E. ROSE
731 Sidcup Rd, **London SE9 3SA**
TEL   081 859 4754
OPEN   8.30–5.30 Mon–Sat. Closed
        Thur.

Specialise in restoring antique clocks and
barometers.
PROVIDE Free Estimates.
SPEAK TO Ron Rose.
Mr Rose is a FBHI.

GREENWICH CONSERVATION WORKSHOPS
Spread Eagle Antiques of Greenwich,
8–9 Nevada Street, **London SE10 9JL**
TEL   081 305 1666
OPEN   10–5.30 Mon–Sat.

Specialise in restoring furniture.
PROVIDE Home Inspections. Refundable
Estimates. Free/Chargeable
Collection/Delivery Service.
SPEAK TO Richard Moy.
SEE Oil Paintings.

RELCY ANTIQUES
9 Nelson Road, **London SE10 9JB**
TEL   081 858 2812
FAX   081 293 4135
OPEN   10–6 Mon–Sat.

Specialise in restoring 18th and 19th
century English and Continental
furniture.
PROVIDE Home Inspections.
Free/Chargeable Estimates.
Collection/Delivery Service by
arrangement.
SPEAK TO Robin Challis.
SEE Collectors (Scientific Instruments),
Oil Paintings, Silver.

A. FAGIANI
30 Wagner Street, **London SE15 1NN**
TEL　071 732 7188
OPEN　8–5.30 Mon–Fri.

Specialise in repairing and restoring antique English and Continental furniture and polishing.

PROVIDE Home Inspections. Free Estimates. Free Collection/Delivery Service.

SPEAK TO Mr. A. Fagiani

J. T. GROSSE LTD
12 Verney Road, **London SE16 3DH**
TEL　071 231 7969
OPEN　7.30–5.30 Mon–Fri; Sat By Appointment.

Specialise in renovation of antique and other quality furniture.

PROVIDE Home Inspections. Free Estimates. Free Collection/Delivery Service.

SPEAK TO A. F. Grosse.

This family business has been established since 1911.

NEWCOMBE & SON
89 Maple Rd, Penge, **London SE20 8UL**
TEL　081 778 0816
OPEN　7.15–5.30 Mon–Fri.

Specialise in repairing and restoring antique clocks and barometers including silvering and gilding service, enamel and painted clock faces, brass and wood frets, clock hands in brass or steel.

PROVIDE Home Inspections. Free Estimates. Free Collection/Delivery Service.

SPEAK TO Mike Newcombe.

GLEN'S ANTIQUE RESTORATION
Unit 134, 62 Tritton Road, **London SE21 8DE**
TEL　081 761 5609
FAX　081 761 5609
OPEN　9–6 Mon–Fri.

Specialise in restoring painted furniture, gilding and wood-carving, French polishing.

PROVIDE Home Inspections. Free Estimates. Chargeable Collection/Delivery Service.

SPEAK TO Glen Beckford.

SEE Oil Paintings.

N. BLOOM & SON (ANTIQUES) LTD
Harrod's Fine Jewellery Room, **London SW1 1XL**
TEL　071 730 1234 ext. 4062 or 4072
FAX　071 581 0470
OPEN　9–6 Mon–Sat, 9–8 Wed.

Specialise in restoring carriage clocks, good mechanical watches.

PROVIDE Free Estimates.

SPEAK TO Heidi McKeown.

Members of LAPADA.

SEE Silver.

OSSWOSKI WORKSHOP
83 Pimlico Road, **London SW1W 8PH**
and at 595 Kings Road, **London SW6 2EL**
TEL　071 730 3256 and 731 0334
OPEN　10–6 Mon–Fri; 10–1 Sat.

Specialise in restoring and gilding 18th century giltwood mirrors, furniture and carvings. Water-gilding only; no oil-gilding, small repairs or touching-up jobs.

PROVIDE Free Estimates.

SPEAK TO Mark or Matthew Ossowski.

JOANNA PIOTROWSKA
A. & J. Restoration, Chenil Galleries
G1/G2, 181–183 Kings Road, **London SW3 5EB**
TEL   071 352 2704 and 081 578 9688
OPEN   10.30–6 Mon–Sat.
Specialise in restoring mirrors and furniture, gilding, lacquering and painting.
PROVIDE Home Inspections. Free Estimates. Free Collection/Delivery Service.
SPEAK TO Joanna Piotrowska.

JOHN HEAP
No.1 The Polygon, **London SW4**
TEL   071 627 4498
OPEN   By Appointment.
Specialise in restoring painted antique furniture, gesso work and gilding.
PROVIDE Home Inspections. Free Estimates. Free Collection/Delivery Service.
SPEAK TO John Heap.
SEE Porcelain, Silver.

DAVID ALEXANDER ANTIQUES & KATE THURLOW
102 Waterford Road, **London SW6 2HA**
TEL   071 731 4644
OPEN   By Appointment.
Specialise in restoring 16th–17th century European furniture.
PROVIDE Home Inspections. Chargeable Collection/Delivery Service.
SPEAK TO Kate Thurlow or Rodney Robertson.

BIG BEN CLOCKS
5 Broxholme House, New Kings Road, **London SW6 4AA**
TEL   071 736 1770
FAX   071 384 1957
OPEN   9–5 Mon–Fri.

Specialise in repairing and overhauling all types of antique clocks. They are not undertaking restoration work at present.
PROVIDE Home Inspections. Chargeable Collection/Delivery Service.
SPEAK TO Roger Lascelles.

I. & J. L. BROWN LTD
636 Kings Road, **London SW6 2DU**
TEL   071 736 4141
OPEN   9–5.30 Mon–Sat.
Specialise in restoring English country and French Provincial furniture. Also undertake chair rush work.
PROVIDE Free/Chargeable Estimates. Free/Chargeable Collection/Delivery Service.
SPEAK TO Peter Baker-Place.
SEE Furniture **Hereford and Worcester**.

JOHN CLAY ANTIQUES
263 New Kings Road, **London SW6 4RB**
TEL   071 731 5677
OPEN   9–6 Mon–Sat.
Specialise in restoring antique furniture.
PROVIDE Home Inspections. Refundable Estimates. Chargeable Collection/Delivery Service.
SPEAK TO John Clay.

PETER L. JAMES
681 Fulham Road, **London SW6 5PZ**
TEL   071 736 0183
OPEN   7.30–5.30 Mon–Fri.
Specialise in restoring lacquer, painted and gilded furniture and mirror frames.
PROVIDE Home Inspections. Refundable Estimates. Chargeable Collection/Delivery Service.
SPEAK TO Peter L. James.
SEE Oil Paintings.

CHRISTOPHER J. LEWIS
464A Fulham Road, **London SW6 6HY**
TEL   071 386 5669
OPEN   10–6 Mon–Fri.

Specialise in restoring all aspects of furniture, except for upholstery, as well as offering a design and construction service.

PROVIDE Home Inspections. Refundable Estimates.

SPEAK TO Christopher Lewis.

MICHAEL MARRIOTT LTD
588 Fulham Road, **London SW6 5NT**
TEL   071 736 3110
FAX   071 731 2632
OPEN   9.30–5.30 Mon–Fri.

Specialise in restoring furniture, including traditional upholstery.

PROVIDE Home Inspections in London , outside London for major restorations only. Free Estimates.
Collection/Delivery Service.

SPEAK TO Michael Marriott.

SEE Oil Paintings.

AUBREY BROCKLEHURST
124 Cromwell Road, **London SW7 4ET**
TEL   071 373 0319
OPEN   9–1, 2–5.30 Mon–Fri; 10–1 Sat.

Specialise in restoring and repairing antique English and French clocks and antique furniture.

PROVIDE Home Inspections. Free Estimates. Chargeable Collection/Delivery Service.

SPEAK TO Aubrey Brocklehurst, Ms. Gill or Mrs. Leonard.

Mr. Brocklehurst is a FBHI and a member of BADA.

R. HORNSBY
33 Thurloe Place, **London SW7 2HQ**
TEL   071 225 2888
FAX   071 225 2888
OPEN   8.30–6 Mon–Fri; 8.30–2 Sat.

Specialise in restoring furniture including French polishing, chair repairs, cabinet work and repairs, traditional upholstery.

PROVIDE Home Inspections. Free Estimates. Collection/Delivery Service Available.

SPEAK TO Mr. R. Gough.

Established 1890.

M. TURPIN LTD
21 Manson Mews, **London SW7 5AF**
TEL   071 736 3417
FAX   071 408 1869
OPEN   By Appointment.

Specialise in restoring 17th–early 19th century furniture and giltwood mirrors.

PROVIDE Home Inspections. Chargeable/Refundable Estimates. Chargeable Collection/Delivery Service.

SPEAK TO M Turpin.

SEE **London W1**

CAPITAL CLOCKS
190 Wandsworth Road, **London SW8 2JU**
TEL   071 720 6372
OPEN   9–5 Tues–Sat.

Specialise in restoring pre-1900 clocks, longcase, bracket and carriage, restoration of barometers, new mercury tubes, Boulle and enamel work.

PROVIDE Free Estimates. Chargeable Collection/Delivery Service.

SPEAK TO Robert McMillan.

PETER & FRANCES BINNINGTON
65 St. Johns Hill, **London SW11 1SX**
TEL   071 223 9192
FAX   071 924 1668
OPEN   8.30–5.30 Mon–Fri.

Specialise in restoring all kinds of antique furniture, including surfaces decorated in marquetry, paint, carving and gilding.

PROVIDE Home Inspections. Free Estimates. Chargeable Collection/Delivery Service.
SPEAK TO Joanne Neal.
SEE Porcelain.

RUPERT BEVAN
75 Lower Richmond Road, **London SW15 1ET**
TEL   081 780 1190
OPEN   9–6 Mon–Fri.

Specialise in restoring gilded furniture and mirror frames.

PROVIDE Home Inspections. Free Estimates. Chargeable Collection/Delivery Service.
SPEAK TO Rupert Bevan.
SEE Oil Paintings.

ROGER BOARD DESIGNS
273 Putney Bridge Road, **London SW15 2PT**
TEL   081 789 0046
FAX   081 789 0047
OPEN   9–6 Mon–Fri.

Specialise in restoring antique furniture and panelling.

PROVIDE Home Inspections. Free Estimates. Free Local Collection/Delivery Service.
SPEAK TO Roger Board.

DELIA BRAIN
136 Putney Bridge Road, **London SW15 2NQ**
TEL   081 874 1678
OPEN   9–5 Mon–Fri.

Specialise in restoring 18th and 19th century painted furniture and specialist paint techniques such as marbling and graining.

PROVIDE Home Inspections. Free/Refundable Estimates. Chargeable Collection/Delivery Service.
SPEAK TO Delia Brain.

Ms. Brain also restores and retouches scenic wallpaper on site.

THE CLOCK CLINIC LTD
85 Lower Richmond Road, **London SW15 1EU**
TEL   081 788 1407
OPEN   9–6 Tues–Fri; 9–1 Sat.

Specialise in restoring antique clocks, barometers and barographs.

PROVIDE Chargeable Home Inspections. Free Estimates in shop. Chargeable Collection/Delivery Service.
SPEAK TO Robert Pedler.
Mr. Pedler is a FBHI.

ALAN S. STONE
3 Wadham Road, **London SW15**
TEL   081 870 1606
OPEN   9–4.30 Mon–Fri; 9–2.30 Sat.

Specialise in restoring 18th and 19th century furniture.

PROVIDE Home Inspections. Free Estimates. Free Collection/Delivery Service.
SPEAK TO Alan S. Stone.

THORNHILL GALLERIES LTD
78 Deodar Road, **London SW15 2NJ**
TEL   081 874 5669 or 2101
FAX   081 877 0313

Specialise in restoring English and French panelling and period wooden chimney-pieces.

PROVIDE Home Inspections. Free Estimates. Free/Chargeable Collection/Delivery Service.

SPEAK TO Mr G. Wakefield or Mrs V. Haigh.

SEE Porcelain.
Established 1880.

WEAVER NEAVE & DAUGHTER
17 Lifford Street, **London SW15 1NY**
TEL   081 785 2464
OPEN   9–6 Mon–Fri.

Specialise in all cane and rush work for antique furniture.

PROVIDE Home Inspections. Free Estimates. Collection/Delivery Service by arrangement.

SPEAK TO Rosslyn Neave.

E. & A. WATES LTD
82–84 Mitcham Lane, **London SW16 6NR**
TEL   081 769 2205
FAX   081 677 4766
OPEN   9–6 Mon–Sat; 9–7 Thur.

Specialise in repairing fine furniture including re-upholstery, French polishing, caning and carving.

PROVIDE Home Inspections. Free/Refundable Estimates.

SPEAK TO Mr. R. D. Wates.
Established 1900.

CARVERS & GILDERS
9 Charterhouse Works, Eltringham Street, **London SW18 1TD**
TEL   081 870 7047
FAX   081 874 0470
OPEN   By Appointment.

Specialise in restoring wood-carving and gilding, particularly of ornate applied ornament. Also design and make new pieces.

PROVIDE Home Inspections. Free Estimates.

SPEAK TO Anna Baker.

SERENA CHAPLIN
32 Elsynge Road, **London SW18 2HN**
TEL   081 870 9455
OPEN   By Appointment.

Specialise in restoring mirror frames and other gilded objects as well as restoring and conserving antique lacquer such as screens, cabinets and trays.

PROVIDE Free Estimates.

SPEAK TO Serena Chaplin.

Ms. Chaplin also runs gilding courses.
SEE Oil Paintings.

COMPTON HALL RESTORATION
Unit A, 133 Riverside Business Centre, Haldane Place, **London SW18 4UQ**
TEL   081 874 0762
OPEN   9–5 Mon–Fri.

Specialise in restoring painted furniture, lacquer, gilding, papier mâché, penwork.

PROVIDE Home Inspections. Free Estimates. Collection/Delivery Service by arrangement.

SPEAK TO Lucinda Compton, Jane or Henrietta Hohler.

They are members of BAFRA and UKIC.
SEE Silver.

102

PLOWDEN & SMITH LTD
190 St Ann's Hill, **London SW18 2Rt**
TEL   081 874 4005
FAX   081 874 7248
OPEN   9–5.30 Mon–Fri.

Specialise in restoring and conserving fine furniture and upholstery.

PROVIDE Home Inspections. Free Estimates. Chargeable Collection/Delivery Service.
SPEAK TO Bob Butler.

They also advise on conservation strategy, environmental control and micro-climates for collections as well as installing, mounting and displaying temporary and permanent exhibitions.
SEE Oil Paintings, Silver, Porcelain.

CONNOLLY LEATHERS
Wandle Bank, **London SW19 1DW**
TEL   081 542 5251 and 543 4611
FAX   081 543 7455
OPEN   9–12.45, 1.30–4 Mon–Fri.

Specialise in restoring any leather furniture, cleaning and renovating, matching aged leather including gold-embossed leather.

PROVIDE Home Inspections. Chargeable Estimates. Free Collection/Delivery Service.
SPEAK TO Mr. Humpage or Mr. Carron.

They will also restore automobile upholstery for classic and vintage cars.

W. R. HARVEY & CO. (ANTIQUES) LTD
5 Old Bond Street, **London W1X 3TA**
TEL   071 499 8385
FAX   071 495 0209
OPEN   10–5.30 Mon–Sat.

Specialise in restoring fine English period (1650–1830) furniture and works of art.

PROVIDE Home Inspections. Free Estimates. Free Collection/Delivery Service.
SPEAK TO A. D. or G. M. Harvey or David Watkinson.

They are members of BADA and the Guild of Master Craftsmen. This workshop is included on the register of conservators maintained by the Conservation Unit of the Museums and Galleries Commission.

RICHARD KERLEY
6 York Mansions, 84 Chiltern Street, **London W1M 1PT**
TEL   071 486 6483
OPEN   By Appointment.

Specialise in restoring furniture; Boulle work and carving, English water-gilding. Also copy chairs and mirror frames to match client's own pieces.

PROVIDE Home Inspections. Chargeable Estimates. Chargeable Collection/Delivery Service.
SPEAK TO Richard Kerley.

L. NEWLAND & SON
17 Picton Place, **London W1M 5DE**
TEL   071 935 2864
OPEN   10.30–2, 3.30–6 Mon–Fri.

Specialise in repairing and restoring antique watches and clocks. jewellery, enamels, ivory, piquet, tortoiseshell, amber.

PROVIDE Home Inspections. Free Estimates. Free Collection/Delivery Service.
SPEAK TO Mr. Newland.
SEE Silver.

B. V. M. SOMERSET
The Dial, Kings Head PH, 13 Westmoreland Street, **London W1M 7HH**
TEL   071 935 2201
OPEN   11–8 daily.

Specialise in restoring antique clocks and watches. Clock cases can be repaired; also French polishing.

PROVIDE Home Inspections. Free
Collection/Delivery Service.
SPEAK TO B. Somerset.

Mr. Somerset is a MBHI.

M. TURPIN LTD
27 Bruton Street, **London W1X 7DB**
TEL   071 493 3275
OPEN   10–5 Mon–Fri.

Specialise in repairing 17th–early 19th
century furniture and giltwood mirrors.

PROVIDE Home Inspections.
Chargeable/Refundable Estimates.
Chargeable Collection/Delivery Service.
SPEAK TO J. Mann.

SEE **London SW7.**

JOHN WALKER
64 South Molton Street, **London
W1Y 1HH**
TEL   071 629 3487
OPEN   8.30–5.15 Mon–Fri.

Specialise in repairing and restoring
antique and modern clocks and watches.

PROVIDE Home Inspections. Free
Estimates. Chargeable
Collection/Delivery Service.
SPEAK TO John Walker or Steve Martin.

This family firm was established in 1830.
Fellow of BHI.
SEE Silver.

G. D. WARDER & SONS LTD
14 Hanway Place, **London W1P 9DG**
TEL   071 636 1867
OPEN   9–4.30 Mon–Fri.

Specialise in water-gilding and carving,
gilding and restoration of period
mirrors, antique furniture, frames and
bijoutiers. Reproduction Regency
mirrors made to order.

PROVIDE Free Estimates. Chargeable
Collection/Delivery Service.
SPEAK TO David or Robert Warder.

H. J. HATFIELD & SON
42 St.Michael's Street, **London W2 1QP**
TEL   071 723 8265
FAX   071 706 4562
OPEN   9–1, 2–5 Mon–Fri.

Specialise in restoring English and
French 17th–19th century furniture.

PROVIDE Home Inspections. Free
Estimates.
SPEAK TO Philip Astley-Jones.
SEE Silver.

WILLIAM MANSELL
24 Connaught Street, **London W2 2AF**
TEL   071 723 4154
OPEN   9–6 Mon–Fri and Sat a.m.

Specialise in repairing and restoring
antique clocks, wrist watches, pocket
watches. silverware and antique
jewellery.

PROVIDE Home Inspections. Free
Estimates. Free Collection/Delivery
Service.
SPEAK TO Bill Salisbury.

This is a small established business which
dates back to 1864.
SEE Silver.

THE OLD CINEMA
160 Chiswick High Road, **London
W4 1PR**
TEL   081 995 4166
OPEN   10–6 daily.

Specialise in comprehensive restoration
and upholstery service for antique and
Victorian furniture.

PROVIDE Free Estimates. Free
Collection/Delivery Service.
SPEAK TO Martin Hanness.

BADGER ANTIQUES
12 St. Mary's Road, **London W5 5ES**
TEL   081 567 5601
OPEN   10–6 Mon–Sat.
Specialise in restoring furniture, clocks and pocket watches.
PROVIDE Home Inspections. Free Estimates. Free Collection/Delivery Service.
SPEAK TO Michael Allders.

C. J. G. GILDERS & CARVERS
Unit 10, Sandringham Mews, **London W5 5DF**
TEL   081 579 2341
FAX   081 571 9022
OPEN   10–5 Mon–Sat.
Specialise in restoring antique mirrors and gilt furniture.
PROVIDE Home Inspections. Free Estimates. Free Collection/Delivery Service within London.
SPEAK TO Chris Gostonski or Richard Kosmala.
SEE Oil Paintings.

ROY BENNETT
22 Cuckoo Lane, **London W7 3EY**
TEL   081 840 6911
OPEN   By Appointment.
Specialise in restoring antique clocks and watches.
PROVIDE Free Estimates, Chargeable Collection/Delivery Service.
SPEAK TO Roy Bennett.
Member of the BWCMG.

DON HOLMES ANTIQUES
47c Earls Court Road, (in Abingdon Villas), **London W8 6EE**
TEL   071 937 6961 or 020 888 0254
OPEN   2–7 Fri; 9.30–5.30 Sat or By Appointment.
Specialise in restoring and repairing 18th and 19th century furniture, mainly mahogany.
PROVIDE Home Inspections. Refundable Estimates. Chargeable Collection/Delivery Service.
SPEAK TO Don or Sarah Holmes.

THE ROWLEY GALLERY LTD
115 Kensington Church Street, **London W8 7LN**
TEL   071 727 6495
OPEN   9–5 Mon–Fri; 9–7 Thur.
Specialise in restoring antique frames, gilding and veneering.
PROVIDE Home Inspections, Free Estimates, Free Collection/Delivery Service.
SPEAK TO A. J. Savill.
This firm was founded in 1898.
SEE Oil Paintings.

ARTHUR SEAGER
25A Holland Street, **London W8 4NA**
TEL   071 937 3262
FAX   071 937 3262
OPEN   10–5.30 Mon–Sat.
Specialise in restoring 17th and 18th century oak furniture.
PROVIDE Home Inspections. Free Estimates. Free/Chargeable Collection/Delivery Service.
SPEAK TO Arthur Seager.

TITIAN STUDIO
326 Kensal Road, **London W10 5BN**
TEL   081 960 6247 and 969 6126
OPEN   9–6 Mon–Fri.
Specialise in carving, gilding, furniture restoration and lacquer polishing.
PROVIDE Home Inspections. Free/Chargeable Estimates. Chargeable Collection/Delivery Service.
SPEAK TO Rod Titian or Elizabeth Porter.

IGOR TOCIAPSKI
39 Ledbury Road, **London W11 2AA**
TEL   071 229 8317
OPEN   10–5 Tues–Fri.
Specialise in repairing antique clocks.
PROVIDE Home Inspections. Free
Estimates. Chargeable
Collection/Delivery Service.
SPEAK TO Igor Tociapski.

WARWICK DE WINTER c/o
WYNYARDS ANTIQUES
5 Ladbroke Road, **London W11 3PA**
TEL   071 221 7936
OPEN   10–6 Tues–Fri; 1.30–6 Mon and
       Sat.
Specialise in repairing and restoring
furniture, upholstery, re-caning, rush
seating.
PROVIDE Home Inspections. Free
Estimates. Free/Chargeable
Collection/Delivery Service.
SPEAK TO Warwick de Winter.

ROSEMARY COOK RESTORATION
78 Stanlake Road, **London W12 7HJ**
TEL   081 749 7977
OPEN   By Appointment.
Specialise in restoring painted furniture,
caning and rush seating.
PROVIDE Home Inspections. Free
Estimates. Free Collection/Delivery
Service in London.
SPEAK TO Rosemary Cook.
SEE Porcelain, Silver.

COUTTS GALLERIES
75 Blythe Road, **London W14 OHD**
TEL   071 602 3980
OPEN   10–5 Mon–Fri.
Specialise in restoring decorative antique
furniture, including gilding, lacquer
work, cabinet work and restoration of
antique frames.

PROVIDE Home Inspections. Free
Estimates. Free Collection/Delivery
Service.
SPEAK TO Seabury Burdett-Coutts.
SEE Oil Paintings.

BAROMETER FAIR AT:
CARTOGRAPHIA LTD
Pied Bull Yard, Bury Place, **London
WC1A 2JR**
TEL   071 404 4521 or 4050
OPEN   By Appointment.
Specialise in restoring antique mercury
and aneroid barometers.
PROVIDE Local Delivery Service.
SPEAK TO John Forster.

PAUL FERGUSON
Unit 20, 21 Wren Street, **London
WC1X OHF**
TEL   071 278 8759
FAX   071 278 8759
OPEN   9–5.30 Mon–Fri.
Specialise in restoring carved and gilded
furniture, girandoles, torchères.
PROVIDE Home Inspections. Free
Estimates. Collection/Delivery Service
by arrangement.
SPEAK TO Paul Ferguson.
SEE Oil Paintings.

S. H. JEWELL
26 Parker Street, **London WC2B 5PH**
TEL   071 405 8520
OPEN   9–5.30 Mon–Fri; Sat By
       Appointment.
Specialise in 19th and 20th century
English furniture repairs and polishing,
table–lining and upholstery.
PROVIDE Home Inspections. Free
Estimates. Chargeable
Collection/Delivery Service.
SPEAK TO S. H. Jewell.

DAVID NEWELL
55 Shelton Street, **London WC2H 9HE**
TEL   071 836 1000
OPEN   By Appointment.

Specialises in restoring antique clocks and watches, particularly French Clocks. Barometers and barographs are also restored.

PROVIDES Free Estimates.
SPEAK TO David Newell.
Mr Newell is a FBHI.
SEE Collectors (Mechanical Music).

ALBION ANTIQUES
643 Stockport Road, Longsight, **Greater Manchester M12 4QA**
TEL   061 225 4957
OPEN   9–6 Mon–Fri or By Appointment.

Specialise in restoring antique and period furniture and timber items.

PROVIDE Chargeable Home Inspections. Refundable Estimates. Chargeable Collection/Delivery Service.
SPEAK TO Tony Collins.

CASEMENTS THE CABINETMAKERS
Slack Lane Works, Pendlebury, Salford, **Greater Manchester M27 2QT**
TEL   061 794 1610
OPEN   8–6 Mon–Fri; 8–1 Sat.

Specialise in antique restoration, including veneering, French polishing and turning. One-off copy pieces.

PROVIDE Home Inspections. Refundable Estimates. Chargeable Collection/Delivery Service.
SPEAK TO D. Casement.

J. G. TREVOR–OWEN
181–193 Oldham Rd, Rochdale, **Greater Manchester OL16 5QZ**
TEL   0706 48138
OPEN   1.30–7 Mon–Fri or By Appointment.

Specialise in restoring clocks and small items of furniture.

PROVIDE Home Inspections. Refundable Estimates.
SPEAK TO J. G. Trevor-Owen.
SEE Oil Paintings, Collectors (Musical Instruments).

TREEN ANTIQUES
Treen House, 72 Park Road, Prestwich, **Greater Manchester M25 8FA**
TEL   061 740 1063
FAX   061 720 7244
OPEN   By Appointment.

Specialise in restoring antique English furniture, particularly regional furniture with an emphasis on finishes and coating technology.

PROVIDE Home Inspections. Free Estimates. Free Local Collection/Delivery.
SPEAK TO Simon Feingold.
Members of BAFRA, GADAR, UKIC and RFS.

R. W. BAXTER
Joel House, 43 Hoghton Street, Southport, **Merseyside PR9 OPG**
TEL   0704 537377
OPEN   9–10, 2–5.30 Mon–Fri.

Specialise in restoring antique clocks, carriage, longcase, bracket, French. Brass dials resilvered and pocket watches and modern clocks and watches repaired.

PROVIDE Home Inspections. Free Estimates. Free Collection/Delivery Service.
SPEAK TO R. W. Baxter.
Mr Baxter is a FBHI. This workshop is

included on the register of conservators maintained by the Conservation Unit of the Museums and Galleries Commission.

MICHAEL BENNETT
5 Warren Road, Hoylake, Wirral, **Merseyside L47 2AR**
TEL   051 632 2101 and 4331
FAX   051 632 6220
OPEN   9–5.30 Mon–Fri and By Appointment.

Specialise in invisible repairing of late 17th–early 19th century furniture with emphasis on blending in both colour and patina repairs. Also Boulle and marquetry work.
PROVIDE Home Inspections. Free Estimates. Free Collection/Delivery Service.
SPEAK TO Michael Bennett.

THE CLOCK SHOP
7 The Quadrant, Hoylake, Wirral, **Merseyside L47 2AY**
TEL   051 632 1888
OPEN   9–5.30 Mon–Fri.

Specialise in restoring antique clocks.
PROVIDE Home Inspections. Free Estimates. Collection/Delivery Service by arrangement.
SPEAK TO Kevin Whay.
Mr Whay is a MBHI and MBWCG.

WELLINGTON CRAFTS (1980)
121A/123A St John's Road, Waterloo, Liverpool, **Merseyside L22 9QE**
TEL   051 920 5511
OPEN   9.30–5 Mon, Tues; 9.30–2 Wed; 9.30–5.30 Thur–Sat.

Specialise in cane, rush and bergère restoration.

PROVIDE Home Inspections. Refundable Estimates. Chargeable Collection/Delivery Service.
SPEAK TO Neville Hymus.
SEE Oil Paintings.

PILGRIMS PROGRESS
1A–3A Bridgewater Street, Liverpool, **Merseyside L1 0AR**
TEL   051 708 7515
FAX   051 709 1465
OPEN   9–5 Mon–Fri; 1–4 Sat.

Specialise in restoring antique furniture including cabinet work, French polishing, re-upholstery.
PROVIDE Home Inspections. Free Estimates. Free/Chargeable Collection/Delivery Service.
SPEAK TO Selwyn Hyams.

BARNT GREEN ANTIQUES
93 Hewell Road, Barnt Green, Birmingham, **West Midlands B45 8NL**
TEL   021 445 4942
OPEN   9–5.30 Mon–Fri; 9–1 Sat.

Specialise in restoring and conserving antique furniture and longcase clocks, gilding.
PROVIDE Home Inspections. Free Estimates. Chargeable Collection/Delivery Service.
SPEAK TO Mr. N. Slater.
Members of BAFRA.

GEOSTRAN ANTIQUES
Middle Lane, Whitacre Heath, Coleshill, Birmingham, **West Midlands B46 2HX**
TEL   0675 81483
OPEN   10–5 Mon–Fri or By Appointment.

Specialise in restoring antique clocks and small furniture.
PROVIDE Home Inspections. Free Estimates. Free/Chargeable Collection/Delivery Service.
SPEAK TO Anthony Potter.
They are CMBHI.

HAMPTON UTILITIES (B'HAM) LTD
15 Pitsford Street, Hockley, Birmingham, **West Midlands B18 6LJ**
TEL   021 554 1766
OPEN   9–5 Mon–Thur; 9–4 Fri.
Specialise in restoring and repairing mirror frames including gilding.
PROVIDE Free Estimates. Chargeable Collection/Delivery Service.
SPEAK TO B. Levine.
SEE Oil Paintings, Silver.

HARBORNE PLACE UPHOLSTERY
22–24 Northfield Road, Harborne, Birmingham, **West Midlands B17 OSU**
TEL   021 427 5788
OPEN   9–6 Mon–Sat.
Specialise in all types of furniture restoration and upholstery including deep buttoning using traditional materials.
PROVIDE Home Inspections. Refundable Estimates. Free Collection/Delivery Service.
SPEAK TO Peter Hubbard.

GEOFFREY HASSALL ANTIQUES
20 New Road, Solihull, **West Midlands B91 3DP**
TEL   021 705 0068
OPEN   9 30–1, 2–5.30 Tues–Sat.
Specialise in restoring all periods of furniture.
PROVIDE Home Inspections. Free Estimates. Free/Chargeable Collection/Delivery Service.
SPEAK TO Geoffrey Hassall.

JOHN HUBBARD ANTIQUES
224–226 Court Oak Road, Harborne, Birmingham, **West Midlands B32 2EG**
TEL   021 426 1694
FAX   021 428 1214
OPEN   9–6 Mon–Sat.
Specialise in restoring 18th and 19th century fine furniture and decorative items including carving, veneering, polishing and leather lining.
PROVIDE Home Inspections. Refundable Estimates. Collection/Delivery Service.
SPEAK TO John Hubbard or David Taplin.
SEE Oil Paintings, Porcelain, Silver.

THE OLD CLOCK SHOP
32 Stephenson Street, Birmingham, **West Midlands B2 4BH**
TEL   021 632 4864
OPEN   9.30–5 Mon–Fri; 10–3 Sat.
Specialise in restoring wrist watches including Patek Phillipe, Rolex, precision pocket watches, also longcase, bracket and carriage clocks.
PROVIDE Home Inspections. Free Estimates. Chargeable Collection/Delivery Service.
SPEAK TO M. L. or S. R. Durham.
They are a MBHI.

OSBORNES ANTIQUES
91 Chester Road, New Oscott, Sutton Coldfield, **West Midlands B73 5BA**
TEL   021 355 6667
FAX   021 354 7166
OPEN   9–1 Mon; 9–1, 2–5 Tues/Wed; 9–1, 2–5.30 Thur/Fri; 9.15–12 Sat.
Specialise in repairing and restoring antique barometers, scientific glass blowing and manufacture of replacement barometer parts.
PROVIDE Free Estimates.
SPEAK TO Mrs. Osborne.
Member of BSSG.

109

H. AKSERALIAN
79 Mollison Way, Edgware, **Middlesex**
HA8 5QU
TEL   081 952 6432 evenings.
OPEN   By Appointment.

Specialise in chair caning, repairs to cane work, re-seating, staining cane work and sea-grass seating including bergère suites.
PROVIDE Home Inspections. Free Estimates. Chargeable Collection/Delivery Service.
SPEAK TO Harry Akseralian.

ANTIQUE RESTORATIONS
45 Windmill Road, Brentford,
Middlesex TW8 0QQ
TEL   081 568 5249
OPEN   8–5 Mon–Fri.

Specialise in restoring and conserving painted and gilded furniture, Oriental lacquer and Japanning.
PROVIDE Home Inspections. Free Chargeable Estimates. Free Local Collection/Delivery Service.
SPEAK TO Reginald Dudman.

ARTBRY'S ANTIQUES
44 High Street, Pinner, **Middlesex**
HA5 5PW
TEL   081 868 0834
OPEN   9.15–5.30 Mon–Sat;
            9.15–1 Wed.

Specialise in restoring bracket, longcase and carriage clocks.
PROVIDE Home Inspections. Free Estimates. Free Collection/Delivery Service.
SPEAK TO Mr. A. H. Davies.

R. BECKFORD
4 Elms Lane, Wembley, **Middlesex**
HA0 2NH
TEL   081 904 4735
OPEN   9.30–6.00 Mon–Fri.

Specialise in repairing and restoring all types of furniture, polishing and refinishing.
PROVIDE Home Inspections. Free Estimates. Chargeable Collection/Delivery Service.
SPEAK TO R. Beckford.

CHURCH LANE RESTORATIONS
1 Church Lane, Teddington, **Middlesex**
TW11 8PA
TEL   081 977 2526
OPEN   7.30–5 Mon–Thur; 7.30–4 Fri.

Specialise in restoring period furniture and French polishing.
PROVIDE Home Inspections. Free Estimates. Free Collection/Delivery Service.
SPEAK TO Mr. Vincent.
They are members of LAPADA.

R. V. MORGAN & CO.
Unit 41, 26–28 The Queensway, Ponders End, Enfield, **Middlesex EN3 5UU**
TEL   081 805 0353
OPEN   8–5.30 Mon–Fri; 8–3 Sat.

Specialise in all aspects of furniture restoration, specialist cabinetmaking and French polishing.
PROVIDE Home Inspections. Free/Chargeable Estimates. Chargeable Collection/Delivery Service.
SPEAK TO Mr. R. V. Morgan.

PHELPS LTD
133–135 St. Margarets Road, Twickenham, **Middlesex TW1 1RG**
TEL   081 892 1778
FAX   081 892 3661
OPEN   9–5.30 Mon–Sat.

Specialise in restoring 19th and early 20th century furniture.

PROVIDE Home Inspections. Free
Estimates. Chargeable
Collection/Delivery Service.
SPEAK TO R. Phelps.

ARK ANTIQUE RESTORATIONS
Morton Peto Road, Gapton Hall
Industrial Estate, Great Yarmouth,
Norfolk NR3 0LT
TEL   0493 653357
FAX   0493 658405
OPEN   9–5.30 Mon–Fri; 9–1 Sat.

Specialise in restoring fine English and
Continental furniture and clocks.

PROVIDE Home Inspections. Chargeable
Estimates. Free Local
Collection/Delivery Service.
SPEAK TO Ben Deveson.

'AS TIME GOES BY'
Wrights Court, Elm Hill, Norwich,
Norfolk NR3 1HQ
TEL   0603 666508
FAX   0263 732718
OPEN   9.30–5 Mon–Fri; 10–4 Sat.

Specialise in restoring antique clocks.

PROVIDE Home Inspections. Free
Estimates. Free/Chargeable
Collection/Delivery Service.
SPEAK TO Stephen or Catherine Phillips.
Member of the BHI.

DAVID BARTRAM FURNITURE
The Raveningham Centre, Castell Farm,
Beccles Road, Raveningham, Nr.
Norwich, **Norfolk NR14 6NU**
TEL   050 846 721
OPEN   10–6 daily.

Specialise in comprehensive antique
restoration service covering furniture,
gilding, upholstery and clocks.
PROVIDE Home Inspections. Free
Estimates. Free Collection/Delivery
Service.
SPEAK TO David Bartram.

Mr Bartram is a member of BAFRA and
UKIC. This workshop is included on
the register of conservators maintained
by the Conservation Unit of the
Museums and Galleries Commission.
SEE Silver.

ERIC BATES & SONS
Melbourne House, Bacton Road, North
Walsham, **Norfolk NR28 0RA**
TEL   0692 403221
OPEN   8.30–4.30 Mon–Fri.

Specialise in restoring antique furniture
and upholstery. They also hand-make
period style oak furniture.

PROVIDE Home Inspections. Refundable
Estimates. Collection/Delivery Service
by arrangement.
SPEAK TO Eric Bates.
SEE also **Norfolk.**

BROCKDISH ANTIQUES (M. & L. E. PALFREY)
Commerce House, Brockdish, Diss,
Norfolk IP21 4JL
TEL   03975 498
OPEN   9–5.30 Mon–Sat; closed Wed.

Specialise in sympathetic restoration of
antique furniture including antique
upholstery, using only traditional
methods.

PROVIDE Home Inspections. Free
Estimates. Free Collection/Delivery
Service.
SPEAK TO Michael Palfrey.

This is a three-generation family
business.

J. C. DAWES
The Street, Corpusty, Norwich, **Norfolk WR11 6QP**
TEL   026387 512
FAX   026387 512
OPEN   By Appointment.

Specialise in conservation of carved,

moulded, veneered wood or parquetry, stained and polished using traditional or modern methods, working when necesary with other specialist art conservators.

PROVIDE Home Inspections. Refundable/Chargeable Estimates. Chargeable Collection/Delivery Service.
SPEAK TO J. C. Dawes.

TONY GROVER, FAKENHAM ANTIQUES CENTRE
14 Norwich Road, Fakenham, **Norfolk NR21 8AZ**
TEL   0328 862941 or 0953 83654
OPEN   10–5 Mon–Sat.
Specialise in restoring antique English bracket and longcase clocks.
PROVIDE Home Inspections. Free Estimates. Chargeable Collection/Delivery Service
SPEAK TO Tony Grover.

PETER HOWKINS
39–40 King Street, Great Yarmouth, **Norfolk NR30 2PQ**
TEL   0493 851180
OPEN   9–5.30 Mon–Sat or by appointment.
Specialise in restoring antique furniture.
PROVIDE Home Inspections.
SPEAK TO Peter Howkins, Thomas Burn or Matthew Higham.
Member of NAG.
SEE Silver (different address).

HUMBLEYARD FINE ART
3 Fish Hill, Holt, **Norfolk NR25 6BD**
TEL   0263 713362
OPEN   10–5 Mon–Thur and 10–5 Sat.
Specialise in repairing and restoring barometers.

PROVIDE Home Inspections. Free Estimates. Chargeable Collection/ Delivery Service.
SPEAK TO James Layte.
SEE Collectors.

JASPER ANTIQUES
11A Hall Road, Snettisham, King's Lynn, **Norfolk PE31 7LU**
TEL   0485 541485 and 540604)
OPEN   10.30–1 Mon, Wed, Fri; 10.30–1, 2–4 Sat.
Specialise in repair service for clocks and watches.
PROVIDE Home Inspections. Free Estimates. Free Collection/Delivery Service.
SPEAK TO Mrs. A. A. Norris.
SEE Porcelain, Silver.

RODERICK LARWOOD
The Oaks, Station Road, Larling, Norwich, **Norfolk NR16 2QS**
TEL   0953 717937
OPEN   8–6 Mon–Fri.
Specialise in restoring 18th century furniture, brass inlay.
PROVIDE Home Inspections. Free Local Estimates. Free Collection/Delivery Service.
SPEAK TO Roderick Larwood.
Member of BAFRA.

LAWRENCE & CABLE
6 Merchants Court, St George's Street, Norwich, **Norfolk NR3 1AB**
TEL   0603 632064
OPEN   9–5 Mon–Fri.
Specialise in restoring and conserving painted furniture.
PROVIDE Home Inspections. Free Estimates. Free/Chargeable Collection/Delivery Service.
SPEAK TO Penny Lawrence or Tim Cable.

This workshop is included on the register of conservators maintained by the Conservation Unit of the Museums and Galleries Commission.
SEE Oil Paintings, Silver.

PARRISS
20 Station Road, Sheringham, **Norfolk NR26 8RE**
TEL   0263 822661
OPEN   9.30–1, 2.15–5 Mon–Fri.
Specialise in repairing antique clocks.
PROVIDE Home Inspections. Chargeable Estimates. Free/Chargeable Collection/Delivery Service.
SPEAK TO J. H. Parriss.

R. PINDER
20 Recreation Road, Hethersett, Norwich, **Norfolk NR9 3EF**
TEL   0603 8118641
OPEN   By Appointment.
Specialise in restoring and repairing antique English and French clocks and barometers. He also repairs case work.
PROVIDE Home Inspections. Free/Chargeable Estimates. Free/Chargeable Collection/Delivery Service.
SPEAK TO R. Pinder.
Mr Pinder is a member of the BHI and the BWCMG.

THOMAS TILLETT & CO.
17 Saint Giles Street, Norwich, **Norfolk NR2 1JL**
TEL   0603 625922 or 620372
FAX   0603 620372
OPEN   9–5.30 Mon–Sat.
Specialise in repairing antique and modern watches.
PROVIDE Home Inspections. Free Estimates. Free Collection/Delivery Service.
SPEAK TO Mr. T. Scally or Lorraine Scally.
This firm was established in 1908.
SEE Silver.

WICKENDEN CLOCKS
53 Gorse Rd, Thorpe St. Andrew, Norwich, **Norfolk NR7 OAY**
TEL   0603 32179
OPEN   9–5 Sun–Sat.
Specialise in restoring clocks and barometers.
PROVIDE Home Inspections. Free Estimates. Free Local Collection/Delivery Service.
SPEAK TO Eric Wickenden.
SEE Collectors (Musical Items).

R. C. WOODHOUSE
10 Westgate, Hunstanton, **Norfolk PE36 5AL**
TEL   0485 532903
OPEN   11–5 Wed, Fri, Sat or By Appointment.
Specialise in restoring all types of clocks, especially longcases. Also restore barometers.
PROVIDE Home Inspections. Free Estimates (domestic clocks). Free Collection/Delivery Service.
SPEAK TO R. C. Woodhouse
Member of the UKIC and MBHI.

CLASSIC UPHOLSTERY
Estate Yard, Upper Harlestone, Northampton, **Northamptonshire NN7 4EH**
TEL   0604 584556
OPEN   8.30–5 Mon–Fri.
Specialise in traditionally restoring and renovating upholstered furniture.
PROVIDE Home Inspections. Free Estimates. Free Collection/Delivery Service.
SPEAK TO Mark Austin.
Member of the Association of Master Upholsterers.

DOMENICO LUCISANO 'THE WOODCARVER'
The Grange Farm, Sywell,
Northamptonshire NN6 0BE
TEL   0604 755068
OPEN   8–5 Mon–Fri.
Specialise in any restoration involving woodcarving.
PROVIDE Home Inspections. Free Estimates. Chargeable Collection/Delivery Service.
SPEAK TO Domenico Lucisano.

BRYAN PERKINS ANTIQUES
52 Cannon Street, Wellingborough,
Northamptonshire NN8 4DT
TEL   0933 228812
OPEN   9–5.30 Mon–Fri; 10–12.30 Sat.
Specialise in restoring antique furniture and French polishing, especially chests of drawers and mahogany dining tables.
PROVIDE Home Inspections. Free Estimates. Chargeable Collection/Delivery Service.
SPEAK TO B. or J. Perkins.

J. A. & T. HEDLEY
3 St Mary's Chare, Hexham,
Northumberland NE46 1NQ
TEL   0434 602317
OPEN   9–5 Mon–Sat; 9–12 Thur.
Specialise in restoring antique furniture and French polishing.
PROVIDE Free Estimates. Chargeable Collection/Delivery Service.
SPEAK TO D. Hall or W. H. Jewitt
SEE Oil Paintings.

JOHN SMITH OF ALNWICK LTD
West Cawledge Park, Alnwick,
Northumberland NE66 2HJ
TEL   0665 604363
OPEN   10–5 Sun–Sat.
Specialise in restoring antique English and Continental furniture.

PROVIDE Home Inspections. Chargeable Estimates. Chargeable Collection/Delivery Service.
SPEAK TO Mr. Watson.

T. S. BARROWS & SON
Hamlyn Lodge, Station Road, Ollerton,
Nr. Newark, **Nottinghamshire NG22 9BN**
TEL   0623 823600
OPEN   8.30–5 Mon–Fri.
Specialise in restoring furniture, French polishing, cabinet-making.
PROVIDE Home Inspections. Chargeable Collection/Delivery Service.
SPEAK TO Norman Barrows.
A three-generation family business.

FLORENCE CONSERVATION & RESTORATION
102 Nottingham Road, Long Eaton,
Nottingham, **Nottinghamshire NG10 2BZ**
TEL   0602 733625
OPEN   8–5 Mon–Fri; 9–12 Sat.
Specialise in restoring gesso frames, gilding and gold leafing. They also repair and restore marquetry, painted and inlaid furniture.
PROVIDE Home Inspections. Refundable Estimates. Chargeable Collection/Delivery Service.
SPEAK TO Ron Florence.
SEE Oil Paintings, Porcelain.

GOODACRE ENGRAVING LTD
Thrumpton Avenue (off Chatsworth Avenue), Meadow Lane, Long Eaton,
Nottingham, **Nottinghamshire NG10 2GB**
TEL   0602 734387
FAX   0602 461193
OPEN   8.30–5 Mon–Thur; 8.30–1.30 Fri.
Specialise in restoration of antique dials

and movements including painted dials.
PROVIDE Free Estimates.
Can produce castings on a one-off basis.

COUNTRY CHAIRMEN
Home Farm, Ardington, Wantage,
Oxfordshire OX12 8PY
TEL   0235 833614
OPEN   8.30–5.30 Mon–Fri; 10–1 Sat.
Specialise in restoring and repairing
antique furniture, rush and cane seating
of chairs.
PROVIDE Home Inspections. Free
Estimates. Free Collection/Delivery
Service.
SPEAK TO Tony Handley.

LA CHAISE ANTIQUE
30 London Street, Faringdon,
Oxfordshire SN7 7AA
TEL   0367 240427
OPEN   9.30–5.30 Mon–Sat.
Specialise in restoring and
re-upholstering 18th and 19th century
furniture using traditional materials,
deep buttoning, leather table-liners.
PROVIDE Home Inspections. Free
Estimates. Free Collection/Delivery
Service.
SPEAK TO Roger Clark.
Member of the Guild of Master
Craftsmen.

**WOOLF LEIGH c/o LAURIE LEIGH
ANTIQUES**
36 High Street, Oxford, **Oxfordshire
OX1 4AN**
TEL   0865 244197 or 0608 810607
OPEN   By Appointment.
Specialise in repairing and restoring
British antique longcase and bracket
clocks including casework.
SPEAK TO Woolf Leigh.

**GERALD MARSH ANTIQUE
CLOCKS LTD**
Jericho House, North Aston,
Oxfordshire OX5 4HX
TEL   0869 40086
OPEN   9.30–5 Mon–Sat. (This branch
       opens January 1992.)
Specialise in restoring antique English
and French clocks, watches and
barometers.
PROVIDE Home Inspections. Free
Estimates. Free Collection/Delivery
Service.
SPEAK TO Gerald Marsh
Member of Worshipful Company of
Clockmakers, Craftsman of British
Horological Institute, Member of
NAWCC (USA) and BADA.
SEE **Hants**.

PETER A. MEECHAM
The Malt House, Milton-Under-
Wychwood, **Oxfordshire OX7 6JJ**
TEL   0993 830215
FAX   0993 830039
OPEN   8.30–5 Mon–Fri.
Specialise in restoring and repairing
antique and tower clocks.
PROVIDE Home Inspections. Free
Estimates. Free Collection/Delivery
Service.
SPEAK TO P. A. Meecham.
Craft Member BHI.

ROSEMARY AND TIME
42 Park Street, Thame, **Oxfordshire
OX9 3HR**
TEL   084421 6923
OPEN   9–12.30, 1.30–6 Mon–Sat.
Specialise in restoring clocks and all
mechanical items.
PROVIDE Home Inspections. Free
Estimates. Chargeable
Collection/Delivery Service.
SPEAK TO Tom Fletcher.

115

TERENCE C. J. WALSH
Park Farmhouse, Hook Norton,
Banbury, **Oxfordshire OX15 5LR**
TEL   0608 730293
OPEN   Mon–Sat daily.

Specialise in restoring 17th–19th century
furniture including Boulle and
marquetry. They also do upholstery
including four–poster beds and
headboards.

PROVIDE Home Inspections. Chargeable
Collection/Delivery Service.
SPEAK TO Terence Walsh.

WEAVES & WAXES
53 Church Street, Bloxham, Banbury,
Oxfordshire OX15 4ET
TEL   0295 721535
FAX   0295 271867
OPEN   9–1, 2–5.30 Tues–Fri; 9–1,
        2–4 Sat.

Specialise in restoring antique furniture
including polishing, veneering, general
repairs, gilding, rush and cane seating,
clocks, brass facsimiles, upholstery,
leather repairs.

PROVIDE Home Inspections.
Free/Chargeable Estimates. Chargeable
Collection/Delivery Service.
SPEAK TO Laurie Grayer.

SEE Collectors (Dolls, Toys).

PETER WIGGINS
Raffles, Southcombe, Chipping Norton,
Oxfordshire OX7 5QH
TEL   0608 642652
OPEN   9–6 Mon–Fri.

Specialise in restoring barometers and
clocks.

PROVIDE Home Inspections. Free
Estimates. Chargeable
Collection/Delivery Service.
SPEAK TO Peter Wiggins.

SEE Collectors (Scientific Instruments).

WITNEY RESTORATIONS
Workshop : Unit 17, Hanborough
Business Park, Main Road, Long
Hanborough, **Oxfordshire OX7 2LH**
Accounts and Enquiries : 96–100 Corn
Street, Witney, **Oxfordshire OX8 7BU**
TEL   0993 703902 accounts and
        enquiries
        0993 883336 workshop
FAX   0993 779852
OPEN   9.30–5 Mon–Fri.

Specialise in restoring and conserving
fine antique furniture, clocks as well as
decorative furniture and objects.
PROVIDE Home Inspections. Free
Estimates. Chargeable
Collection/Delivery Service.
SPEAK TO Mr. A. Smith or Mrs. J. Jarrett.

RICHARD HIGGINS
The Old School, Longnor, Nr.
Shrewsbury, **Shropshire SY5 7PP**
TEL   074373 8162
OPEN   8–6 Mon–Fri.

Specialise in restoring antique furniture
including Boulle, marquetry, rosewood
and mahogany, also bracket, longcase
and carriage clocks.
PROVIDE Home Inspections.
Free/Chargeable Estimates.
Collection/Delivery Service by
arrangement.
SPEAK TO Richard Higgins.
Member of BAFRA and UKIC. This
workshop is included on the register of
conservators maintained by the
Conservation Unit of the Museums and
Galleries Commission.

F. C. MANSER & SON LTD
53–54 Wyle Cop, Shrewsbury,
Shropshire SY1 1XJ
TEL   0743 351120
FAX   0743 271047
OPEN   9–5.30 Mon, Tues, Wed, Fri;
        9–10 Thur; 9–5 Sat.
Specialise in restoring clocks,
barometers, Boulle work.

PROVIDE Home Inspections. Free
Estimates. Chargeable
Collection/Delivery Service.
SPEAK TO Paul Manser.
Members of LAPADA and the Guild of
Master Craftsmen.
SEE Porcelain, Silver.

C. J. PRITCHARD
143a Belle Vue Road, Shrewsbury,
Shropshire SY3 7NN
TEL   0743 362854
OPEN   8.15–1, 2.15–4 Mon–Fri.
Specialise in restoring and conserving
antique furniture.
PROVIDE Home Inspections. Refundable
Estimates. Chargeable
Collection/Delivery Service.
SPEAK TO Mr. A. W. Jones.

**ST. MARY'S ANTIQUES &
CABINETMAKERS**
2 Lower Bar, Newport, **Shropshire
TF10 1BQ**
TEL   0952 811549
OPEN   9–6 Mon–Fri; 9–12 Sat.
Specialise in restoring antique furniture.
PROVIDE Home Inspections. Free
Estimates. Free/Chargeable
Collection/Delivery Service.
SPEAK TO Ray Edwards.

T. R. BAILEY
11 St Andrew's Road, Stogursey,
Bridgwater, **Somerset TA5 1TE**
TEL   0278 732887
OPEN   By Appointment.
Specialise in restoring small items of
English furniture.
PROVIDE Free Estimates.
Collection/Delivery Service by
arrangement.
SPEAK TO Tim Bailey.
SEE Silver.

J. BURRELL
Westerfield House, Seavington St. Mary,
Ilminster, **Somerset TA19 OQR**
TEL   0460 40610
OPEN   By Appointment.
Specialise in restoring antique furniture,
including structural repairs, veneering,
marquetry, lacquer work, carving, wax
polishing.
PROVIDE Home Inspections. Refundable
Estimates. Chargeable
Collection/Delivery Service.
SPEAK TO J. Burrell.
Member of BAFRA.

CASTLE HOUSE
Unit 1, Bennetts Field Estate, Moor
Lane, Wincanton, **Somerset BA9 9DT**
TEL   0963 33884
OPEN   8.30–5.30 Mon–Fri.
Specialise in restoring antique and
Continental furniture, Boulle work,
marquetry and period finishes.
PROVIDE Home Inspections.
Free/Chargeable Estimates.
Free/Chargeable Collection/Delivery
Service.
SPEAK TO Michael Durlee.
Member of BAFRA.

CLARE HUTCHISON
1A West Street, Ilminster, **Somerset
TA19 9AA**
TEL   0460 53369
OPEN   10–5.30 Mon–Fri; 10–1 Sat.
Specialise in restoring antique mirror
frames.
PROVIDE Free Estimates.
SPEAK TO Clare Hutchison.
SEE Oil Paintings.

JENNIFER M. JOHN
Myrtle Cottage, Merryfield Lane, Ilton,
Ilminster, **Somerset TA19 9EZ**
TEL   0460 53963
OPEN   9–5 Mon–Sat or By
Appointment.

Specialise in cane seating including
medallions, blind and close caning as
well as seating in sea-grass, rush and
string.

PROVIDE Home Inspections. Free
Estimates. Free Local Collection/
Delivery Service.

SPEAK TO Jennifer John.

Member of the Basket Makers
Association.

EDWARD VENN ANTIQUE
RESTORATIONS
52 Long Street, Williton, Taunton,
Somerset TA4 4QU
TEL   0984 32631
OPEN   8.30–5.30 Mon–Fri.

Specialise in restoring barometers,
longcase clocks and antique furniture up
to 1900. They also replace mirror glass
and restore frames.

PROVIDE Chargeable Estimates.
Chargeable Collection/Delivery Service

SPEAK TO Mr. Venn

THE ANTIQUE RESTORATION
STUDIO
The Old Post Office, Haughton,
Staffordshire ST18 9JH
TEL   0785 780424
FAX   0785 780157
OPEN   9–5 Mon–Fri.

Specialise in restoring antique and
modern furniture.

PROVIDE Home Inspections. Free
Estimates. Free Collection/Delivery
Service.

SPEAK TO D. P. Albright.

SEE Porcelain, Oil Paintings, Carpets.

ANTIQUES WORKSHOP
43–45 Hope Street, Hanley, Stoke-on-
Trent, **Staffordshire ST1 5BT**
TEL   0782 273645
OPEN   9–5 Mon–Fri; 10–4 Sat.

Specialise in repairing and restoring oak
and mahogany and French polishing of
the latter.

PROVIDE Home Inspections. Free
Estimates. Chargeable
Collection/Delivery Service.

SPEAK TO Howard Oakes.

JALNA ANTIQUES
'Jalna', Coley Lane, Little Haywood, Nr.
Stafford, **Staffordshire ST18 OUP**
TEL   0889 881381
OPEN   9–5 Sun–Sat.

Specialise in restoring upholstery,
carving, veneering and French
polishing.

PROVIDE Home Inspections. Free
Estimates. Free Collection/Delivery
Service.

SPEAK TO Geoff Hancox.

A. C. PRALL RESTORATIONS
Highfield Farm, Uttoxeter Road,
Draycott, **Staffordshire ST11 9AE**
TEL   0782 399022
OPEN   9–7 Mon–Fri.

Specialise in restoring Georgian
furniture and clocks including longcase,
mantel.

PROVIDE Free Estimates.
Free/Chargeable Collection/Delivery
Service..

SPEAK TO Mr. Prall.

GRAHAM WHEELER PERIOD
INTERIORS
24 Radford Street, Stone, **Staffordshire
ST15 8DA**
TEL   0785 875000
FAX   0785 875015
OPEN   9–5 Mon–Fri.

Specialise in restoring antique furniture
and creating period interiors.

PROVIDE Home Inspections. Refundable Estimates. Chargeable Collection/Delivery Service.
SPEAK TO Graham Wheeler.

ROGER & SYLVIA ALLAN
The Old Red Lion, Bedingfield, Eye, **Suffolk IP23 7LQ**
TEL   0728 76 491
OPEN   By Appointment.

Specialise in restoring antique furniture, carved objects and treen.
PROVIDE Home Inspections. Free Estimates.
SPEAK TO Roger Allan.
SEE Oil Paintings, Silver.

ANTIQUE CLOCKS BY SIMON CHARLES
The Limes, 72 Melford Rd, Sudbury, **Suffolk CO10 6LT**
TEL   0787 75931
OPEN   10–6 Mon–Sat.

Specialise in restoring early English clocks including movements and cases.
PROVIDE Home Inspections. Free Estimates. Chargeable Collection/Delivery Service.
SPEAK TO Simon Charles.
Member of BWCMG.

BALLYBEG RESTORATIONS & HARCOURT ANTIQUES
101 Kingsway, Mildenhall, **Suffolk IP28 7HS**
TEL   0638 712378
OPEN   By Appointment.

Specialise in restoring antique furniture including upholstery, gilding, painted furniture, marquetry, veneering, French polishing.

PROVIDE Home Inspections. Free Estimates. Free Collection/Delivery Service.
SPEAK TO Mr. P. B. Bailey.

BED BAZAAR
29 Double Street, Framlingham, Woodbridge, **Suffolk IP13 9BN**
TEL   0728 723756
FAX   0728 724626
OPEN   By Appointment.

Specialise in restoring antique brass and iron beds and supply mattresses and bed-spring bases.
PROVIDE Home Inspections. Free Estimates. Chargeable Collection/Delivery Service.
SPEAK TO Ben Goodbrey.

JOHN GAZELEY ASSOCIATES FINE ART
17 Fonnereau Road, Ipswich, **Suffolk IP1 3JR**
TEL   0473 252420
OPEN   By Appointment.

Specialise in gilding and repairing mirror frames as well as making reproduction frames.
PROVIDE Free Estimates
SPEAK TO Dr. John Gazeley
SEE Oil Paintings.

E. T. MANSON
8 Market Hill, Woodbridge, **Suffolk IP12 4LU**
TEL   0394 380235
OPEN   10–5 Thur and Sat or By Appointment.

Specialise in restoring antique clocks including wheel and pinion cutting, remaking of missing parts, repeating work.
PROVIDE Home Inspections. Free Estimates. Free Collection/Delivery Service.
SPEAK TO E. T. Manson.

THE MENDLESHAM FURNITURE WORKSHOP
Elms Farm, Mendlesham, Stowmarket,
Suffolk IP14 5RS
TEL　　0449 767107
OPEN　　By Appointment.

Specialise in restoring English antique furniture, particularly Mendlesham chairs, woodcarving, French polishing and some upholstery work.

PROVIDE Home Inspections. Chargeable Estimates. Chargeable Collection/Delivery Service.
SPEAK TO Roy Clement-Smith.

Member of the Guild of Master Craftsmen.

NETTLE HALL RESTORATION
Unit 1, Corner Farm, Sibton,
Saxmundham, **Suffolk IP17 2NE**
TEL　　072 879 550 and 205.
OPEN　　9–5 Mon–Sat.

Specialise in restoring and conserving antique furniture, inlay work, marquetry, cabinetmaking, French polishing, gilding.
PROVIDE Home Inspections. Free Estimates. Chargeable Collection/Delivery Service.
SPEAK TO Thomas Mark Spirling.

PEASENHALL ART & ANTIQUES GALLERY
Peasenhall, Nr. Saxmundham, **Suffolk IP17 2HJ**
TEL　　072 879 224
OPEN　　9–6 Sun–Sat.

Specialise in restoring antique furniture. They also make and repair walking sticks.

PROVIDE Local Home Inspections. Free Estimates. Free Local Collection/Delivery Service.
SPEAK TO Mike Wickins.
SEE Oil Paintings.

PEPPERS PERIOD PIECES
23 Churchgate Street, Bury St.Edmunds,
Suffolk IP33 1RG
TEL　　0284 768786
OPEN　　10–5 Mon–Sat.

Specialise in restoring furniture and clocks.

PROVIDE Home Inspections. Refundable Estimates. Free/Chargeable Collection/Delivery Service.
SPEAK TO M. E. Pepper.

Their restorers are West Dean trained.

A. G. SMEETH
Clock House, Locks Lane, Leavenheath,
Suffolk CO6 4PF
TEL　　0206 262187
OPEN　　By Appointment.

Specialise in restoring antique clocks and furniture.

PROVIDE Home Inspections. Free Estimates. Free Collection/Delivery Service.
SPEAK TO A. G. Smeeth.

MICHAEL ADDISON ANTIQUES
28–30 Godstone Road, Kenley, **Surrey CR8 5JE**
TEL　　081 668 6714
OPEN　　10–5 Mon–Sat.

Specialise in restoring antique furniture and upholstery.

PROVIDE Home Inspections. Free Estimates. Free Collection/Delivery Service.
SPEAK TO M. Addison.

A. E. BOOTH & SON
9 High Street, Ewell, Epsom, **Surrey KT17 1SG**
TEL　　081 393 5245
OPEN　　9–5 Mon–Fri.

Specialise in repairs to dining chairs, antique and reproduction furniture, including polishing, restoration of clocks, gilding and upholstery.

PROVIDE Home Inspections. Free/Refundable Estimates. Free Collection/Delivery Service.

SPEAK TO D.J.Booth.

Member of BAFRA.

B. S. ANTIQUES
39 Bridge Road, East Molesey, **Surrey KT8 9ER**

TEL   081 941 1812
OPEN   10–5 Mon–Sat; closed Wed.

Specialise in repairing and restoring antique clocks and barometers.

PROVIDE Home Inspections. Free Estimates. Collection/Delivery Service by arrangement.

SPEAK TO Stephen Anderman.

IAN CALDWELL
9A The Green, Dorking Road, Tadworth, **Surrey KT20 5SQ**

TEL   0737 813969
OPEN   10–5.30 daily; closed Wed.

Specialise in restoring furniture including gilding, lacquer work and upholstery.

PROVIDE Home Inspections. Free Collection/Delivery Service.

SPEAK TO Ian Caldwell.

Member of LAPADA.

THE CLOCK SHOP
64 Church Street, Weybridge, **Surrey KT13 8DL**

TEL   0932 840407 and 855503
OPEN   9.45–5.45 Mon–Sat.

Specialise in restoring antique dial clocks and barometers including casework.

PROVIDE Home Inspections. Free Estimates. Free Collection/Delivery Service.

SPEAK TO Mr. Forster.

COURTLANDS RESTORATION
Courtlands, Park Road, Banstead, **Surrey SM7 3EF**

TEL   0737 352429
OPEN   8–7 Mon–Sat.

Specialise in restoring antique furniture including traditional and French polishing, simulation effects, cabinetmaking, turning and carving, veneer repairs, gilding, metal repairs.

PROVIDE Home Inspections. Free Estimates. Free Collection/Delivery Service.

SPEAK TO David Sayer.

Member of BAFRA.

SEE Porcelain.

ROGER A. DAVIS
19 Dorking Rd, Great Bookham, **Surrey KT23 4PU**

TEL   0372 457655 and 453167
OPEN   9.30–5.30 Tues, Thur, Sat.

Specialise in restoring antique clocks.

PROVIDE Home Inspections. Free Estimates. Free Collection/Delivery Service.

SPEAK TO Roger Davis.

Member of BHI and BWCMG.

DAVID EMBLING
45 Fairfield, Farnham, **Surrey GU9 8AG**

TEL   0252 712660
OPEN   8–1, 2–5 Mon–Fri.

Specialise in restoring antique and modern furniture, French polishing, lacquering, gilding.

PROVIDE Home Inspections. Free Estimates. Chargeable Collection/Delivery Service.

SPEAK TO David Embling.

SEE Oil Paintings.

G. & R. FRASER SINCLAIR
11 Orchard Works, Streeters Lane,
Beddington, **Surrey SM6 7ND**
TEL   081 669 5343
OPEN   8–5.30 Mon–Fri.

Specialise in restoring 18th century English furniture.

PROVIDE Home Inspections. Free Estimates. Free Collection/Delivery Service.
SPEAK TO Glen Sinclair.

Member of BAFRA.

GILLETT & JOHNSTON (CROYDON) LTD
28 Sanderstead Road, South Croydon,
Surrey CR2 0PA
TEL   081 686 2694
FAX   081 681 4028
OPEN   9–5 Mon–Fri.

Specialise in refurbishment of old tower clocks and bells on churches, cathedrals, town halls and other public buildings. Also stable clocks.

PROVIDE Home Inspections. Free Estimates. Chargeable Collection/Delivery Service.
SPEAK TO S. J. Coombs or C. L. Edwards.

HEARN–COOPER LTD
46 Park Hill Road, Wallington, **Surrey SM6 0SB**
TEL   081 395 5498
OPEN   8.30–5.30 Mon–Fri; Sat By Appointment.

Specialise in restoring Oriental lacquer and European lacquered furniture.

PROVIDE Home Inspections. Estimates. Collection/Delivery Service Available.
SPEAK TO Richard Hearn-Cooper.

HEATH-BULLOCK
8 Meadrow, Godalming, **Surrey GU7 3HN**
TEL   0483 422562
FAX   0483 426077
OPEN   10–1, 2–4 Mon–Sat.

Specialise in restoring and upholstering antique furniture. They have a long tradition in leather upholstery.

PROVIDE Home Inspections. Free Estimates. Chargeable Collection/Delivery Service.
SPEAK TO Roger Heath-Bullock.

MICHAEL HEDGECOE
Rowan House, 21 Burrow Hill Green,
Chobham, Woking, **Surrey GU24 8QS**
TEL   0276 858206
OPEN   8–5 Mon–Fri.

Specialise in restoring top quality English and French 18th and 19th century furniture. Also best quality upholstery.

PROVIDE Home Inspections. Free Estimates. Chargeable Collection/Delivery Service.
SPEAK TO Michael Hedgecoe.

Member of LAPADA.

E HOLLANDER LTD
The Dutch House, Horsham Road,
South Holmwood, Dorking, **Surrey RH5 4NF**
TEL   0306 888921
OPEN   8–4.50 Mon–Fri; Sat By Appointment.

Specialise in restoring 17th–19th century clocks and watches as well as barometers.

PROVIDE Home Inspections. Free Estimates. Collection/Delivery Service by arrangement.
SPEAK TO David Pay.

Member of BADA and BHI.

HOROLOGICAL WORKSHOPS
204 Worplesdon Road, Guildford,
Surrey GU2 6UY
TEL   0483 576496
OPEN   8.30–5.30 Mon–Fri; 9–12.30 Sat.
Specialise in repairing antique clocks,
watches and barometers and restoring
turret clocks.
PROVIDE Home Inspections, Free
Estimates. Chargeable
Collection/Delivery Service.
SPEAK TO Mr. M. D. Tooke.
Member of BADA.

JOHN KENDALL
156 High St, Old Woking, **Surrey
GU21 9JH**
TEL   0483 771310
OPEN   9–5 Mon–Fri.
Specialise in restoring clocks, especially
17th century, barometers and frames,
restoring furniture including marquetry.
PROVIDE Home Inspections. Free
Estimates. Chargeable
Collection/Delivery Service.
SPEAK TO John Kendall.

RICHARD LAWMAN–WARWICK ANTIQUE RESTORATIONS
32 Beddington Lane, Croydon, **Surrey
CR0 4TB**
TEL   081 688 4511
OPEN   9–6 Tues–Sat.
Specialise in restoring fine furniture,
leathering, caning, rushing, upholstery
and clock restoration.
PROVIDE Home Inspections. Free
Estimates. Free Collection/Delivery
Service.
SPEAK TO Richard Lawman.
Member of the Guild of Master
Craftsmen. This workshop is included
on the register of conservators
maintained by the Conservation Unit of
the Museums and Galleries
Commission.

MANOR ANTIQUES & RESTORATIONS
2 New Shops, High Street, Old Woking,
Surrey GU22 9JW
TEL   0483 724666
OPEN   10–5 Mon–Fri; 10–4.30 Sat.
Specialise in restoring furniture
including French polishing, inlay work,
chair-caning and rush work. They also
carry out clock repairs.
PROVIDE Home Inspections. Free
Estimates. Collection/Delivery Service.
SPEAK TO Alan Wellstead or Paul
Thomson.
Member of the Guild of Master
Craftsmen.
SEE Oil Paintings.

SIMON MARSH RESTORATIONS
The Old Butchers Shop, High St,
Bletchingley, **Surrey RH1 4PA**
TEL   0883 743350
OPEN   By Appointment.
Specialise in restoring fine furniture.
PROVIDE Home Inspections.
Free/Refundable Estimates. Chargeable
Collection/Delivery Service.
SPEAK TO Mrs. Marsh.
Member of BAFRA.

TIMOTHY NAYLOR LTD
88 Sheen Road, Richmond, **Surrey
TW9 1UF**
TEL   081 332 0444
OPEN   8–5.30 Mon–Fri.
Specialise in restoring 18th century
English furniture including marquetry
and carving.
PROVIDE Home Inspections. Free
Estimates. Collection/Delivery Service
by arrangement.
SPEAK TO Timothy Naylor.

N. J. NEWMAN
22 Eastcroft Road, West Ewell, **Surrey KT19 9TX**
TEL   081 393 0538
OPEN   By Appointment.

Specialise in restoring English and Continental furniture.

PROVIDE Home Inspections. Free/Chargeable Estimates. Chargeable Collection/Delivery Service.
SPEAK TO Nick Newman.

Member of BAFRA. This workshop is included on the register of conservators maintained by the Conservation Unit of the Museums and Galleries Commission.

SAGE ANTIQUES & INTERIORS
High Street, Ripley, **Surrey GU23 6BB**
TEL   0483 224396
FAX   0483 211996
OPEN   9.30–5.30 Mon–Sat.

Specialise in restoring furniture 1600–1840; oak, walnut, mahogany, fruitwood.

PROVIDE Free Estimates. Free Collection/Delivery Service.
SPEAK TO Howard or Chrissie Sage.

They are members of LAPADA and the Guild of Master Craftsmen.
SEE Oil Paintings, Porcelain.

R. SAUNDERS
71 Queens Road, Weybridge, **Surrey KT13 9UQ**
TEL   0932 842601
OPEN   9.15–5 Mon–Sat; closed Wed.

Specialise in repairing good quality English furniture pre-1830.

PROVIDE Home Inspections. Free Estimates. Free Collection/Delivery Service.
SPEAK TO J. B. Tonkinson.

SEE Oil Paintings, Porcelain, Silver.

MICHAEL SCHRYVER ANTIQUES
The Granary, 10 North Street, Dorking, **Surrey RH4 1DN**
TEL   0306 881110
FAX   0306 76168
OPEN   8.30–5.30 Mon–Fri; 8.30–12.30 Sat.

Specialise in restoring fine quality period furniture including metalwork, period and contemporary upholstery.

PROVIDE Home Inspections. Free Estimates. Free Collection/Delivery Service.
SPEAK TO Michael Schryver.

SURREY CLOCK CENTRE
3 Lower Street, Haslemere, **Surrey GU27 2NY**
TEL   0428 651313
OPEN   9–5 Wed; 9–1 Sat.

Specialise in restoring antique clocks and barometers.

PROVIDE Home Inspections. Free Estimates. Chargeable Collection/Delivery Service.
SPEAK TO C. Ingrams or S. Haw.

CHARLES WRIGHT
Lark Rise, Glendine Avenue, East Horsley, **Surrey KT24 5AY**
TEL   04865 2904
OPEN   By Appointment.

Specialise in restoring furniture of all periods.

PROVIDE Chargeable Home Inspections. Free Estimates.
SPEAK TO Charles Wright.

Mr.Wright was Head of the Furniture Conservation Department at the Victoria and Albert Museum for 36 years.

BRAGGE & SONS
Landgate House, Rye, **East Sussex
TN31 7LH**
TEL   0797 223358
FAX   0797 225143
OPEN   By Appointment.

Specialise in restoring 18th century English and French furniture.

PROVIDE Home Inspections. Free Estimates. Free Collection/Delivery Service.

SPEAK TO J. Bragge.

W. BRUFORD & SON LTD
11–13 Cornfield Road, Eastbourne, **East Sussex BN21 3NA**
TEL   0323 25452
OPEN   9–1, 2–5.30 Mon–Fri; 9–1, 2–5 Sat.

Specialise in repairing and restoring 19th century bracket and carriage clocks and pocket watches.

PROVIDE Free Estimates.

SPEAK TO N. Bruford or J. Burgess.

SEE Silver.

JOHN COWDEROY ANTIQUES
42 South Street, Eastbourne, **East Sussex BN21 4XB**
TEL   0323 20058
FAX   0323 410163
OPEN   9.30–1, 2.30–5 Mon–Tues, Thur–Fri; 9.30–1 Wed & Sat.

Specialise in restoring antique English and French clocks. They also undertake furniture restoration and French polishing.

PROVIDE Home Inspections. Free Estimates. Chargeable Collection/Delivery Service.

SPEAK TO John, Ruth, David or Richard Cowderoy.

Members of BADA and West Dean trained.

SEE Collectors (Mechanical Music).

EASTBOURNE CLOCKS
9 Victoria Drive, Eastbourne, **East Sussex BN20 8JR**
TEL   0323 642650
OPEN   8.30–12.30, 2–5 Mon–Fri; 8.30–12.30 Sat.

Specialise in restoring and repairing antique and good quality clocks. They will make clocks and movements to order.

PROVIDE Home Inspections. Free Estimates. Free Collection/Delivery Service.

SPEAK TO Philip Wardale.

Craft Member of BHI.

FIRELEAD LTD
Banff Farm, Upper Clayhill, Uckfield Rd, Ringmer, Lewes, **East Sussex BN8 5RR**
TEL   0273 890918
FAX   0273 890691
OPEN   8.00–5.30 Mon–Fri By Appointment.

Specialise in full antique restoration including re-leathering writing surfaces, upholstery, re-silvering mirrors, keys made for old locks, marquetry repairs, water-gilding. Also duplicate items to match other pieces.

PROVIDE Local Home Inspections. Local Free Estimates. Chargeable Collection/Delivery Service.

SPEAK TO David Gilbert.

SEE Oil Paintings.

GOLDEN FISH GILDING & RESTORATION
94 Gloucester Road, Brighton, **East Sussex BN1 4AP**
TEL   0273 691164
FAX   0273 691164
OPEN   9–5 Mon–Fri.

Specialise in gilding and restoring mirror frames and furniture including carving.

PROVIDE Home Inspections. Free

Estimates. Free Collection/Delivery Service.
SPEAK TO Marianne Hatchwell.
Also teaches gilding techniques.
SEE Oil Paintings, Porcelain.

PROVIDE Local Home Inspections. Free Estimates.
SPEAK TO D. J. Matthews.
Member of the Guild of Master Craftsmen.

JOHN HARTNETT & SON
2 Victoria Street, Brighton, **East Sussex BN1 3FP**
TEL   0273 28793
OPEN   9–6 Mon–Fri.

Specialise in restoring fine furniture including French polishing, upholstery, leather insets, lacquer and japanning, marquetry and inlay, caning and rushing, carving, gilding.
PROVIDE Home Inspections. Free Estimates. Chargeable Collection/Delivery Service.
SPEAK TO John Hartnett.

MORE RESTORATIONS
The Old Booking Hall, Hove Park Villas, Hove, **East Sussex BN3 6HP**
TEL   0273 25380
OPEN   8.30–5 Mon–Fri.

Specialise in restoring period (1700–1850) English furniture and some continental marquetry. They also restore English dial clocks, barometers, barographs and their case work.
PROVIDE Home Inspections. Free Estimates. Collection/Delivery Service by arrangement.
SPEAK TO Arthur Moore.

SIMON HATCHWELL ANTIQUES
94 Gloucester Rd, Brighton, **East Sussex BN1 4AP**
TEL   0273 691164
OPEN   9–1.30, 2.30–5 Mon–Fri; Sat By Appointment.

Specialise in restoring barometers, furniture and clocks.
PROVIDE Home Inspections. Free Estimates. Free Local Collection/Delivery Service.
SPEAK TO Simon Hatchwell.
Member of LAPADA.

THE OLD BAKERY FURNISHING COMPANY
Punetts Town, Nr. Heathfield, **East Sussex TN21 9DS**
TEL   0435 830608
OPEN   9–5 Mon–Fri; 9–1 Sat.

Specialise in restoring antique furniture, including tapestry work and traditional upholstery.
PROVIDE Free/Chargeable Home Inspections. Estimates. Chargeable Collection/Delivery Service.
SPEAK TO Ann Spencer.

D. J. MATTHEWS
20–21 Newark Place, Brighton, **East Sussex BN2 2NT**
TEL   0273 602427
OPEN   7.30–5 Mon–Fri.

Specialise in restoring antique furniture, particularly that which has a painted finish, including trays, small boxes, screens and papier mâché items.

R. J. ROSSI
Hillsview, Lion Hill, Stone Cross, Pevensey, **East Sussex BN24 5ED**
TEL   0323 768929
OPEN   By Appointment.

Specialise in restoring giltwood frames and gilding and will make frames to customers' specifications.
PROVIDE Home Inspections. Free

Estimates. Collection/Delivery Service by arrangement.
SPEAK TO R. J. Rossi.

Estimates. Chargeable Collection/Delivery Service.
SPEAK TO C.Houston.
Member of BHI.

PETER SEMUS CRAFTING ANTIQUES
The Warehouse, Gladstone Land, Portslade, **East Sussex BN41 1LJ**
TEL 0273 420154
FAX 0273 430355
OPEN 8–6 Mon–Fri.
Specialise in restoring antique furniture, making bespoke furniture and reproduction furniture.
PROVIDE Home Inspections. Refundable Estimates. Free Collection/Delivery Service.
SPEAK TO Peter Semus.

CAROL BANKS
September Cottage, 88 Victoria Road, Shoreham-by-Sea, **West Sussex BN4 5WS**
TEL 0273 461647 after 5pm.
OPEN By Appointment.
Specialise in restoring ornate gilt mirror frames and decorated and painted furniture.
PROVIDE Local Home Inspections. Free Estimates.
SPEAK TO Carol Banks.
SEE Porcelain.

YELLOW LANTERN ANTIQUES LTD
34 & 34B Holland Road, Hove, **East Sussex BN3 1JL**
TEL 0273 771572
OPEN 9.30– 1, 2.15–5.30 Mon–Fri; 9–1, 2.15–4.30 Sat.
Specialise in cleaning of ormolu and bronze and restoring furniture.
PROVIDE Home Inspections. Free Estimates. Free Collection/Delivery Service.
SPEAK TO Mr. or Mrs. B. R. Higgins.
Members of LAPADA.
SEE Silver.

RICHARD & SUE BEALE CONSERVATION
West Chiltington, **West Sussex**
TEL 0798 813380
OPEN 9.30–5 Mon–Fri.
Specialise in conserving and restoring antique furniture including English japanned, Oriental lacquer, French vernis Martin, gilded and painted furniture, frames and related objets d'art.
PROVIDE Home Inspections. Free Estimates. Chargeable Collection/Delivery Service.
SPEAK TO Richard or Sue Beale.

ANTIQUE CLOCK RESTORATION
23 Greenacres Ring, Angmering, **West Sussex BN16 4BU**
TEL 0903 786203
OPEN 9–5 Mon–Sat.
Specialise in repairing and restoring English and French antique clocks and pocket watches.
PROVIDE Home Inspections. Free

T. P. BROOKS
Sycamores, School Lane, Lodsworth, Petworth, **West Sussex GU28 9DH**
TEL 07985 248
OPEN 9–6 Mon–Fri or By Appointment.
Specialise in restoring 17th to 19th century clocks and barometers.
PROVIDE Home Inspections. Free

Estimates. Free Collection/Delivery Service.

SPEAK TO Mr. T. P. Brooks.

Member of BHI and UKIC. This workshop is included on the register of conservators maintained by the Conservation Unit of the Museums and Galleries Commission.

P. G. CASEBOW
Pilgrims, Millhouse, Worthing, **West Sussex BN13 3DE**
TEL   0903 64045
OPEN   By Appointment.

Specialise in restoring period furniture, fretwork, inlay and marquetry.

PROVIDE Home Inspections. Free Estimates. Chargeable Collection/Delivery Service.

SPEAK TO Peter Casebow.

Member of BAFRA.

SONIA DEMETRIOU
The Studio, Tillington Cottage, Tillington, Petworth, **West Sussex GU28 ORA**
TEL   0798 44113
OPEN   9.30–6 Mon–Fri.

Specialise in cleaning and restoring all types of decorated
furniture and objets d'art including japanned work and Tole Ware.

PROVIDE Local Home Inspections. Free Local Estimates.

SPEAK TO Sonia Demetriou.

GARNER & CO.
Stable Cottage, Steyning Road, Wiston, **West Sussex BN44 3DD**
TEL   0903 814565
OPEN   By Appointment (Tel Mon–Fri 9–5.30).

Specialise in conserving fine period (1600–1850) English and Continental

furniture and works of art including painted furniture and gilded frames. They also restore clocks and dials.

PROVIDE Home Inspections. Estimates.

SPEAK TO Sid Garner.

SEE Porcelain, Silver.

NOEL & EVA-LOUISE PEPPERALL
Dairy Lane Cottage, Walberton, Arundel, **West Sussex BN18 0PT**
TEL   0243 551282
OPEN   By Appointment.

Specialise in restoring antique furniture, including painted furniture and gilding.

PROVIDE Home Inspections. Free Estimates. Chargeable Collection/Delivery Service.

SPEAK TO Noel or Eva-Louise Pepperall.

Mr. Pepperall is a member of BAFRA. This workshop is included on the register of conservators maintained by the Conservation Unit of the Museums and Galleries Commission.

ALBERT PLUMB
31 Whyke Lane, Chichester, **West Sussex PO19 2JS**
TEL   0243 788468
OPEN   9.30–5 Mon–Sat.

Specialise in antique furniture restoration.

PROVIDE Home Inspections. Free Estimates. Chargeable Collection/Delivery Service.

SPEAK TO Albert Plumb.

SEE Display.

THAKEHAM FURNITURE
Rock Road, Storrington, **West Sussex RH20 3AE**
TEL   0903 745464
OPEN   8.30–5 Mon–Fri.

Specialise in restoring 18th and 19th century furniture including marquetry, veneering, cabinetwork and French polishing.

PROVIDE Home Inspections. Free/ Chargeable Estimates. Free/ Chargeable Collection/Delivery Service.

SPEAK TO Mr. Chavasse.

Member of BAFRA.

WEST DEAN COLLEGE
West Dean, Chichester, **West Sussex PO18 00Z**

TEL   0243 63 301
FAX   0243 63 342
OPEN   9–5 Mon–Fri.

Specialise in training conservators and restorers in the fields of antique furniture and antique clocks . They will also undertake restoration work.

PROVIDE Local Home Inspections. Free Estimates.

SPEAK TO Peter Sarginson.

SEE Books, Porcelain, Silver.

DAVID WESTON
East Lodge, Woldringfold, Lower Beeding, Horsham, **West Sussex RH13 6NJ**

TEL   0403 891617
OPEN   By Appointment.

Specialise in restoring composition frames and gilding.

PROVIDE Free Estimates.

SPEAK TO David Weston.

Also make reproduction composition frames.

WILSON ANTIQUES
57–59 Broadwater Road, Worthing, **West Sussex BN14 8AH**

TEL   0903 202059
OPEN   9–5 Mon–Sat.

Specialise in restoring antique furniture.

PROVIDE Home Inspections. Free Estimates. Free Collection/Delivery Service.

SPEAK TO Frank Wilson.

ABERCROMBIES
140–142 Manor House Road, Jesmond, Newcastle-upon-Tyne, **Tyne & Wear NE2 2NA**

TEL   091 281 7182
FAX   091 281 7183
OPEN   10–6 Tues–Fri; 10–4 Sat.

Specialise in traditional re-upholstery and furniture restoration.

PROVIDE Home Inspections. Free Estimates. Collection/Delivery Service.

SPEAK TO Mr. C. N. Stell.

The showroom has an extensive collection of archive wallpaper and fabrics.

ANNA HARRISON ANTIQUES
Grange Park, Great North Road, Gosforth, Newcastle-upon-Tyne, **Tyne & Wear NE3 2DQ**

TEL   091 284 3202
FAX   091 284 6689
OPEN   10–5 Mon–Sat.

Specialise in restoring furniture and upholstery.

PROVIDE Home Inspections. Free Estimates. Chargeable Collection/Delivery Service.

SPEAK TO Anna Harrison.

OWEN HUMBLE ANTIQUES
11–12 Clay Road, Jesmond, Newcastle-upon-Tyne, **Tyne & Wear NE2 4RP**

TEL   091 281 4602
OPEN   10–5 Mon–Sat.

Specialise in restoring 18th and 19th century furniture.

PROVIDE Home Inspections. Free Estimates. Free Collection/Delivery Service.

SPEAK TO Michael Humble.

Member of LAPADA.

T. P. ROONEY CLOCKMAKER & RESTORER
191 Sunderland Road, Harton Village,
South Shields, **Tyne & Wear NE34 6AQ**
TEL   091 456 2950
OPEN   By Appointment.

Specialise in restoring and repairing antique and quality clocks, except turret and carriage, and will hand–make traditional clocks to commission.
PROVIDE Home Inspections. Free Estimates. Free Collection/Delivery Service.
SPEAK TO T. P. Rooney.
This workshop is included on the register of conservators maintained by the Conservation Unit of the Museums and Galleries Commission.

W. MAHONEY CLOCK & WATCH RESTORATION
15 Meadow Road, Newbold-on-Avon,
Nr. Rugby, **Warwickshire CV21 1ER**
TEL   0788 546985
OPEN   9–6 Mon–Sat.

Specialise in restoring clocks and watches including movement, dials, cases, silvering dials, painted dials, recutting wheels, pinions.
PROVIDE Home Inspections. Chargeable Estimates. Chargeable Collection/Delivery Service.
SPEAK TO William Mahoney.

TAYLOR & BROOK RE-UPHOLSTERY LTD
5 Greenhill Street, Stratford upon Avon,
Warwickshire CV37 6LF
TEL   0789 269604
OPEN   9–5 Mon–Sat.

Specialise in re-upholstering antique and quality traditional furniture, re-caning and supply of all upholstery sundries and materials for DIY.

PROVIDE Home Inspections, Free Estimates, Free Collection/Delivery Service all within a 10–mile radius.
SPEAK TO Collin Brook.

TIME IN HAND
11 Church Street, Shipston-on-Stour,
Warwickshire CV36 4AP
TEL   0608 62578
OPEN   9–1, 2–5.30 Mon–Sat.
        SPEAK TO Francis Bennett.

Specialise in restoring fine clocks, barometers and antique mechanisms.
PROVIDE Home Inspections. Free Estimates. Chargeable Collection/Delivery Service.
Member of BHI.

PERCY F. WALE
32 & 34 Regent Street, Leamington Spa,
Warwickshire CV32 3 5EG
TEL   0926 421288
OPEN   9–1, 2–5.30 Mon–Sat.

Specialise in restoring fine old and antique furniture, including cabinet repairs, French polishing, desk-lining and re-upholstery.
PROVIDE Home Inspections. Free Estimates. Chargeable Collection/Delivery Service.
SPEAK TO Peter G. Barton.

BRADFORD FURNITURE WORKSHOPS
Unit 20, Longs Yard, Trowbridge Road,
Bradford-on-Avon, **Wiltshire BA15 1EE**
TEL   02216 4551
OPEN   9–5.30 Mon–Fri; 9–12 Sat.

Specialise in restoring antique and general furniture, cabinet work and French polishing.
PROVIDE Home Inspections. Refundable Estimates. Free Collection/Delivery Service.
SPEAK TO I. Blackshaw.

130

CHAIRPERSONS OF MARSHFIELD
40 High Street, Marshfield, Nr.
Chippenham, **Wiltshire SN14 8LP**
TEL 0225 891431
OPEN By Appointment.

Specialise in cane and rush seating. Also
repair wicker, rattan, bamboo and
willow chairs and can arrange for chair
frames to be repaired.
PROVIDE Home Inspections. Free
Estimates. Free Delivery/Collection
Service to Bath/Bristol.
SPEAK TO Michael Pitts.

PHILIP HAWKINS
The Old School Workshop, High Street,
Maiden Bradley, Warminster, **Wiltshire
BA12 7JG**
OPEN By Appointment.

Specialise in restoring early oak, country
and period furniture.
PROVIDE Home Inspections. Free
Estimates. Free Collection/Delivery
Service.
SPEAK TO Philip Hawkins.
Member of BAFRA.

MAC HUMBLE ANTIQUES
7–9 Woolley Street, Bradford-on-Avon,
Wiltshire BA15 1AD
TEL 02216 6329
OPEN 9–6 Mon–Sat.

Specialise in restoring 18th and 19th
century furniture and decorative objects.
PROVIDE Home Inspections. Refundable
Estimates. Free Collection/Delivery
Service.
SPEAK TO Mac Humble.
SEE Carpets, Silver.

ROD NAYLOR
208 Devizes Road, Hilperton,
Trowbridge, **Wiltshire BA14 7QP**
TEL 0225 754497
OPEN By Appointment.

Specialise in restoring quality wooden
items, particularly carving. Also supply
hard-to-find items for restorers such as
three-dimensional copying machines,
embossed lining paper.
PROVIDE Home Inspections. Free
Estimates. Free Collection/Delivery
Service.
SPEAK TO Rod Naylor.
SEE Display, Porcelain.

RESTORATIONS UNLIMITED
Pinkney Park, Malmesbury, **Wiltshire
SN16 0NX**
TEL 0666 840888
OPEN 9–12.30, 1.30–5 Mon–Fri; 9.30–
12 Sat.

Specialise in restoring period furniture,
veneering, inlay, woodturning, rush and
cane seating and will also make furniture
to match existing pieces. They also
repair and restore clocks.
PROVIDE Home Inspections. Free
Estimates. Free Collection/Delivery
Service.
SPEAK TO David Ellis.
SEE Oil Paintings, Porcelain.

SHENSTONE RESTORATIONS
23 Lansdown Road, Swindon, **Wiltshire
SN1 3NE**
TEL 0793 644980
OPEN By Appointment.

Specialise in restoring smaller decorative
items including marquetry, inlay and
veneering. They work in bone, mother-
of-pearl, ebony and ivory and its
substitutes. They also do Boulle
marquetry and marble restoration.
PROVIDE Local Home Inspections.

Chargeable Estimates. Chargeable
Collection/Delivery Service.
SPEAK TO Blair Shenstone.
SEE Silver.

JOHN TIGHE
One Oak, Lights Lane, Alderbury,
Salisbury, **Wiltshire SP5 3AL**
TEL   0722 710231
OPEN   By Appointment.

Specialise in restoring 18th and 19th
century furniture and gilding.

PROVIDE Home Inspections. Free
Estimates.
SPEAK TO John Tighe.
Member of BAFRA.

TIME RESTORED & CO.
18–20 High Street, Pewsey, **Wiltshire
SN9 5AQ**
TEL   0672 63544
FAX   0672 63544
OPEN   By Appointment.

Specialise in restoring antique English
and French clocks and barometers.

PROVIDE Home Inspections. Free
Estimates. Free Collection/Delivery
Service.
SPEAK TO J. H. Bowler-Reed.
SEE Collectors (Mechanical Music).

CHRIS WADGE CLOCKS
142 Fisherton Street, Salisbury,
Wiltshire SP2 7QT
TEL   0722 334467
OPEN   9–5 Tues–Sat.

Specialise in repairing most types of
clocks, especially anniversary clocks
1880–1970. They also repair barometers,
barographs and pocket watches.

PROVIDE Home Inspections. Free
Estimates. Chargeable
Collection/Delivery Service.
SPEAK TO Chris or Patrick Wadge.

PAUL WINSTANLEY
213 Devizes Road, Salisbury, **Wiltshire
SP2 9LT**
TEL   0722 337383
OPEN   8.30–5.30 Mon–Fri.

Specialise in restoring antique furniture,
particularly marquetry and veneers.

PROVIDE Home Inspections. Free
Estimates. Chargeable
Collection/Delivery Service.
SPEAK TO Paul Winstanley.

ALVERTON ANTIQUES
7 South Parade, Northallerton, **North
Yorkshire DL7 0SE**
TEL   0609 780402
OPEN   10–5.30 Wed, Fri, Sat or By
           Appointment.

Specialise in repairing and restoring
British longcase clocks.

PROVIDE Home Inspections. Free
Estimates. Chargeable
Collection/Delivery Service.
SPEAK TO Mrs. Matson.

HAWORTH ANTIQUES
Harrogate Road, Huby, Nr. Leeds,
North Yorkshire LS17 0EF
and 26 Cold Bath Road, Harrogate,
North Yorkshire HG2 0NA
TEL   0423 734293
           0423 521401
OPEN   9–6 Tues–Sat or By
           Appointment.

Specialise in restoring clocks including
white and brass dial movements and
casework.

PROVIDE Home Inspections. Free
Estimates. Chargeable
Collection/Delivery Service.
SPEAK TO Glynn or June White.
Member of BWCMG.

DAVID MASON & SON
7–9 Westmoreland Street, Harrogate,
North Yorkshire H91 5AY
TEL   0423 567305
OPEN   9–5 Mon–Sat.
Specialise in repair of clocks, watches
and barometers.
PROVIDE Home Inspections. Free
Estimates. Chargeable
Collection/Delivery Service.
SPEAK TO John Mason.
Member of NAG, Yorkshire
Goldsmiths Association, FGA.
SEE Silver.

NIDD HOUSE ANTIQUES
Nidd House, Bogs Lane, Harrogate,
North Yorkshire. HG1 4DY
TEL   0423 884739
OPEN   9–5 Mon–Fri or By
        Appointment.
Specialise in restoring furniture and
upholstery, cane and rush seats, leaf and
powder gilding, gesso work, inlay.
PROVIDE Home Inspections. Free Local
Estimates. Chargeable
Collection/Delivery Service.
SPEAK TO Mr. D. Preston.
A member of the Guild of Master
Craftsmen and the UKIC. This
workshop is included on the register of
conservators maintained by the
Conservation Unit of the Museums and
Galleries Commission.
SEE Collectors (Scientific Instruments),
Porcelain, Silver.

JOHN PEARSON ANTIQUE CLOCK RESTORATION
Church Cottage, Birstwith, Harrogate,
North Yorkshire HG3 2NG
TEL   0423 770828
OPEN   By Appointment.
Specialise in dial restoration, complete
clock restoration including movement,
case and dial.

PROVIDE Home Inspections. Refundable
Estimates. Collection/Delivery Service.
SPEAK TO John Pearson.

T. L. PHELPS
8 Mornington Terrace, Harrogate, **North
Yorkshire HG1 5DH**
TEL   0423 524604
OPEN   8.30–6 Mon–Fri or By
        Appointment.
Specialise in restoring fine English and
Continental furniture.
PROVIDE Home Inspections. Free
Estimates. Chargeable
Collection/Delivery Service.
SPEAK TO Timothy Phelps.
Member of BAFRA.

ANDREW G. PODMORE & SON
49a East Mount Road, York, **North
Yorkshire YO2 2BD**
TEL   0904 627717
OPEN   8.30–5 Mon–Fri.
Specialise in restoring antique furniture,
French polishing and upholstery.
PROVIDE Home Inspections. Free
Estimates. Free/Chargeable
Collection/Delivery Service.
SPEAK TO David Podmore.

G. SHAW RESTORATIONS
Jansville, Quarry Lane, New Park,
Harrogate, **North Yorkshire HG1 3HR**
TEL   0423 503590
OPEN   7–6 Mon–Fri or By
        Appointment.
Specialise in restoring antique furniture
and copying furniture to customers'
requirements.
PROVIDE Home Inspections. Free
Estimates.
SPEAK TO G. or M. G. S. Shaw.

DOVETAIL RESTORATIONS
112–114 London Road, Sheffield, **South Yorkshire S2 4LR**
TEL   0742 700273
OPEN   9–4.30 Mon–Sat.
Specialise in restoring furniture, including French polishing and stripping by hand.
PROVIDE Home Inspections. Free Estimates. Free Collection/Delivery Service.
SPEAK TO Darren Beedle.

JULIE GODDARD ANTIQUES
7–9 Langsett Road South, Oughtibridge, Sheffield, **South Yorkshire S30 3GY**
TEL   0742 862261
OPEN   By Appointment; closed Wed.
Specialise in restoring antique furniture.
PROVIDE Home Inspections. Free Estimates. Chargeable Collection/Delivery Service.
SPEAK TO Julie Goddard.

A. E. JAMESON & CO.
257 Glossop Road, Sheffield, **South Yorkshire S10 2GZ**
TEL   0742 723846
OPEN   8–6 Mon–Fri; 9.30–5 Sat.
Specialise in restoring Georgian and Victorian furniture.
PROVIDE Home Inspections. Chargeable Estimates. Free Collection/Delivery Service.
SPEAK TO Mr Jameson.
Established 1883.

GEARY ANTIQUES
114 Richardshaw Lane, Pudsey, Leeds, **West Yorkshire LS28 6BN**
TEL   0532 564122
OPEN   10–5.30 Mon–Sat; closed Wed.
Specialise in conserving and restoring furniture and upholstery and allied skills.
PROVIDE Home Inspections. Free Estimates. Free Collection/Delivery Service.
SPEAK TO J. A. Geary.

THOMAS H. KEARNEY & SONS
Treasure House Antiques, 123 University Street, Belfast, **Co. Antrim BT7 1HP.**
TEL   0232 231055
OPEN   8–6 Mon–Fri.
Specialise in restoring antique furniture of all types, upholstery, polishing.
PROVIDE Home Inspections. Free Estimates.
SPEAK TO Thomas Kearney.

FIONA CHICHESTER–CLARK
186 Loughgall Road, Portadown, Craigavon, **Co. Armagh BT62 4EQ**
TEL   0762 335848
OPEN   8–5 Mon–Fri.
Specialise in restoring antique English and Irish furniture and cane seating.
PROVIDE Home Inspections. Free Estimates. Free Collection/Delivery Service.
SPEAK TO Fiona Chichester-Clark.

T. M. TUKE
18 Main Street, Greyabbey, Newtownards, **Co. Down**
TEL   024774 416
FAX   024774 250
OPEN   11–5 Mon–Sat; closed Thur.
Specialise in restoring antique clocks, longcase, bracket and carriage, and pocket and wrist watches.
PROVIDE Home Inspections. Free Estimates. Free Collection/Delivery Service.
SPEAK TO Tom Tuke.
Mr. Tuke is a MBHI.
SEE Silver.

K. & M. NESBITT
21 Tobermore Road, Magherafelt, **Co. Londonderry BT45 5HB**
TEL 0648 32713
OPEN By Appointment.
Specialise in restoring antique clocks and watches.
PROVIDE Home Inspections. Free Estimates. Chargeable Collection/Delivery Service.
SPEAK TO Mr. K. Nesbitt.

THE CLOCK CENTRE
71 York Road, Dun Laoghaire, **Co. Dublin**
TEL 2803667
OPEN 9.30–5 Mon–Fri; 9.30–1 Sat.
Specialise in restoring and repairing clocks but not watches.
PROVIDE Home Inspections. Free Estimates.
SPEAK TO Patrick Healey.

T. J. MITCHELL LTD
4 Lower Pembroke, Dublin 1, **Co. Dublin**
TEL 766881
OPEN 9–12.45, 2–5.30 Mon–Fri.
Specialise in restoring English and Irish furniture.
PROVIDE Home Inspections. Refundable Estimates. Collection/Delivery Service by arrangement.
SPEAK TO Tommy Mitchell.

ST JAMES'S GALLERY LTD
18–20 Le Bordage, St Peter Port, **Guernsey, Channel Islands**
TEL 0481 720070
OPEN 9–5.30 Mon–Sat or By Appointment.
Specialise in restoring 18th and 19th century English and Continental furniture, Edwardian furniture and clock repairs.

PROVIDE Home Inspections. Chargeable Estimates. Collection/Delivery Service by arrangement.
SPEAK TO Mr. or Mrs. Whittam.
SEE Porcelain.

CHISHOLME ANTIQUES
5 Orrock Place, Hawick, **Borders TD9 0HQ**
TEL 0450 76928
OPEN 9–6 Mon–Fri.
Specialise in restoring antique furniture including veneering, tortoiseshell, ivory, gilding and composition work, rush seating, caning and upholstery.
PROVIDE Home Inspections. Free Estimates. Chargeable Collection/Delivery Service.
SPEAK TO Mr. Roberts.
SEE Carpets.

JUDITH LIVINGSTONE
Willowbrae, 3 Pittenweem Road, Anstruther, **Fife KY10 3DS**
TEL 0333 310 425
OPEN By Appointment.
Specialise in restoring antique furniture, veneering, French polishing, carving and mouldings.
PROVIDE Home Inspections. Free/Chargeable Estimates.
SPEAK TO Judith Livingstone.
Member of SSCR.

PETER DAVIS
Unit 5, Glen Nevis Place, Fort William, **Highland PH33 6DA**
TEL 0397 704039
OPEN 8–5 Mon–Fri.
Specialise in hand-made furniture and furniture repair and restoration, wood-turning.

PROVIDE Home Inspections. Free Estimates. Chargeable Collection/Delivery Service. SPEAK TO Peter Davis.

GILES PEARSON
Brightmony House, Auldern, **Highland IV12 5HZ**
TEL   0667 55550
OPEN   9–6 daily.

Specialise in rush and cane-work for chairs, stools and bergère suites.
PROVIDE Home Inspections. Free Estimates. Collection/Delivery Service by arrangement.
SPEAK TO Giles Pearson.
SEE Silver.

STABLE WORKSHOP
Fodderty by Dingwall, **Highland IV15 9UE**
TEL   0997 21606
OPEN   9–5 Mon–Sat.

Specialise in restoring antique furniture and will make furniture on commission.
PROVIDE Chargeable Estimates. Free Local Collection/Delivery Service.
SPEAK TO Dennis Manson.

G. A. WHITE
High Street, Nairn, **Highland IV12 4QD**
TEL   0667 52201
FAX   0667 56033
OPEN   9–5.30 Mon–Fri.

Specialise in restoring antique furniture and upholstery.
PROVIDE Home Inspections. Free Estimates. Chargeable Collection/Delivery Service.
SPEAK TO W. G. White.

PAUL COUTS LTD
Linkfield House, 8–10 High Street, Musselburgh, **Lothian EH21 7BN**
TEL   031 665 7759
FAX   031 665 0836
OPEN   9–5 Mon–Fri; Sat a.m. By Appointment.

Specialise in conserving and restoring fine English furniture.
PROVIDE Home Inspections. Free/Chargeable Estimates. Chargeable Collection/Delivery Service.
SPEAK TO Julian Labarre.

ANSELM FRASER
The Carthouse, Crauchie, East Linton, **Lothian EH40 3EB**
TEL   0620 860067
OPEN   9–4.30 Mon–Fri.

Specialise in restoring antique furniture including veneer repairs, wood carving and turning, Boulle and marquetry work, inlays, gilding, gesso mouldings, grain simulation, metal repairs, French polishing, simple upholstery, carcase repairs.
PROVIDE Home Inspections. Free Estimates. Free/Chargeable Collection/Delivery Service.
SPEAK TO Anselm Fraser.

HAMILTON & INCHES
87 George Street, Edinburgh, **Lothian EH2 3EY**
TEL   031 225 4898
FAX   031 220 6994
OPEN   9–5 Mon–Fri; 9–12.30 Sat.

Specialise in repairing clocks and watches.
PROVIDE Home Inspections. Free Estimates. Chargeable Collection/Delivery Service.
SPEAK TO Densil Skinner.

Member of NAG.
SEE Silver.

HOUNDWOOD ANTIQUES RESTORATION
7 West Preston Street, Edinburgh, **Lothian EH8 9PX**
TEL   031 667 3253
OPEN   By Appointment.

Specialise in restoring antique furniture.

PROVIDE Home Inspections. Free Estimates. Chargeable Collection/Delivery Service.

SPEAK TO Mr A Gourlay.

SEE Porcelain, Silver.

SIMON LOWMAN
112 Gilmore Place, Edinburgh, **Lothian EH3 9PL**
TEL   031 229 2129
OPEN   9–6 Mon–Fri.

Specialise in repairing and restoring 18th century English and French bracket and longcase clocks as well as carriage clocks.

PROVIDE Home Inspections. Free Estimates. Chargeable Collection/Delivery Service.

SPEAK TO Simon Lowman.

Member of BHI.

TRIST & McBAIN
9 Cannongate Venture, New Street, Edinburgh, **Lothian EH8 8VH**
TEL   031 557 3828
OPEN   8.30–5.30 Mon–Fri; By Appointment Sat.

Specialise in conserving and restoring period furniture including Boulle, marquetry, wood turning, French polishing . They also do cane and rush seating and desk leathers.

PROVIDE Home Inspections. Free Estimates. Free Collection/Delivery Service.

SPEAK TO William Trist or Andrew McBain.

WHYTOCK & REID
Sunbury House, Belford Mews, Edinburgh **Lothian EH4 3DN**
TEL   031 226 4911
FAX   031 226 4595
OPEN   9–5.30 Mon–Fri; 9–12.30 Sat.

Specialise in restoring 18th and 19th century furniture, re-upholstery, polishing and gilding.

PROVIDE Home Inspections. Free Estimates. Collection/Delivery Service available.

SPEAK TO David Reid.

SEE Carpets.

KENNETH CHAPPELLE ANTIQUE CLOCK RESTORER
26 Otago Lane, Glasgow, **Strathclyde G12 8PB**.
TEL   041 334 7766
OPEN   8.30–4.30 Mon–Fri; 8.30–1 Sat.

Specialise in restoring fine antique clocks.

PROVIDE Home Inspections. Free Estimates. Chargeable Collection/Delivery Service.

SPEAK TO Kenneth Chappelle.

Mr Chappelle is a FBHI, a member of BADA and West Dean trained.

DAPHNE FRASER
Glenbarry, 58 Victoria Road, Lenzie, Glasgow, **Strathclyde G66 5AP**
TEL   041 776 1281
OPEN   By Appointment.

Specialise in restoring ornate mirror frames.

PROVIDE Free Estimates.

SPEAK TO Daphne Fraser.

SEE Collectors (Dolls, Toys), Oil Paintings.

ROBERT HOWIE & SON
19 High Street, Mauchline, **Strathclyde**
TEL   0290 50556
OPEN   8–5 Mon–Fri.

Specialise in restoring painted furniture, specialised finishes.

PROVIDE Home Inspections. Free Estimates. Chargeable Collection/Delivery Service.
SPEAK TO Robert Howie.

PIERS KETTLEWELL CABINETMAKERS
10 Robertson Street, Barrhead, **Strathclyde G78 1QW**
TEL   041 881 8166
OPEN   By Appointment.

Specialise in restoring antique furniture and making furniture to commission.

PROVIDE Home Inspections. Free Estimates. Collection/Delivery Service by arrangement.
SPEAK TO Piers Kettlewell.

FRAN MALLOY
Suite 1, 66 Dora Street, Glasgow, **Strathclyde G40 4DP**
TEL   041 551 0616
OPEN   8.30–6 Mon–Sat.

Specialise in restoring antique furniture of all periods.

PROVIDE Home Inspections. Free/Chargeable Estimates. Free/Chargeable Collection/Delivery Service.
SPEAK TO Fran Malloy.

THE OLD CURIOSITY SHOP
27–29 Crown Street, Ayr, **Strathclyde KA8 8AG**
TEL   0292 280222
OPEN   8–5 Mon–Fri; 10–4 Sat.

Specialise in restoring antique furniture, repairs, re-upholstery and polishing.

PROVIDE Home Inspections. Refundable Estimates. Free Collection/Delivery Service locally.
SPEAK TO Brian Kelly.

GREYCROFT ANTIQUES
Station Road, Errol, **Tayside PH2 7SN**
TEL   08212 221
OPEN   11–5 Mon–Sat.

Specialise in restoring pre-1840 furniture sympathetically.

PROVIDE Home Inspections. Refundable Estimates.
SPEAK TO David or June Pickett.

KINGS OF KINBUCK
Old Mill, Kinbuck, **Tayside FK15 0NQ**
TEL   0786 822915
FAX   0786 822915
OPEN   10–5 Mon–Fri; 10–2 Sat.

Specialise in restoring upholstered items including chaises longues, Victorian and Edwardian sofas and chairs.

PROVIDE Free Estimates. Free Collection/Delivery Service.
SPEAK TO Hilda King.

NEIL LIVINGSTONE
3 Old Hawkhill, Dundee, **Tayside DD1 5EU**
TEL   0382 25517
OPEN   9–5 Mon–Fri.

Specialise in restoring antique furniture and wood carving.

PROVIDE Free Estimates. Chargeable Collection/Delivery Service.
SPEAK TO Neil Livingstone.

SEE Collectors (Arms and Armour), Oil Paintings, Silver.

IRENA ANTIQUES
111 Broad Street, Barry, **South Glamorgan CF6 8SX**
TEL   0446 747626 or 732517
OPEN   10–4 Mon–Fri.

Specialise in restoring antique furniture including painted and lacquer work. Their specialist service includes trompe l'oeil, marbling, gold leaf and gilding and painting of Pontypool tin ware.

PROVIDE Free Estimates. Free Collection/Delivery Service.
SPEAK TO Irena Halabuda.

Mrs. Halabuda is a specialist in painted work in the manner of Angelica Kauffmann.
SEE Porcelain.

TIM BRAMELD
Howell's House, Grosmont, **Gwent NP7 8BP**
TEL   0981 240 940
OPEN   By Appointment.

Specialise in repairing and restoring antique clocks, particularly regulators.

PROVIDE Home Inspections. Free Estimates. Chargeable Collection/Delivery Service.
SPEAK TO Tim Brameld.

SNOWDONIA ANTIQUES
Station Road, Llanrwst, **Gwynedd LL26 QEP**
TEL   0492 640789
OPEN   9–5.30 Mon–Sat or By Appointment.

Specialise in restoring period furniture and longcase clocks.

PROVIDE Home Inspections. Chargeable Estimates. Chargeable Collection/Delivery Service.
SPEAK TO Mr. J. Collins.

Silver, Jewellery, Objects of Vertu and Metalwork

The two words conservation and restoration are occasionally a cause for some disagreement: the first is usually preferred by museums and their staff, while the second is more generally used by the trade and collectors. The two words, however, are not incompatible, and most people involved in the buying, selling, collecting or custodianship of works of art are slowly beginning to realise this. The main trouble lies in the view one takes of an object: as a collector, you might buy a cream jug made in 1730 and, not unreasonably, use it for cream or milk whenever you felt so inclined. This is, after all, the use for which it was designed, and the passing of time has not changed the object into anything noticeably different – so in one sense, it is not at all foolish to pursue the maker's original intention. The museum curator, however, is likely to view the matter in an entirely different light and consider the same cream jug as an object to be handled only on the rarest occasions, and then only with cotton gloves. It should no longer be used, but should rather become part of a collection only to be viewed behind glass as if it were the most fragile of objects.

There is no doubt that all objects, whether old or new, get a certain amount of hammering when in general use, and silver, which is after all a tough and durable material, is bound to be used – and sometimes abused. But there is an astonishing amount of silver around that is in an extraordinarily good state of preservation. The point here, however, is what to do about it when it is not! One can argue, on a question of semantics, that to conserve an object, either silver or jewellery, is to stabilise it, clean it gently, remove any lingering acids and then leave it entirely alone whilst keeping it in a controlled environment for the public to view. On the other hand, to restore it, you could argue that you strip it right down and, with a lot of ingenuity, bring it back to what it looked like when it was new. Neither pole is really correct: both conservation and restoration need the most sympathetic understanding

140

from the restorer and it requires tremendous experience and judgement to be able to do as little as possible or as little as necessary to any object of gold, silver or jewellery. Nobody really wants their 200-year-old object to come back from the restorer looking 'new', gleaming and with all that fine patination removed. Rather, it should come back with the barest minimum of change but once again ready for use or display.

Over-restoration is a dreadful thing, and sometimes the line between what one can safely do and what will utterly spoil the piece can be very fine. It is always a good idea to talk over the problem with the restorer before he starts work, so that you both have a clear idea of what is required.

The main conservation work that you can carry out on your own silver or jewellery is cleaning. There is no particular mystique about this, but few people seem to clean their silver satisfactorily and even fewer seem to clean their jewellery at all!

If jewellery is antique and gem-set, then the chances are it is foiled – that is to say that the stones are in settings which are closed at the back and probably have some foil behind them to enhance the colour of the stone. If this is the case, do not, in any circumstances, use any liquid to clean the pieces: serious cleaning is best left to an expert restorer/ conservator. If, on the other hand, the stones are in an open setting and held in by claws, as is the case with most 20th century rings for example, then a good soak in ammonia followed by a gentle scrub with a tiny toothbrush will bring the ring to life again and you will be quite stunned at the amount of filth that will come out of the back of it. Open-set brooches and necklaces can be treated in the same way, but it is the constantly worn finger jewellery that tends to attract the most dirt.

The best maxim for silver is this: 'Polish the furniture but clean the silver'. Silver does not need lots of 'elbow grease' expended upon it and probably the best cleaner is Goddards Silver Foam, a proprietary mixture of rouge and other substances which you can use with a wet sponge or a soft toothbrush for any chased work. Rinse this off and then wash thoroughly with a liquid soap and very hot water, again using the toothbrush assiduously in any decoration in order to remove all possible traces of the cleaner. Dry with a dry linen tea-cloth while the object is still really hot from the water, and that should be enough. If you have any residue of pink powder in the decoration, jolly well scrub it again!

The same form of cleaning is recommended for Old Sheffield Plate and the use of very hot water is even more efficacious because the piece virtually dries itself against the linen cloth and needs very little rubbing – though gently rubbed it must be, otherwise you will get rather unsightly water spots left on it. These aren't harmful, just unattractive. Of course, many pieces of Old Sheffield Plate have almost no silver left on them at all and have been reduced to almost entirely copper objects. The value having thus been destroyed, it is up to the owner to decide whether to re-plate the piece using the modern electro-plating technique, or simply to leave it alone. It is purely a matter of personal taste and neither course of action is going to bring back the value it would have had if it were mint or nearly mint. If you are in any doubt about how badly worn a piece of Old Sheffield Plate is, it might be best to talk to a dealer or restorer and get his view.

A good restorer with, perhaps, the further advice of a dealer or auctioneer, should hopefully be able to guide you as to how much, if anything, should be done to an object, but, as has already been stated, in general terms, the less that is done, the better.

Brand Inglis

IAN & DIANNE McCARTHY
Arcadian Cottage, 112 Station Road,
Clutton, **Avon BS18 4RA**
TEL   0761 53188
OPEN   By Appointment.
Specialise in restoring metalware,
including table lamps.
PROVIDE Home Inspections. Free
Estimates. Chargeable
Collection/Delivery Service.
SPEAK TO Ian or Dianne McCarthy.
SEE Furniture, Porcelain.

ANNE FINNERTY
62 Gainsborough Road, Southcote,
Reading, **Berkshire RG3 3BZ**
TEL   0734 588274
OPEN   By Appointment.
Specialise in restoring antique beadwork,
pearl and bead re-threading.
PROVIDE Home Inspections. Free
Estimates. Postal Collection/Delivery
Service.
SPEAK TO Anne Finnerty.

HAMILTON HAVERS
58 Conisboro Avenue, Caversham
Heights, Reading, **Berkshire RG4 7JE**
TEL   0734 473379
OPEN   By Appointment.
Specialise in restoring Boulle, marquetry,
ivory, tortoiseshell, mother-of-pearl,
brass, lapis-lazuli and malachite objets
d'art.
PROVIDE Free/Chargeable Estimates.
SPEAK TO Hamilton Havers.
SEE Furniture.

STYLES SILVER
12 Bridge Street, Hungerford, **Berkshire
RG17 OEH**
TEL   0488 683922
Specialise in repairing and cleaning
English 18th–20th century silverware

PROVIDE Local Home Inspections. Local
Free Estimates. Local Free
Collection/Delivery Service.
SPEAK TO Derek Styles.

JOHN ARMISTEAD
Malham Cottage, Bellingdon, Nr.
Chesham, **Buckinghamshire HP5 2UR**
TEL   024 029 209
OPEN   9–5 Mon–Fri.
Specialise in repairing metalwork,
including brass beds, candlesticks,
chandeliers, fire irons, polishing, plating,
casting.
PROVIDE Home Inspections, Free
Estimates.
SPEAK TO John Armistead.

BUCKIES JEWELLERS
31 Trinity Street, **Cambridge CB2 1TB**
TEL   0223 357910
OPEN   9.45–5 Tues–Sat.
Specialise in repairing and restoring
jewellery and silverware.
PROVIDE Home Inspections. Refundable
Estimates. Chargeable
Collection/Delivery Service.
SPEAK TO Peter R. Buckie.

IAN FALCON HAMMOND
50 Kings Road, Eaton Socon, St Neots,
Cambridgeshire PE19 3DB
TEL   0480 212794
OPEN   By Appointment.
Specialise in restoring Oriental and
European ivories, tortoiseshell, mother-
of-pearl.
PROVIDE Home Inspections. Chargeable
Estimates. Chargeable
Collection/Delivery Service.
SPEAK TO Ian Hammond.

PETER JOHN
38 St Mary's Street, Eyresbury, St.
Neots, **Cambridgeshire PE19 2TA**
TEL   0480 216297
OPEN   9–5 Mon–Sat.
Specialise in restoring antique jewellery.
PROVIDE Home Inspections. Free
Estimates. Chargeable
Collection/Delivery Service.
SPEAK TO Kym or Peter John.
SEE Furniture.

A. ALLEN ANTIQUE RESTORERS
Buxton Rd, Newtown, Newmills, Via
Stockport, **Cheshire SK12 3JS**
TEL   0663 745274
OPEN   8–5 Mon–Fri; 9–12 Sat.
Specialise in restoring Boulle work, inlay,
gilding and metalwork.
PROVIDE Home Inspections.
Free/Chargeable Estimates.
Collection/Delivery Service.
SPEAK TO Tony Allen.
SEE Furniture, Oil Paintings.

THE TEXTILE RESTORATION STUDIO
20 Hargreaves Road, Timperley,
Altrincham, **Cheshire WA15 7BB**
TEL   061 904 9944
FAX   061 903 9144
OPEN   9.30–5 Mon–Fri.
Specialise in cleaning, conserving and
repairing of antique fans.
They also undertake framing and
mounting for display.
PROVIDE Home Inspections. Free
Estimates. Collection/Delivery Service
by arrangement.
SPEAK TO Jacqueline Hyman.
SEE Carpets, Collectors (Dolls).

ST. AUSTELL ANTIQUES CENTRE
(formerly The Furniture Store)
37/39 Truro Road, St. Austell, **Cornwall PL25 5JE**
TEL   0726 63178 and 0288 81548
OPEN   10–5 Mon–Sat or By
         Appointment.
Specialise in restoring metalwork.
PROVIDE Home Inspections. Free
Estimates. Free Local
Collection/Delivery Service.
SPEAK TO Roger Nosworthy
SEE Furniture.

MACLAREN CHAPPELL (RESTORATIONS) LTD
King Street, Bakewell, **Derbyshire DE4 1DZ**
TEL   0629 812496
FAX   0629 814531
OPEN   9–6 Mon–Fri.
Specialise in restoring copper and
brassware.
PROVIDE Home Inspections. Free
Estimates. Free Local
Collection/Delivery Service.
SPEAK TO W. N. Chappell.
SEE Furniture, Porcelain.

THE LANTERN SHOP
4 New Street, Sidmouth, **Devon EX10 8AP**
TEL   0395 516320
OPEN   9.45–12.45, 2.15–4.45 Mon–Sat;
         closed Mon and Sat p.m.
Specialise in restoring antique items of
lighting and conversion to electricity.
PROVIDE Home Inspections. Free
Estimates. Chargeable
Collection/Delivery Service.
SPEAK TO Julia Creeke.
SEE Oil Paintings, Porcelain.

D. J. JEWELLERY
166–168 Ashley Road, Parkstone, Poole,
Dorset BH14 9BY
TEL 0202 745148
OPEN 9.30–5 Mon–Sat.
Specialise in repairing antique jewellery.
PROVIDE Home Inspections. Free
Estimates. Chargeable
Collection/Delivery Service.
SPEAK TO Dennis O Sullivan.
SEE Furniture.

GEORGIAN GEMS
28 High Street, Swanage, **Dorset
BH19 2NU**
TEL 0929 424697
OPEN 9.30–1, 2.15–5 Sun–Sat; closed
Sun summer; closed Mon p.m.,
Thur winter.
Specialise in repairing antique jewellery.
PROVIDE Home Inspections. Free
Estimates. Chargeable
Collection/Delivery Service.
SPEAK TO Brian Parker.
Member of the Gemmological
Association.

HEIRLOOMS ANTIQUE JEWELLERS
21 South Street, Wareham, **Dorset
BH20 4LR**
TEL 0929 554207
OPEN 9–5 Mon–Sat; closed Wed.
Specialise in restoring and repairing
antique jewellery and silver, except
watches.
PROVIDE Free Estimates.
SPEAK TO Michael or Gabrielle Young.

MICHAEL MALLESON
Trent Smithy, Rigg Lane, Trent,
Sherborne **Dorset DT9 4SS**
TEL 0935 850957
OPEN 9–5 Mon–Fri or By
Appointment.

Specialise in restoring, repairing and
reproducing period wrought ironwork.
PROVIDE Home Inspections. Refundable
Estimates. Chargeable
Collection/Delivery Service.
SPEAK TO Michael Malleson.

GEO. A. PAYNE & SON LTD
742 Christchurch Road, Boscombe,
Bournemouth, **Dorset BH7 6BZ**
TEL 0202 394954
OPEN 9–5.30 Mon–Sat.
Specialise in repairing and restoring
jewellery and silverware.
PROVIDE Home Inspections. Free
Estimates. Chargeable
Collection/Delivery Service.
SPEAK TO Nicholas G. Payne.
Fellows of the Gemmological
Association and members of NAG.

DAVANA INTERIORS
88 Hythe Hill, Colchester, **Essex
CO1 2NH**
TEL 0206 577853
OPEN 8–5 Mon–Fri.
Specialise in restoring antique lights and
antique metalware.
PROVIDE Home Inspections, Free
Estimates.
SPEAK TO Mr. D. Donnelly.

MILLSIDE ANTIQUE RESTORATION
Parndon Mill, Parndon Mill Lane,
Harlow, **Essex CM20 2HP**
TEL 0279 428148
FAX 0279 415075
OPEN 10–5 Mon–Fri.
Specialise in cleaning and restoring
enamels, including snuff boxes and
cloisonné work as well as ivory
enamelling.
PROVIDE Home Inspections.
Free/Chargeable Estimates. Chargeable
Collection/Delivery Service.

SPEAK TO David Sparks or Angela
Wickliffe-Philp.
SEE Oil Paintings, Porcelain.

SPEAK TO Mr. Porter.
Established since 1844.
SEE Furniture.

KEITH BAWDEN
Mews Workshop, Montpellier Retreat,
Cheltenham, **Gloucestershire GL50 2XS**
TEL   0242 230320
OPEN   7–4.30 Mon–Fri.

Specialise in conserving and restoring all
aspects of metalwork.

PROVIDE Free Estimates. Home
Inspections. Local Collection/Delivery
Service.

SPEAK TO Keith Bawden.

SEE Furniture, Oil Paintings, Porcelain.

ATELIER FINE ART CASTINGS
LTD
Hulfords Lane, Nr. Hartley Witney,
Hampshire. RG27 8AG
TEL   025 126 4388
OPEN   9–5.30 Mon–Fri.

Specialise in restoring bronze art work
and bronze casting.

PROVIDE Home Inspections. Free
Estimates. Chargeable
Collection/Delivery Service.

SPEAK TO Mrs. A. Wills.

Work can be collected in London from
The Sladmore Gallery, 32 Bruton Place,
London W1X 7AA, TEL 071 499 0365.

A. W. PORTER
High Street, Hartley Witney, Nr.
Basingstoke, **Hampshire RG27 8NY**
TEL   025 126 2676
FAX   025 126 2064
OPEN   9–5.30 Mon–Fri; 9.30–5 Sat.

Specialise in restoring jewellery and
silverware.

PROVIDE Home Inspections. Free
Estimates. Chargeable
Collection/Delivery Service.

STANLEY THORNE
Hursley Antiques, Hursley, Nr.
Winchester, **Hampshire SO21 2JY**
TEL   0962 75488
OPEN   10–6 Mon–Sat.

Specialise in repairs and restoration to
brass, copper, spelter, bronze, pewter,
commissions taken, vases lamped, brass
or lead liners made, lanterns made to
pattern or sketch.

PROVIDE Local Home Inspections. Free
Estimates. Local Free
Collection/Delivery Service.

SPEAK TO Stanley Thorne.

HOWARDS OF BROADWAY
27A The High Street, Broadway,
Hereford & Worcester WR12 7DP
TEL   0386 858924
OPEN   9.30–5.30 Sun–Sat.

Specialise in repairing antique and
modern silver and jewellery. They will
remodel antique or modern pieces to
either customers' own designs or those
by their own designer.

PROVIDE Home Inspections. Free
Estimates. Free Collection/Delivery
Service.

SPEAK TO Robert Allport.

W. B. GATWARD & SON LTD
20 Market Place, Hitchin, **Hertfordshire
SG5 1DU**
TEL   0462 434273
OPEN   9.15–5.15 Mon–Sat; closed Wed.

Specialise in repairing and restoring
antique jewellery and silver.

PROVIDE Local Home Inspections. Free
Estimates. Chargeable
Collection/Delivery Service.
SPEAK to Miss Gatward or Mr. Hunter.
SEE Furniture.

WILLIAM H. STEVENS
8 Eton Avenue, East Barnet,
Hertfordshire EN4 8TU
TEL   081 449 7956
OPEN   9–5.30 Mon–Fri.

Specialise in restoring Japanese and
Chinese works of art including enamels,
lacquer, ivory, horn, mother-of-pearl,
soapstone and jade. They also restore
Blue John.
PROVIDE Home Inspections. Free
Estimates. Free Collection/Delivery
Service.
SPEAK TO John Robin or Daniel Stevens.
This is the fifth generation of a family
firm founded in 1836.
SEE Porcelain.

D. W. WINDSOR
Marsh Lane, Ware, **Hertfordshire,
SG12 9QL**
TEL   0920 466499
FAX   0920 460327
OPEN   9–1, 2–5 Mon–Fri.

Specialise in restoring exterior lighting.
PROVIDE Home Inspections. Free
Estimates. Chargeable
Collection/Delivery Service.
SPEAK TO Mr.D.Laws.

BEEBY & POWELL
2–6 Basement, Victoria Street,
Rochester, **Kent ME1 1XH**
TEL   0634 830764
OPEN   By Appointment.

Specialise in restoring antique silver and
gold objects.
PROVIDE Home Inspections. Free
Estimates. Free Collection/Delivery
Service.

SPEAK TO Jonathan Beeby or Jim Powell.
Member of the Guild of Master
Craftsmen.

SARGEANT RESTORATIONS
21 The Green, Westerham, **Kent
TN16 1AX**
TEL   0959 62130
OPEN   8.30–5.30 Mon–Sat.

Specialise in restoring, cleaning and
wiring metal chandeliers, candelabra
and general light fittings.
PROVIDE Home Inspections. Free
Estimates. Chargeable
Collection/Delivery Service.
SPEAK TO Ann, David or Denys Sargeant.

THE HOLME FIRE CO. LTD
Holme Hill, Holme, Nr. Carnforth,
Lancashire LA6 1RD
TEL   0524 781423
OPEN   10–5 Mon–Sat; 12–4 Sun.

Specialise in restoring and refinishing
cast iron especially on kitchen ranges
and fireplaces, and on-site repair service
where necessary.
PROVIDE Home Inspections. Free
Estimates. Chargeable
Collection/Delivery Service.
SPEAK TO Tom Smurthwaite.

CHARLES HOWELL JEWELLER
2 Lord Street, Oldham, **Lancashire
OL1 3EY**
TEL   061 624 1479
OPEN   9.15–5 Sun, Mon, Thur, Fri, Sat.

Specialise in restoring Victorian and
Edwardian jewellery and silverware.
PROVIDE Free Estimates.
SPEAK TO Mr.N.G.Howell.
Member of NAG.

WILLIAM DICKENSON
Home Farm, Burley On The Hill,
Oakham, **Leicestershire LE15 7SX**
TEL   0572 757333
OPEN   By Appointment.
Specialise in cleaning brass and copper
objects.
PROVIDE Home Inspections. Chargeable
Estimates. Chargeable
Collection/Delivery Service.
SPEAK TO William Dickenson.
SEE Furniture.

BARRY M. WITMOND
42 Wragby Road, Bardney, **Lincolnshire
LN3 5XL**
TEL   0526 398338 and 071 409 2335
OPEN   By Appointment.
Specialise in restoring English and
Continental silver plate.
PROVIDE Home Inspections.
Free/Chargeable Estimates.
Collection/Delivery Service available.
SPEAK TO Barry Witmond.

DAVID TURNER
4 Atlas Mews, Ramsgate Street, **London
E8 2NA**
TEL   071 249 2379
OPEN   10–6 Mon–Fri.
Specialise in restoring metalwork and
metal light fittings.
PROVIDE Home Inspections. Free
Estimates. Free Collection/Delivery
Service.
SEE Furniture, Porcelain.

RUPERT HARRIS
Studio 5, 1 Fawe Street, **London E14 6PD**
TEL   071 987 6231 and 515 2020
FAX   071 987 7994
OPEN   9–6 Mon–Fri.
Specialise in conserving fine and
decorative metalwork. Advice also given
on display, storage, environmental
control, security of outdoor sculpture,
emergency and disaster planning and
salvage.
PROVIDE Home Inspections. Chargeable
Estimates. Chargeable
Collection/Delivery Service.
SPEAK TO Rupert Harris.
Mr. Harris is a member of UKIC and
IIC. This workshop is included on the
register of conservators maintained by
the Conservation Unit of the Museums
and Galleries Commission.
SEE Porcelain.

EDWARD BARNARD & SONS LTD
54 Hatton Garden, **London EC1N 8HN**
TEL   071 405 5677
FAX   071 405 6604
OPEN   9–5 Mon–Fri.
Specialise in repairing and restoring
antique and modern silver and gold
ware.
PROVIDE Home Inspections. Free
Estimates. Free Collection/Delivery
Service in Central London.
SPEAK TO C. Ashenden or J. Padgett.

THE CONSERVATION STUDIO
Unit 17, Pennybank Chambers, 33–35 St
Johns Square, **London EC1M 4DS**
TEL   071 251 6853
OPEN   9.30–5 Mon–Fri.
Specialise in restoring enamels including
snuff boxes, jewellery and watch dials.
They will also repair objects in ivory and
tortoiseshell.
PROVIDE Home Inspections (large items
only). Refundable Estimates.
Chargeable Collection/Delivery Service.
SPEAK TO Sandra Davison.
SEE Furniture, Porcelain.

Silver, Metalwork & Enamels

R. HOLT & CO. LTD
98 Hatton Garden, **London EC1N 8NX**
TEL   071 405 5286 or 0197
FAX   071 430 1279
OPEN   9.30–5.30 Mon–Fri.
Specialise in cutting and re-cutting gemstones and restoring and repairing gemset items and carvings.
PROVIDE Home Inspections. Free estimates.
SPEAK TO R. Holt or M. R. Howard.
Members of Guild of Master Craftsmen, British Jewellers Association and the Gemmological Association of Great Britain.

KEMPSON & MAUGER
Studio 26, 63 Clerkenwell Road, **London EC1M 5NP**
TEL   071 251 0578
OPEN   By Appointment.
Specialise in restoring enamel on precious metals.
PROVIDE Free Estimates.
SPEAK TO Mr. Hamilton.

C. J. VANDER LTD
Dunstan House, 14A St. Cross Street, **London EC1N 8XD**
TEL   071 831 6741
FAX   071 831 9695
OPEN   9–5.30 Mon–Fri.
Specialise in repairing and restoring high quality antique and second-hand silver and Victorian electroplate.
PROVIDE Free Estimates.
SPEAK TO Mr. R. F. H. Vander.
This firm was established in 1886.

DON BAKER
3 Canonbury Park South, **London N1 2JR**
TEL   071 226 2314
OPEN   By Appointment.
Specialise in restoring Indian miniatures.
PROVIDE Free Estimates.
SPEAK TO Don Baker.

PETER CHAPMAN ANTIQUES
Incorporating CHAPMAN RESTORATIONS
10 Theberton Street, **London N1 0QX**
TEL   071 226 5565
FAX   081 348 4846
OPEN   9.30–6 Mon–Sat.
Specialise in repairing bronze and other metalwork and will convert objects into lamps.
PROVIDE Home Inspections. Refundable Estimates. Chargeable Collection/Delivery Service.
SPEAK TO Peter Chapman or Tony Holohan.
SEE Furniture, Oil Paintings, Porcelain.

CHARLOTTE DE SYLLAS
28 Park Avenue North, **London N8 7RT**
TEL   081 348 7181
OPEN   By Appointment.
Specialise in restoring hard stone carvings particularly jade.
PROVIDE Home Inspections. Free Estimates. Collection/Delivery Service by arrangement.
SPEAK TO Charlotte de Syllas.
Charlotte de Syllas can also be commissioned to make one–off pieces of jewellery.

W. PAIRPOINT & SONS LTD
10 Shacklewell Road, **London N16 7TA**
TEL   071 254 6362
FAX   071 254 7175
OPEN   8.30–5.30 Mon–Fri.
Specialise in restoring Old Sheffield and EPNS plate.

PROVIDE Free Estimates, Free Collection/Delivery Service within the London area.
SPEAK TO Eric Soulard.
SEE Furniture.

WAKELEY & WHEELER LTD
10 Shacklewell Road, **London N16 7TA**
TEL 071 254 6362
FAX 071 254 7175
OPEN 8.30–9.30 Mon–Fri.

Specialise in restoring and repairing antique and other silverware.
PROVIDE Free Estimates
SPEAK TO F. J. P. Legget
They have been established for 200 years.

ROCHEFORT ANTIQUES LTD
32–34 The Green, **London N21 1AX**
TEL 081 886 4779 or 363 0910
OPEN 10–6 Mon, Tues, Thur, Sat.

Specialise in restoring silver.
PROVIDE Home Inspections. Free Estimates. Chargeable Collection/Delivery Service.
SPEAK TO L. W. Stevens-Wilson.
SEE Furniture, Porcelain.

STAMFORD SILVER REPAIRS
The Workshop, Scope Antiques Emporium, 64–66 Willesden Lane.
London NW6 7SX
TEL 071 328 5833
OPEN 10–6 Mon–Sat.

Specialise in repairing silver including removing dents and engravings, replacing missing parts. They will also repair good quality brass and copper objects.
PROVIDE Free Estimates.
SPEAK TO Donald Stamford.

WELLINGTON GALLERY
1 St. John's Wood High Street, **London NW8 7NG**
TEL 071 586 2620
OPEN 10–5.30 Mon–Sat.

Specialise in restoring silver and Sheffield plate.
PROVIDE Home Inspections. Free Estimates. Chargeable Collection/Delivery Service.
SPEAK TO Mrs. Maureen Barclay or Mr. K. J. Barclay.
They are members of LAPADA.
SEE Porcelain, Oil Paintings, Furniture.

B. C. METALCRAFTS
69 Tewkesbury Gardens, **London NW9 0QU**
TEL 081 204 2446
OPEN By Appointment.

Specialise in restoring and repairing antique lighting decor and all types of conversion to electricity.
SPEAK TO F. Burnell or M. A. Burnell.
They are members of LAPADA.
SEE Furniture.

CRAWLEY STUDIOS
Unit 17, Carew Street, **London SE5 9DF**
TEL 071 733 1276
FAX 071 733 1014
OPEN 9–6.15 Mon–Fri.

Specialise in restoring Tole and papier mâché objects.
PROVIDE Home Inspections. Free Estimates. Chargeable Collection/Delivery Service.
SPEAK TO Marie Louise Crawley.
Ms Crawley is a member of BAFRA and UKIC.
SEE Furniture.

VERDIGRIS ART METALWORK RESTORERS
Arch 280 or 290, Crown Street, **London SE5 OUR**
TEL   071 703 8373
OPEN   9–5 Mon–Fri.

Specialise in restoring bronzes, chandeliers, door furniture, ormolu, pewter and spelter, monumental bronzes, including modern works.
PROVIDE Free Estimates.
SPEAK TO Gerard Bacon.

R. WILKINSON & SON
5 Catford Hill, **London SE6 4NU**
TEL   081 314 1080
FAX   081 690 1524
OPEN   9–5 Mon–Fri.

Specialise in restoring chandeliers.
PROVIDE Home Inspections. Free Estimates. Chargeable Collection/Delivery Service.
SPEAK TO Peter Prickett, Jane Milnes or David Wilkinson.
SEE Porcelain.

THE FAN MUSEUM
12 Crooms Hill, **London SE10 8ER**
TEL   081 858 7879 or 305 1441
OPEN   By Appointment.

Specialise in conserving and restoring all types of fans.
PROVIDE Home Inspections. Free Estimates. Postal Collection/Delivery Service.
SPEAK TO Mrs. Alexander.

RELCY ANTIQUES
9 Nelson Road, Greenwich, **London SE10 9JB**
TEL   081 858 2812
FAX   081 293 4135
OPEN   10–6 Mon–Sat.

Specialise in restoring antique metalwork including copper, brass, silver and ormolu.
PROVIDE Home Inspections. Free/Chargeable Estimates. Collection/Delivery Service by arrangement.
SPEAK TO Robin Challis.
SEE Collectors (Scientific Instruments), Furniture, Oil Paintings.

N. BLOOM & SON (ANTIQUES) LTD
Harrod's Fine Jewellery Room, **London SW1X 7XL**
TEL   071 730 1234 ext. 4062 or 4072
FAX   071 581 0470
OPEN   Mon–Sat 9–6, Wed 9–8.

Specialise in restoring old jewellery, antique and Victorian silver, enamel repairs.
PROVIDE Free Estimates.
SPEAK TO Heidi McKeown.
Member of LAPADA.
SEE Furniture.

SOMLO ANTIQUES
7 Piccadilly Arcade, **London SW1Y 6NA**
TEL   071 499 6526
FAX   071 499 0603
OPEN   10–5.30 Mon–Fri.

Specialise in repairing vintage wrist watches, antique pocket watches, technical and decorative enamel watches.
PROVIDE Home Inspections. Free/Chargeable Estimates.
SPEAK TO George Somlo.

BOURBON–HANBY ANTIQUES
Chelsea Antiques Market, 245–253 Kings Road, **London SW3 5EL.**
TEL   071 352 2106
OPEN   10–6 Mon–Sat.

Specialise in repairing antique jewellery.
PROVIDE Home Inspections. Free
Estimates. Free Collection/Delivery
Service.
SPEAK TO Mr. Barrett.

CHRISTINE SCHELL
15 Cale Street, **London SW3 3QS**
TEL   071 352 5563
OPEN   10–5.30 Mon–Fri; 10–1 Sat.
Specialise in restoring tortoiseshell, silver
and pique work. refurbishing dressing-
table sets and photograph frames.
PROVIDE Home Inspections.
Free/Chargeable Estimates.
SPEAK TO Christine Schell.

JOHN HEAP
No. 1 The Polygon, **London SW4**
TEL   071 627 4498
OPEN   By Appointment.
Specialise in restoring enamels, cane
handles.
PROVIDE Home Inspections. Free
Estimates. Free Collection/Delivery
Service.
SPEAK TO John Heap.
SEE Furniture, Porcelain.

CHRISTOPHER WRAY'S
LIGHTING EMPORIUM
600 Kings Road, **London SW6 2DX**
TEL   071 736 8434
FAX   071 731 3507
OPEN   9.30–6 Mon–Sat.
Specialise in restoring original Victorian
and Edwardian light fittings.
PROVIDE Free Estimates. Chargeable
Collection/Delivery Service.
SPEAK TO Christopher Wray.
SEE China.

COMPTON HALL RESTORATION
Unit A, 133 Riverside Business Centre,
Haldane Place, **London SW18 4UQ**
TEL   081 874 0762
OPEN   9–5 Mon–Fri.

Specialise in restoring Tole, papier
mâché and penwork.
PROVIDE Home Inspections. Free
Estimates. Collection/Delivery Service
by arrangement.
SPEAK TO Lucinda Compton, Jane or
Henrietta Hohler.
Members of BAFRA and UKIC.
SEE Furniture.

PLOWDEN & SMITH LTD
190 St Ann's Hill, **London SW18 2Rt**
TEL   081 874 4005
FAX   081 874 7248
OPEN   9–5.30 Mon–Fri.
Specialise in restoring and conserving
gold and silver.
PROVIDE Home Inspections. Free
Estimates. Chargeable
Collection/Delivery Service.
SPEAK TO Bob Butler.
They also advise on conservation
strategy, environmental control and
micro-climates for collections as well as
installing, mounting and displaying
temporary and permanent exhibitions.
SEE Furniture, Oil Paintings, Porcelain.

BLOOMFIELD CERAMIC
RESTORATIONS LTD
4th Floor, 58 Davies Street, **London
W1Y 1LB**
TEL   071 580 5761
FAX   071 636 1625
OPEN   By Appointment.
Specialise in restoring antique European
and Oriental objets d'art.
PROVIDE Free Estimates.
SPEAK TO Steven P. Bloomfield.
SEE Porcelain.

Silver, Metalwork & Enamels **London–London**

A. & B. BLOOMSTEIN
Bond Street Silver Galleries, 111–112 New Bond Street, **London W1Y OBQ**
TEL   071 493 6180
FAX   071 495 3493
OPEN   9–5 Mon–Fri.
Specialise in restoring antique silver, Victorian plate and old Sheffield plate.
PROVIDE Free Estimates. Free Collection/Delivery Service.
SPEAK TO Alfred Bloomstein.
They are members of LAPADA and BADA.

BRUFORD & HEMING LTD
28 Conduit Street, **London W1R 9TA**
TEL   071 499 7644
FAX   071 493 5879
OPEN   9.30–5.30 Mon–Fri.
Specialise in restoring antique jewellery and antique domestic silver, especially flatware. They also specialise in matching up missing items of antique cutlery.
PROVIDE Home Inspections. Free Estimates. Free Collection/Delivery Service.
SPEAK TO Alan Kinsey.
Members of BADA & NAG, they have traded from the same address since 1858.

HADLEIGH JEWELLERS
30A Marylebone High Street, **London W1M 3PP**
TEL   071 935 4074
OPEN   9.30–5.30 Mon–Fri; 9.30–5 Sat.
Specialise in repairing and restoring antique jewellery and stones.
PROVIDE Home Inspections. Refundable Estimates.
SPEAK TO Mr. J. Aldridge.

GEOFFREY HAGGER
58 Davies Street, **London W1Y 1LB**
TEL   071 409 1418
OPEN   9.30–4 Sun–Sat.
Specialise in restoring all types of jewellery.
PROVIDE Home Inspections. Free Estimates. Free Collection/Delivery Service.
SPEAK TO Geoffrey Hagger.

HARVEY & GORE
4 Burlington Gardens, **London W1X 1LH**
TEL   071 493 2714
FAX   071 493 0324
OPEN   9.30–5 Mon–Fri.
Specialise in restoring antique, period and fine jewellery and antique silver and old Sheffield plate.
PROVIDE Home Inspections. Free/Chargeable Estimates.
SPEAK TO Brian Norman.
Members of BADA, this company was established in 1723.

HENNELL SILVER LTD
12 New Bond Street, **London W1Y OH6**
TEL   071 629 6888
FAX   071 493 8158
OPEN   9.30–5.30 Tues–Sat.
Specialise in restoring modern and antique silver, old Sheffield plate.
PROVIDE Home Inspections. Free Estimates. Free Collection/Delivery Service.
SPEAK TO A. C. Kaufmann.
SEE Collectors (Scientific Instruments).

MYRA ANTIQUES
Bond Street Antiques Centre, 124 New Bond Street, **London W1**
TEL   071 408 1508
FAX   071 409 1317
OPEN   10–5.30 Mon–Fri.

153

Specialise in restoring jewellery.
SPEAK TO Myra Sampson.

L. NEWLAND & SON
17 Picton Place, **London W1M 5DE**
TEL   071 935 2864
OPEN   10.30–2, 3.30–6 Mon–Fri.

Specialise in repairing and restoring jewellery, enamels, ivory, pique, tortoiseshell and amber.

PROVIDE Home Inspections. Free Estimates. Free Collection/Delivery Service.

SPEAK TO Mr. Newland.
SEE Furniture.

W. SITCH & CO. LTD
48 Berwick Street, **London W1V 4JD**
TEL   071 437 3776
OPEN   8.30–5.30 Mon–Fri; 9–10 Sat.

Specialise in restoring late 19th century lighting.

PROVIDE Home Inspections. Free Estimates. Free/Chargeable Collection/Delivery Service.
SPEAK TO Ron Sitch.

JOHN WALKER
64 South Molton Street, **London W1Y 1HH**
TEL   071 629 3487
OPEN   8.30–5.15 Mon–Fri.

Specialise in repairing and restoring antique and modern jewellery.

PROVIDE Home Inspections. Free Estimates. Chargeable Collection/Delivery Service.

SPEAK TO John Walker or Steve Martin.

This family firm was established in 1830. They are FBHI.
SEE Furniture.

YOUNG & STEPHENS LTD
1 Burlington Gardens, **London W1X 1LD**
TEL   071 499 7927
FAX   071 495 0570
OPEN   9.30–5.30 Mon–Fri; 10.30–4.30 Sat.

Specialise in repairing and restoring fine antique and period jewellery.

PROVIDE Home Inspections. Free Estimates. Chargeable Collection/Delivery Service.
SPEAK TO Stephen Burton or Duncan Semmens.

H. J. HATFIELD & SON
42 St. Michael's Street, **London W2 1QP**
TEL   071 723 8265
FAX   071 706 4562
OPEN   9–1, 2–5 Mon–Fri.

Specialise in restoring metalwork and lacquer.

PROVIDE Home Inspections. Free Estimates.
SPEAK TO Philip Astley–Jones.
SEE Furniture.

WILLIAM MANSELL
24 Connaught Street, **London W2 2AF**
TEL   071 723 4154
OPEN   9–6 Mon–Fri; 10–1 Sat.

Specialise in repairing and restoring silverware and antique jewellery.

PROVIDE Home Inspections. Free Estimates. Free Collection/Delivery Service.
SPEAK TO Bill Salisbury.

This business was established in 1864.
SEE Furniture.

S. LAMPARD & SON LTD
32 Notting Hill Gate, **London W11 3HX**
TEL   071 229 5457
OPEN   9–4.30 Mon–Fri.
Specialise in restoring antique jewellery and silver.
PROVIDE Home Inspections. Free Estimates.
SPEAK TO Mr. J. R. Barnett.

ROSEMARY COOK RESTORATION
78 Stanlake Road, **London W12 7HJ**
TEL   081 749 7977
OPEN   By Appointment.
Specialise in restoring painted objects.
PROVIDE Home Inspections. Free Estimates. Free Local Collection/Delivery Service.
SPEAK TO Rosemary Cook.
SEE Furniture, Porcelain.

S. J. SHRUBSOLE LTD
43 Museum Street, **London WC1A 1LY**
TEL   071 405 2712
OPEN   9–5.30 Mon–Fri.
Specialise in repairing antique silver and old Sheffield plate.
PROVIDE Free Estimates. Free Collection/Delivery Service.
SPEAK TO Mr. C. J. Shrubsole.
Member of the Antique Plate Committee, Goldsmith Hall.

HAMPTON UTILITIES (B'HAM) LTD
15 Pitsford Street, Hockley, Birmingham, **West Midlands B18 6LJ**
TEL   021 554 1766
OPEN   9–5 Mon–Thur; 9–4 Fri.
Specialise in restoring and repairing antique and modern silver including plating and gilding.

PROVIDE Free Estimates. Chargeable Collection/Delivery Service.
SPEAK TO B. Levine.
SEE Furniture, Oil Paintings.

JOHN HUBBARD ANTIQUES
224–226 Court Oak Road, Harborne, Birmingham, **West Midlands B32 2EG**
TEL   021 426 1694
FAX   021 428 1214
OPEN   9–6 Mon–Sat.
Specialise in restoring lighting.
PROVIDE Home Inspections. Refundable Estimates. Collection/Delivery Service.
SPEAK TO John Hubbard or David Taplin.
SEE Furniture, Oil Paintings, Porcelain.

RICKETT & CO. ANTIQUES
Church Square, Shepperton, **Middlesex TW17 8JN**
TEL   0932 243571
OPEN   9–5 Mon–Sat.
Specialise in repairing and restoring 18th and 19th century metal items, including fenders, fire grates, fire tools, fire dogs and candlesticks.
PROVIDE Free Estimates.
SPEAK TO A. Spencer.

ROGERS OF LONDON
344 Richmond Road, East Twickenham, **Middlesex TW1 2DU**
TEL   081 891 2122
OPEN   081 891 6418
Specialise in restoring period lighting.
PROVIDE Home Inspections. Chargeable Estimates. Collection/Delivery Service by arrangement.
SPEAK TO Joy or Charles Lolcoma.

WILLIAM ALLCHIN
22–24 St. Benedict's Street, Norwich,
Norfolk NR2 4AQ
TEL   0603 660046
FAX   0603 660046
OPEN   10.30–5 Mon–Sat.

Specialise in restoring period lighting,
including metal chandeliers and wall
brackets.

PROVIDE Home Inspections. Free
Estimates.
SPEAK TO William Allchin.
SEE Porcelain.

DAVID BARTRAM FURNITURE
The Raveningham Centre, Castell Farm,
Beccles Road, Raveningham, Nr.
Norwich, **Norfolk**
TEL   050 846 721
OPEN   10–6 Sun–Sat.

Specialise in comprehensive antique
restoration service including metalwork.

PROVIDE Home Inspections. Free
Estimates. Free Collection/Delivery
Service.
SPEAK TO David Bartram.
SEE Furniture.

PETER HOWKINS
135 King Street, Great Yarmouth,
Norfolk NR30 2PQ
TEL   0493 844639
OPEN   9–5.30 Mon–Sat or By
Appointment.

Specialise in restoring antique jewellery
and silver.

PROVIDE Home Inspections.
SPEAK TO Peter Howkins, Thomas Burn
or Matthew Higham.

Member of NAG.
SEE Furniture (different address).

JASPER ANTIQUES
11A Hall Road, Snettisham, King's
Lynn, **Norfolk PE31 7LU**
TEL   0485 541485 (Home 0485
540604)
OPEN   10.30–1 Mon, Wed, Fri; 10.30–
1, 2–4 Sat.

Specialise in repair service for silver,
silver plating and jewellery.

PROVIDE Home Inspections. Free
Estimates. Free Collection/Delivery
Service.
SPEAK TO Mrs. A. A. Norris.
SEE Furniture, Porcelain.

LAWRENCE & CABLE
6 Merchants Court, St. George's Street,
Norwich, **Norfolk NR3 1AB**
TEL   0603 632064
OPEN   9–5 Mon–Fri.

Specialise in restoring and conserving
objets d'art.

PROVIDE Home Inspections. Free
Estimates. Free/Chargeable
Collection/Delivery Service.
SPEAK TO Penny Lawrence or Tim Cable.

This workshop is included on the register
of conservators maintained by the
Conservation Unit of the Museums and
Galleries Commission.
SEE Furniture, Oil Paintings.

MARIANNE MORRISH
South Cottage Studio, Union Lane,
Wortham Ling, Diss, **Norfolk IP22 ISP**
TEL   0379 643831
OPEN   10–4 Mon–Fri.

Specialise in restoring objets d' art.

PROVIDE Home Inspections. Free
Estimates. Chargeable
Collection/Delivery Service.
SPEAK TO Marianne Morrish

Ms. Morrish is a member of the Guild
of Master Craftsmen.

156

THOMAS TILLETT & CO.
17 Saint Giles Street, Norwich, **Norfolk NR2 1JL**
TEL   0603 625922 or 620372
FAX   0603 620372
OPEN   9–5.30 Mon–Sat.
Specialise in all types of jewellery repairs and restoration.
PROVIDE Home Inspections. Free Estimates. Free Collection/Delivery Service.
SPEAK TO Mr. T. Scally or Lorraine Scally
SEE Furniture.

ARTISTRY & METAL
Sherwood Forge, Oakset Drive, Welbeck, Nr. Worksop,
Nottinghamshire S80 3LW
TEL   0909 486029
OPEN   8–5 Mon–Fri.
Specialise in architectural and interior iron and metalwork repoussage and relevage, fine knives and damascus, restoration and conservation of architectural ironwork, etching.
PROVIDE Home Inspections. Refundable Estimates. Chargeable Collection/Delivery Service.
SPEAK TO F. J. M. Craddock.
Mr. Craddock is a Master Bladesmith and a Member of UKIC and BABA.

HOWARDS OF BURFORD
51 High Street, Burford, **Oxon OX18 4QA**
TEL   0993 823172
OPEN   9.30–5.30 Sun–Sat.
Specialise in repairing and restoring antique and modern silver and jewellery.
PROVIDE Home Inspections. Free Estimates. Free Collection/Delivery Service.
SPEAK TO Robert Light.

F. C. MANSER & SON LTD
53–54 Wyle Cop, Shrewsbury,
Shropshire SY1 1XJ
TEL   0743 351120
FAX   0743 271047
OPEN   9–5.30 Mon–Wed, Fri; 9–1 Thur; 9–5 Sat.
Specialise in restoring light fitings and silverware.
PROVIDE Home Inspections. Free Estimates. Chargeable Collection/Delivery Service.
SPEAK TO Paul Manser.
Members of LAPADA and Guild of Master Craftsmen.
SEE Furniture, Porcelain.

T. R. BAILEY
11 St Andrew's Road, Stogursey, Bridgwater, **Somerset TA5 1TE**
TEL   0278 732887
OPEN   By Appointment.
Specialise in providing fine quality fruitwood and hardwood handles and accessories for silverware.
PROVIDE Free Estimates. Collection/Delivery Service by arrangement.
SPEAK TO Tim Bailey.
SEE Furniture.

ROGER & SYLVIA ALLAN
The Old Red Lion, Bedingfield, Eye,
Suffolk IP23 7LQ
TEL   0728 76 491
OPEN   By Appointment.
Specialise in restoring painted snuff boxes and ceramics.
PROVIDE Home Inspections. Free Estimates.
SPEAK TO Roger Allan.
SEE Furniture, Oil Paintings.

157

BRIAN A. BROOKES
Brookes Forge Flempton, Flempton,
Bury St.Edmunds, **Suffolk IP28 6EN**
TEL   0284 728473
OPEN   2.30–6 Mon–Fri.

Specialise in restoring chandeliers and a
variety of ironwork using castings
produced from clients' patterns. Single
items are also undertaken and brass
castings can be patinated to match
colour and tone of the original. Details
of patterns are accurately copied.

PROVIDE Home Inspections. Free
Estimates. Free Collection/Delivery
Service.

SPEAK TO Brian Brookes.

This workshop is included on the register
of conservators maintained by the
Conservation Unit of the Museums and
Galleries Commission.

SUFFOLK BRASS
Thurston, Bury St.Edmunds, **Suffolk
IP31 3SN**
TEL   0359 30888 and 0379 898670
OPEN   9–6 Mon–Fri; 9–12 Sat.

Specialise in casting brass by the hot wax
or sand process from original brassware
for furniture fittings. Also make hand-
forged iron fittings.

PROVIDE Free Estimates. Free
Collection/Delivery Service (same day).
SPEAK TO Mark Peters or Thane
Meldrum.

CRY FOR THE MOON
31 High Street, Godalming, **Surrey
GU7 1AU**
TEL   0483 426201
FAX   0483 860117
OPEN   9.30–5.30 Mon–Sat.

Specialise in restoring antique and fine
jewellery.

PROVIDE Free Estimates.
SPEAK TO Mr. Hibbert.

**NORMAN FLYNN
RESTORATIONS**
37 Lind Road, Sutton, **Surrey SM1 4PP**
TEL   081 661 9505
OPEN   7.45–3.30 Mon–Fri.

Specialise in restoring antique and
modern enamel. They also specialise in
lamp conversions.

PROVIDE Home Inspections. Free
Estimates. Free Collection/Delivery
Service each week to London.
SPEAK TO Norman Flynn.
SEE Porcelain.

R. SAUNDERS
71 Queens Road, Weybridge, **Surrey
KT13 9UQ**
TEL   0932 842601
OPEN   9.15–5 Mon–Sat; closed Wed.

Specialise in restoring and cleaning
English silver.

PROVIDE Home Inspections. Free
Estimates. Free Collection/Delivery
Service.
SPEAK TO J. B. Tonkinson.
SEE Furniture, Oil Paintings, Porcelain.

SIMPSON DAY RESTORATION
Studio 13, Acorn House, Cherry
Orchard Road, Croydon, **Surrey
CR0 6BA**
TEL   081 681 8339
OPEN   9.30–6 Mon–Fri.

Specialise in restoring Canton enamels.
PROVIDE Free Estimates.
SPEAK TO Sarah Simpson or Sarah Day.
SEE Porcelain.

W. BRUFORD & SON LTD
11–13 Cornfield Road, Eastbourne, **East
Sussex BN21 3NA**
TEL   0323 25452
OPEN   9–1, 2–5.30 Mon–Fri; 9–1, 2–5
       Sat.

Specialise in repairing and restoring
Victorian and Edwardian jewellery and
silver.
PROVIDE Free Estimates.
SPEAK TO N. Bruford or J. Burgess.
Fellow of the Gemmological Association
SEE Furniture.

DAVID CRAIG
Toll Cottage, Station Road, Durgates,
Wadhurst, **East Sussex TN5 6RS**
TEL   089 288 2188
OPEN   9–5.30 Mon–Fri.
Specialise in restoring and enamels.
PROVIDE Chargeable Estimates.
Chargeable Collection/Delivery Service.
SPEAK TO David Sutcliffe.
SEE Porcelain.

RECOLLECTIONS
1A Sydney Street, Brighton, **East Sussex
BN1 4EN**
TEL   0273 681517
OPEN   10.30–5 Mon–Sat.
Specialise in polishing and repairing
metalwork, including brass and copper.
PROVIDE Local Home Inspections. Local
Collection/Delivery Service.
SPEAK TO Bruce Bagley or Peter Tooley.

WELLER & E.T.C.
12 North Street, Eastbourne, **East
Sussex BN21 3HG**
TEL   0323 410972
OPEN   9.15–5 Mon–Fri; 9.15–1 Sat.
Specialise in restoring silver plating,
brass repairs, polishing, lacquering and
engraving trophies.
PROVIDE Home Inspections. Free
Estimates.
SPEAK TO Mr. Rothwell.

YELLOW LANTERN ANTIQUES LTD
34 & 34B Holland Road, Hove, **East
Sussex BN3 1JL**
TEL   0273 771572
OPEN   9.30–1, 2.15–5.30 Mon–Fri; 9–1,
        2.15–4.30 Sat.
Specialise in cleaning ormolu and
bronze.
PROVIDE Home Inspections. Free
Estimates. Free Collection/Delivery
Service.
SPEAK TO Mr or Mrs B. R. Higgins.
Members of LAPADA.
SEE Furniture.

GARNER & CO
Stable Cottage, Steyning Road, Wiston,
West Sussex BN44 3DD
TEL   0903 814565
OPEN   By Appointment (Tel Mon–Fri
        9–5.30).
Specialise in repairing lead and brass
objects as well as conserving and
repairing metal chandeliers.
PROVIDE Home Inspections. Estimates.
SPEAK TO Sid Garner.
SEE Furniture, Porcelain.

WEST DEAN COLLEGE
West Dean, Chichester, **West Sussex
PO18 00Z**
TEL   0243 63 301
FAX   0243 63 342
OPEN   9–5 Mon–Fri.
Specialise in training conservators and
restorers in the field of fine metals, which
they will also restore.
PROVIDE Local Home Inspections. Free
Estimates.
SPEAK TO Peter Sarginson.
SEE Books, Furniture, Porcelain.

159

MARTIN PAYNE ANTIQUES
30 Brook Street, Warwick, **Warwickshire CV34 4BL**
TEL   0926 494948
OPEN   10–5.30 Mon–Sat.
Specialise in repairing antique and collectable silver.
PROVIDE Home Inspections. Free Estimates. Free Collection/Delivery Service.
SPEAK TO Martin Payne.
Member of LAPADA.

HECTOR COLE IRONWORK
The Mead, Great Somerford, Chippenham, **Wiltshire SN15 5JB**
TEL   0249 720485
OPEN   By Appointment – best to phone in the evenings.
Specialise in restoring and renovating antique ironwork using wrought iron. Also make reproductions of medieval ironwork.
PROVIDE Free Estimates.
SPEAK TO Hector Cole.

MAC HUMBLE ANTIQUES
7–9 Woolley Street, Bradford-on-Avon, **Wiltshire BA15 1AD**
TEL   02216 6329
OPEN   9–6 Mon–Sat.
Specialise in restoring metalwork.
PROVIDE Home Inspections. Refundable Estimates. Free Collection/Delivery Service.
SPEAK TO Mac Humble.
SEE Furniture, Carpets.

SHENSTONE RESTORATIONS
23 Lansdown Road, Swindon, **Wiltshire SN1 3NE**
TEL   0793 644980
OPEN   By Appointment.

Specialise in restoring smaller decorative items including marquetry and inlay. They work in bone, mother-of-pearl, ebony and ivory and its substitutes as well as Boulle marquetry.
PROVIDE Local Home Inspections. Chargeable Estimates. Chargeable Collection/Delivery Service.
SPEAK TO Blair Shenstone.
SEE Furniture.

RON FIELD (METALWORK)
Rowhouse House, Wykeham, Scarborough, **North Yorkshire YO13 9QC**
TEL   0723 862640
OPEN   9–5.30 Mon–Fri or By Appointment.
Specialise in repairing and restoring antique and vintage metalwork of all types, including mechanical antiques and particularly items of interior decor.
PROVIDE Home Inspections. Free/Refundable Estimates. Free/Chargeable Collection/Delivery Service.
SPEAK TO Ron Field.
Mr. Field is a Member of the Guild of Master Craftsmen.

DUNCAN GRIMMOND
The Old Granary, Uppercourt Terrace, Ripon, **North Yorkshire HG4 1PD**
TEL   0765 600982
OPEN   10–4 Thur. Other times by appointment.
Specialise in restoring jewellery, silverware, ivory, tortoiseshell, mother-of-pearl, non-wood inlay and non-ferrous metalwork.
PROVIDE Home Inspections by arrangement. Chargeable Collection/Delivery Service.
SPEAK TO Duncan Grimmond.

DAVID MASON & SON
7–9 Westmoreland Street, Harrogate,
North Yorkshire H91 5AY
TEL   0423 567305
OPEN   9–5 Mon–Sat.

Specialise in repairing jewellery.
PROVIDE Home Inspections. Free
Estimates. Chargeable
Collection/Delivery Service.
SPEAK TO John Mason.
Member of NAG, Yorkshire
Goldsmiths Association and FGA.
SEE Furniture.

NIDD HOUSE ANTIQUES
Nidd House, Bogs Lane, Harrogate,
North Yorkshire HG1 4DY
TEL   0423 884739
OPEN   9–5 Mon–Fri or By
        Appointment.

Specialise in restoring lead castings and
pewter work.
PROVIDE Home Inspections. Free Local
Estimates. Chargeable
Collection/Delivery service.
SPEAK TO Mr. D. Preston.
Members of Guild of Master Craftsmen
and UKIC.
This workshop is included on the register
of conservators maintained by the
Conservation Unit of the Museums and
Galleries Commission.
SEE Collectors (Scientific Instruments,)
Furniture, Porcelain.

JAMES DENNIS VANCE
Eastgate Antiques, 30 Eastgate,
Pickering, **North Yorkshire YO18 7DU**
TEL   0751 72954
OPEN   10–5 Mon–Sat.

Specialise in restoring antique metalware
including the repairing and polishing of
copper, brass, pewter and spelter.

PROVIDE Home Inspections.
Free Estimates. Chargeable
Collection/Delivery Service.
SPEAK TO James Vance.

FILLIANS ANTIQUES
2 Market Walk, Huddersfield, **West
Yorkshire HD1 2QA**
TEL   0484 531609
FAX   0484 432688
OPEN   9–5.30 Mon–Sat.

Specialise in restoring antique jewellery
and silver.
PROVIDE Home Inspections. Free
Collection/Delivery Service.
SPEAK TO G. Neary.

T. M. TUKE
18 Main Street, Greyabbey,
Newtownards, **Co. Down**
TEL   024774 416
FAX   024774 250
OPEN   11–5 Mon–Sat; closed Thur.

Specialise in repairing silver and
jewellery.
PROVIDE Home Inspections. Free
Estimates. Free Collection/Delivery
Service.
SPEAK TO Tom Tuke.
Member of BHI.

J. BYRNE & SONS
22 Southend Street, Dublin 2, **Co. Dublin**
TEL   718709
OPEN   9–5.30 Mon–Sat.

Specialise in restoring, repairing and
reproducing jewellery.
PROVIDE Free Estimates.
SPEAK TO Jim or Richard Byrne.

DESMOND TAAFFE
51 Dawson Street, Dublin 2, **Co. Dublin**
TEL   719609
OPEN   9–5.30 Mon–Fri.

Specialise in restoring antique and domestic silver and churchware.

PROVIDE Free Estimates.

SPEAK TO Desmond Taafe.

OLD ST ANDREWS GALLERY
9 Albany Place, St. Andrews, **Fife**
KY16 9HH
and 10 Golf Place, St. Andrews, **Fife**
KY16 9JA
TEL   0334 7840 and 0334 78712
OPEN   10–5 Mon–Fri.

Specialise in repairing silver and jewellery.

PROVIDE Home Inspections, Free Estimates, Free Collection/Delivery Service

SPEAK TO Mr. or Mrs. Brown.

SEE Sporting Equipment (Golf).

GALLERY
48A Union Street, Aberdeen, **Grampian**
AB2 1HS
TEL   0224 625909
OPEN   9–5.30 Mon–Sat.

Specialise in repairing and restoring jewellery. They also make jewellery.

PROVIDE Home Inspections. Free Estimates.

SPEAK TO Michael Gray.

GILES PEARSON
Brightmony House, Auldern, **Highland**
IV12 5HZ
TEL   0667 55550
OPEN   9–6 Sun–Sat.

Specialise in cane handles for silver and silver-plated tea and coffee pots.

PROVIDE Home Inspections. Free Estimates. Collection/Delivery Service by arrangement.

SPEAK TO Giles Pearson.

SEE Furniture.

THURSO ANTIQUES
Drill Hall, 21 Sinclair Street, Thurso,
Highland
TEL   0847 63291
FAX   0847 62824
OPEN   10–5 Mon–Fri; 10–1 Sat.

Specialise in cleaning and redesigning jewellery.

PROVIDE Free Estimates.
Collection/Delivery Service by arrangement.

SPEAK TO G. Atkinson.

SEE Oil Paintings.

HAMILTON & INCHES
87 George Street, Edinburgh, **Lothian**
EH2 3EY
TEL   031 225 4898
FAX   031 220 6994
OPEN   9–5 Mon–Fri; 9–12.30 Sat.

Specialise in restoring gold and silver antique and modern jewellery and objects.

PROVIDE Home Inspections. Free Estimates. Chargeable Collection/Delivery Service.

SPEAK TO Densil Skinner.

Member of NAG.

SEE Furniture.

HOUNDWOOD ANTIQUES
RESTORATION
7 West Preston Street, Edinburgh
Lothian EH8 9PX
TEL   031 667 3253
OPEN   By Appointment.

Specialise in restoring objets d'art including ormolu, bronze and pewter.

PROVIDE Home Inspections. Free Estimates. Chargeable Collection/Delivery Service.

SPEAK TO Mr. A. Gourlay.

SEE Furniture, Porcelain.

C. P. R. ANTIQUES AND SERVICES
96 Main Street, Barrhead, Glasgow,
Strathclyde G78 1SE
TEL　　041 881 5379
OPEN　　10–1, 1.30–5 Mon, Wed–Sat;
　　　　closed Tues.

Specialise in restoring brass, copper,
spelter and pewter, chrome stripped,
spare parts made for certain items.
PROVIDE Free Estimates.
SPEAK TO Mrs. C. Porterfield.

NEIL LIVINGSTONE
3 Old Hawkhill, Dundee, **Tayside**
DD1 5EU
TEL　　0382 25517
OPEN　　9–5 Mon–Fri.

Specialise in repairing jewellery.
PROVIDE Free Estimates. Chargeable
Collection/Delivery Service.
SPEAK TO Neil Livingstone.
SEE Arms and Armour, Furniture, Oil
Paintings.

Carpets, Textiles
and Costumes

TEXTILES

No textile can last for ever. It is the nature of organic materials to change and become weaker with age, so, while a good professional conservator can make a great deal of difference to the life expectancy of an object, it is also up to the collector to take particular care of such vulnerable material. The collector should also realise that some maintenance may be necessary at times, even after conservation work has been carried out, especially if the object is displayed in the open or put to any kind of use.

Protection from high levels of light, from whatever source, is the first and most important requirement, as light affects both the colours of the dyes and the molecular structure of the fibres exposed. Other factors in the ageing process are too much humidity creating conditions in which mould can flourish, too dry an atmosphere which will tend to embrittle fibres, exposure to dust and air pollution in general, mechanical distortion through bad display or storage and attack by insects.

Moth, the carpet beetle, woodworm and silver fish will all attack textiles, either directly as a source of food during development or indirectly when an insect will eat through a fabric which prevents its escape. Constant good house-keeping is necessary to ensure that an infestation does not have a chance to take hold before it is discovered.

When considering the acquisition of a fresh item for a collection, note should be made of the degree of fading and how dirty the object is, whether the fabric seems to be strong or shows signs of deterioration in the form of splits in the weave structure or loss of surface finish. Velvet loses its pile and satin loses the warp face which gives it its special quality. The presence of old repairs should also be noted. In three-dimensional objects the structure, that is the seams and stitching

164

or decorations, should be examined for signs of alteration and previous repair. Too much will make conservation difficult and therefore costly. This must then be balanced against the historical interest and importance of the object. If in doubt a conservator should be consulted.

Conservation has a dual role to play in any intervention, not only to make the object look 'tidy' but also to discover and explain its structure and preserve any information about style and past methods of making things which may be present. For the client, anxious to keep down costs, this investigation may seem unnecessary, but the added historical knowledge gained may well increase the value of the object.

CARPETS

If a carpet needs cleaning and is to be washed the owner must be sure that the colours are fast to water and that the nature of the detergents used will not harm the fibres in any way. The mechanical side of the process should also be as gentle as possible with the object kept flat thoughout.

Re-knotting a carpet, which may be termed restoration as opposed to conservation, usually means the attachment of a support fabric to the back of the object, to which the weak areas of the weave are stitched. It should be discussed with the chosen conservator, as some will not restore on ethical grounds.

The same applies to the cleaning and re-weaving of tapestries. When deciding the amount of work to be carried out on a tapestry the client should be prepared for the cost of removing and replacing any lining present. Washing with a lining can give rise to problems of shrinkage of one against the other and repairs carried out through an old lining are worse than useless.

COSTUMES

This category of textile is the one most likely to give rise to questions of alteration to the structure. The style of a dress may actually be later than the date of manufacture of the fabric. A close look at the seams for signs of new lines of stitch holes or turnings and fold lines can confirm an alteration. Whether or not the second version is as valuable as the first will depend on whether it has been made during the useful life of the object or much later, for fancy dress or theatrical use. If in doubt the problem should be discussed with either a historian of costume or a conservator who specialises in costume.

Cleaning is often difficult as the kinds of fabrics in dress such as velvet, satin, heavy silks and taffetas will be ruined by washing. Dry cleaning of fragile objects is a specialist trade, but a few can be found to undertake the work. This will not be cheap, but properly carried out can make a lot of difference to the appearance of the garment.

The fabric of the costume may be fragile in areas such as beneath the arms or at fastenings and other places of stress and taking it to pieces in order to support the weak areas may be suggested. This should be discussed most carefully as original stitching should not be disturbed unless absolutely necessary. The practice of acquiring a wedding dress in order to alter it for wearing again is understandable, but reprehensible if the garment is a good example of its period.

GENERAL TEXTILES

Conservators cannot perform miracles. They cannot replace what is no longer there. They cannot restore faded colours, nor can they make a very brittle fabric completely strong again. However, much can be done to clean and support printed cottons, samplers, lace and small embroideries. When the object is over a certain size it may be difficult to find a conservator with large enough premises and equipment to cope with it.

Once conserved the best protection for flat textiles is to be attached to a board and framed behind glass. Storage boxes and any paper or coverings should be acid free.

Sheila Landi

**THE TEXTILE RESTORATION
STUDIO**
20 Hargreaves Road, Timperley,
Altrincham, **Cheshire WA15 7BB**
TEL   061 904 9944
FAX   061 903 9144
OPEN   9.30–5 Mon–Fri.

Specialise in cleaning, conserving and
repairing all types of antique textiles
including samplers, canvas and bead
work, tapestry, white work, embroidery,
costume and ecclesiastical furnishings
and vestments.

PROVIDE Home Inspections. Free
Estimates. Collection/Delivery Service
by arrangement.
SPEAK TO Jacqueline Hyman.

SEE Collectors (Dolls), Silver.

ANNABEL WYLIE
Hamilton House, The Green, Great
Bentley, Colchester, **Essex CO7 8LY**
TEL   0206 251518
OPEN   By Appointment.

Specialise in conserving furnishing
textiles, rugs, embroidered pictures,
costumes and accessories.

PROVIDE Home Inspections.
Free/Chargeable Estimates. Chargeable
Collection/Delivery Service.
SPEAK TO Annabel Wylie.

COCOA
7 Queens Circus, Montpellier,
Cheltenham, **Gloucestershire GL50 1RX**
TEL   0242 233588
OPEN   10–5 Mon–Sat.

Specialise in restoring antique lace,
wedding gowns, linens, antique veils.
SPEAK TO P. A. O'Sullivan.

**THE LADIES' WORK SOCIETY
LIMITED**
Delabere House, New Road, Moreton-
in-Marsh, **Gloucestershire GL56 OAS**
TEL   0608 50447
OPEN   10–1, 2–5 Mon–Fri; 10–1, 2–4
        Sat.

Specialise in designing needlework for
period furniture and conserving antique
textiles.

PROVIDE local Home Inspections.
Refundable Estimates. Chargeable
Collection/Delivery Service.
SPEAK TO Stanley Duller.

ERIC PRIDE ORIENTAL RUGS
44 Suffolk Road, Cheltenham,
Gloucestershire GL50 2AQ
TEL   0242 580822
OPEN   10–5 Tues–Fri.

Specialise in cleaning and restoring old
handwoven rugs, carpets, kilims and
tapestries both European and Oriental.

PROVIDE Free Estimates.
SPEAK TO Eric Pride.

ELIZABETH W. TAYLOR
Cirencester Workshops, Brewery Court,
Cirencester, **Gloucestershire GL7 1JH**
TEL   0285 641177
OPEN   9–5 Mon–Fri.

Specialise in restoring Oriental rugs and
carpets.

PROVIDE Free Estimates.
SPEAK TO Elizabeth Taylor.

JUDITH DORE
Textile & Costume Conservation, Castle
Lodge, 271 Sandown Road, Deal, **Kent
CT14 6QU**
TEL   0304 373684
OPEN   By Appointment.

Specialise in the conservation,
identification, display and storage of
textile and costume objects.

167

PROVIDE Home Inspections by arrangement. Free/Chargeable Estimates. Chargeable Collection/Delivery Service. SPEAK TO Judith Doré.

DESMOND & AMANDA NORTH
The Orchard, Hale Street, East Peckham, **Kent TN12 5JB**
TEL   0622 831353
OPEN   By Appointment.
Specialise in cleaning and undertaking some repairs to old Oriental rugs and carpets.
PROVIDE Chargeable Home Inspections. Free Estimates.
SPEAK TO Desmond or Amanda North.

PERSIAN RUG SHOP
Vines Farm, Matthews Lane, West Peckham, Maidstone, **Kent ME18 5JS**
TEL   0732 850228
OPEN   9–5.30 Sun–Sat or By Appointment.
Specialise in cleaning and restoring Oriental rugs and carpets.
PROVIDE Home Inspections. Chargeable Estimates. Chargeable Collection/Delivery Service.
SPEAK TO Rod King.

CAROLINE J. BOOTH, TEXTILE CONSERVATOR
Fold Farm, Higher Eastwood, Todmorden, **Lancashire OL14 8RP**
TEL   0706 816888
OPEN   10–5 Mon–Fri.
Specialise in a full range of services for historic textiles both woven and embroidered, including samplers, materials for dolls' houses and costumes for dolls and automata. Condition and conservation reports provided and advice given on handling, storage and display. Ms. Booth uses traditional

conservation techniques so that any work done is reversible.
PROVIDE Home Inspections. Chargeable Estimates. Chargeable Collection/Delivery Service.
SPEAK TO Caroline Booth.
SEE Collectors (Dolls).

PEARCE RUGS & FRINGES
The Cottage, Hamilton Lane, Scraptoft, Leicester, **Leicestershire LE7 9SB**
TEL   0533 414941
OPEN   By Appointment.
Specialise in cleaning, repairing and renovating Oriental rugs. Can also re-weave, clean and repair other types of carpeting.
PROVIDE Home Inspections. Chargeable Estimates. Chargeable Collection/Delivery Service.
SPEAK TO Mr.B.W. Pearce.
Also supply a mail order service for carpet fringes.

TATTERSALL'S
14 Orange Street, 2 Bear Yard, Orange Street, Uppingham, **Leicestershire LE15 9SQ**
TEL   0572 821171
OPEN   9–5 Mon–Sat; closed Thur.
Specialise in restoring antique and old Persian rugs.
PROVIDE Home Inspections. Free Estimates. Chargeable Collection/Delivery Service.
SPEAK TO Janice Tattersall.
SEE Furniture.

DUNCAN WATTS ORIENTAL RUGS
64 St Marys Road, Market Harborough, **Leicestershire LE16 7DU**
TEL   0858 432314
OPEN   10–5.30 Mon–Sat; closed Wed.
Specialise in restoring Oriental rugs.

PROVIDE Home Inspections. Free
Estimates. Free Collection/Delivery
Service.
SPEAK TO Duncan Watts.

POPPY SINGER
213 Brooke Road, **London E5 8AB**
TEL   081 806 3742
OPEN   By Appointment.

Specialise in conserving furnishing
textiles, rugs, embroidered pictures,
costumes and accessories.

PROVIDE Home Inspections.
Free/Chargeable Estimates. Chargeable
Collection/Delivery Service.
SPEAK TO Poppy Singer.

BEHAR PROFEX LTD
The Alban Building, St. Albans Place,
Upper Street, **London N1 0NX**
TEL   071 226 0144
OPEN   8–6 Mon–Thur; 8–5 Fri.

Specialise in cleaning, conserving and
restoring Oriental and European hand-
made carpets, rugs, textiles and
tapestries.

PROVIDE Home Inspections. Free
Estimates. Collection/Delivery Service.
SPEAK TO Robert Behar.

This family firm has been established 70
years and is a member of the UKIC and
the Guild of Master Craftsmen.

DAVID J. WILKINS ORIENTAL
RUGS
27 Princess Road, **London NW1 8JR**
TEL   071 722 7608
OPEN   9.15–5 Mon–Fri.

Specialise in all types of repairs and
cleaning of Oriental rugs.

PROVIDE Home Inspections. Free
Estimates. Chargeable
Collection/Delivery Service.
SPEAK TO David Wilkins or Gill Lowe.

JOSEPH LAVIAN
Block 'F', 53–79 Highgate Road, **London
NW5 1TL**
TEL   071 482 1234 and 071 485 7955
FAX   071 267 9222
OPEN   9.30–6 Mon–Fri.

Specialise in restoring antique Oriental
carpets, rugs, kelims, Aubussons,
tapestries and textiles.

PROVIDE Home Inspections.
Free/Chargeable Estimates. Chargeable
Collection/Delivery Service.
SPEAK TO Joseph Lavian.

MAYORCAS LTD.
38 Jermyn Street, **London SW1Y 6DN**
TEL   071 629 4195
OPEN   9.30–5.30 Mon–Fri; 10–1 Sat.

Specialise in cleaning and repairing
antique textiles, tapestry, needlework,
silks, damasks.

PROVIDE Discretionary Home
Inspections. Collection/Delivery Service.
SPEAK TO Andrew Morley Stephens.
Members of BADA.

WATTS & CO.
7 Tufton Street, **London SW1P 3QE**
TEL   071 233 0424
FAX   071 233 1130
OPEN   9–5 Mon–Fri.

Specialise in restoring church
embroidery and reproduce antique
textiles.

PROVIDE Free Estimates. Chargeable
Collection/Delivery Service.
SPEAK TO Shelagh Scott.

N. SONMEZ
Chenil Galleries, 181–183 Kings Road,
London SW3 5EB
TEL   071 351 6611
OPEN   10–6 Mon–Sat.

Specialise in restoring antique Persian,
Russian and Turkish carpets.

PROVIDE Home Inspections.
Free/Chargeable Estimates.
SPEAK TO N. Sonmez.

HAROUT BARIN
57A New Kings Road, **London SW6 4SE**
TEL   071 731 0546
FAX   071 384 1620
OPEN   9.30–6 Mon–Sat.

Specialise in cleaning and restoring
Oriental carpets, European tapestries,
Aubussons and needlepoints.

PROVIDE Home Inspections. Free
Estimates. Free Collection/Delivery
Service.
SPEAK TO Harout Barin.

LUNN ANTIQUES LTD
86 New Kings Road, **London SW6 4LU**
TEL   071 736 4638
FAX   071 371 7113
OPEN   10–6 Mon–Sat.

Specialise in restoring antique linen and
lace.

PROVIDE Home Inspections. Free
Estimates. Chargeable
Collection/Delivery Service.
SPEAK TO Mr. or Mrs. Lunn.

THE KILIM WAREHOUSE LTD
28A Pickets Street, **London SW12 8QB**
TEL   081 675 3122
FAX   081 675 8494
OPEN   10–6 Mon–Fri; 10–4 Sat.

Specialise in cleaning and restoring
kilims and flatweaves.

PROVIDE Chargeable Estimates.
SPEAK TO Jose Luczyc-Wyhowska.

RAYMOND BERNADOUT
18 Grosvenor Street, **London W1X 9SD**
TEL   071 355 4531
OPEN   8.30–6 Mon–Fri.

Specialise in restoring carpets, rugs,
tapestries and needlework including
Aubussons.

PROVIDE Home Inspections.
Free/Chargeable Estimates. Chargeable
Collection/Delivery Service.
SPEAK TO Raymond Bernadout.

ESSIE CARPETS
62 Piccadilly, **London W1V 9HL**
TEL   071 493 7766
FAX   071 495 3456
OPEN   9.30–6.30 Sun–Fri; closed Sat.

Specialise in restoring Persian carpets
and Oriental rugs.

PROVIDE Home Inspections. Chargeable
Collection/Delivery Service.
SPEAK TO Mr. Essie.

KENNEDY CARPETS
9A Vigo Street, **London W1X 1AL**
TEL   071 439 8873
FAX   071 437 1201
OPEN   9.30–6 Mon–Sat.

Specialise in restoring decorative
European and Oriental carpets 1850–
1920 and fine 19th century Indian carpets
and rugs.

PROVIDE Free Estimates.
SPEAK TO Mr. M. Kennedy.

**SHAIKH & SON (ORIENTAL RUGS)
LTD**
16 Brook Street, **London W1Y 1AA**
TEL   071 629 3430
OPEN   10.30–6.30 Mon–Sat.

Specialise in repairing and cleaning
Oriental rugs.

PROVIDE Home Inspections. Free
Estimates. Free Collection/Delivery
Service.
SPEAK TO Mr. A. Shaikh.

FRANSES CONSERVATION
11 Spring Street, **London W2 3RA**
TEL   071 262 1153
FAX   071 930 8451
OPEN   9–5 Mon–Fri.

Specialise in cleaning, conserving and
restoring fine carpets, needlework and
tapestries including Aubussons and
Savonneries.

PROVIDE Home Inspections by
arrangement. Free Estimates.
Chargeable Collection/Delivery Service.
SPEAK TO Spencer Franses.

DAVID BLACK
96 Portland Road, **London W11 4LN**
TEL   071 727 2566
FAX   071 229 4599
OPEN   11–6 Mon–Sat.

Specialise in cleaning and repairing
antique and modern Oriental carpets,
textiles and English Arts & Crafts
carpets.

PROVIDE Free Estimates.
SPEAK TO David Black.
Member of BADA.

JACK FAIRMAN (CARPETS) LTD
218 Westbourne Grove, **London
W11 2RH**
TEL   071 229 2262
FAX   071 229 2263
OPEN   10–6 Mon–Fri; 10–1 Sat.

Specialise in cleaning and repairing
Oriental carpets, rugs and tapestries.

PROVIDE Home Inspections. Free Verbal
Estimates. Free Collection/Delivery
Service.
SPEAK TO Serina Page.

KASIA & ELA TEXTILE
RESTORATION STUDIO
Unit 11, Kolbe House, 63 Jeddo Road,
London W12 9EE
TEL   081 740 4977
OPEN   8–5 Mon–Fri.

Specialise in restoring flatweaves
including tapestries, Aubussons,
needlework and kilims.

PROVIDE Home Inspections. Free
Estimates. Free Collection/Delivery
Service within London.
SPEAK TO Kasia Kolendarska or Ela
Sosnowska.

THE NATIONAL TRUST TEXTILE
CONSERVATION WORKROOM
Blickling Hall, Blickling, Norwich,
Norfolk NR11 6NF
TEL   0263 733 471
FAX   0263 734 924
OPEN   9–5.30 Mon–Fri.

Specialise in conserving textiles including
costume and large woven tapestries. Will
also survey collections.

PROVIDE Home Inspections. Chargeable
Estimates.
SPEAK TO Kysnia Marko.

This is the first time conservation services
are being offered to non-Trust clients.

MISS LYNDALL BOND
Textile Conservation Services, 3–4 West
Workshops, Tan Gallop, Welbeck,
Worksop, **Nottinghamshire S80 3LW**
TEL   0909 481655
OPEN   By Appointment.

Specialise in conserving costume.

PROVIDE Home Inspections. Chargeable
Estimates. Chargeable
Collection/Delivery Service.
SPEAK TO Lyndall Bond.

CHRISTOPHER LEGGE ORIENTAL CARPETS
25 Oakthorpe Road, Summertown, Oxford, **Oxfordshire OX2 7BD**
TEL   0865 57572
FAX   0865 54877
OPEN   9.30–5 Mon–Sat.

Specialise in cleaning, conserving, restoring and re-weaving old and antique tribal rugs and carpets.
PROVIDE Home Inspections by arrangement. Free Estimates.
SPEAK TO Christopher or Ann Marie Legge

Also provide courses on rugs and their repair and conservation.

THE ANTIQUE RESTORATION STUDIO
The Old Post Office, Haughton, **Staffordshire ST18 9JH**
TEL   0785 780424
FAX   0785 780157
OPEN   9–5 Mon–Fri.

Specialise in restoring antique and modern textiles.
PROVIDE Home Inspections. Free Estimates. Free Collection/Delivery Service.
SPEAK TO D.P. Albright.
SEE Furniture, Oil Paintings, Porcelain.

THE ROYAL SCHOOL OF NEEDLEWORK
Apartment 12A, Hampton Court Palace, East Molesey, **Surrey KT8 9AU**
TEL   081 943 1432
FAX   081 943 4910
OPEN   9.30–4 Mon–Fri.

Specialise in restoring and conserving antique textiles including large hand-woven tapestries, needlework rugs, samplers and stump work.

PROVIDE Chargeable Home Inspections. Free Estimates at the School. Chargeable Collection/Delivery Service.
SPEAK TO Mrs Elizabeth Elvin.

TEXTILE CONSERVATION CENTRE
Apartment 22, Hampton Court Palace, East Molesey, **Surrey KT8 9AU**
TEL   081 977 4943
OPEN   9–5 Mon–Fri.

Specialise in conserving early, historic and modern textiles. Also train textile conservators.

PROVIDE Chargeable Home Inspections. Free Estimates at the Centre.
SPEAK TO Caroline Clark.

KAREL WEIJAND
Lion & Lamb Courtyard, Farnham, **Surrey GU9 7LL**
TEL   0252 726215
OPEN   9.30–5.30 Mon–Fri or By Appointment.

Specialise in full restoration, repair and cleaning service for antique Oriental rugs, hand-made carpets and textiles.
PROVIDE Home Inspections. Free Estimates. Chargeable Collection/Delivery Service.
SPEAK TO Karel Weijand.
Member of LAPADA.

CLIVE ROGERS ORIENTAL RUGS
22 Brunswick Road, Hove, Brighton, **East Sussex BN3 1DG**
TEL   0273 738257
FAX   0273 738687
OPEN   By Appointment.

Specialise in cleaning, conservation and historical analysis of early tribal and village rugs and kilims and some Near Eastern textiles.

PROVIDE Home Inspections. Free Local Estimates. Chargeable Collection/Delivery Service.
SPEAK TO Clive Rogers or Elizabeth Fereday.

MAJID AMINI
Church House, Church Street, Petworth,
West Sussex GU28 0AD
TEL   0798 43344
FAX   0798 42673
OPEN   9–5 Mon–Sat.
Specialise in cleaning and restoring
Oriental rugs and carpets.
PROVIDE Home Inspections. Free
Estimates.
SPEAK TO Majid Amini.
Mr Amini lectures on Oriental rug care
and restoration at West Dean College.

MAC HUMBLE ANTIQUES
7–9 Woolley Street, Bradford-on-Avon,
Wiltshire BA15 1AD
TEL   02216 6329
OPEN   9–6 Mon–Sat.
Specialise in restoring needlework.
PROVIDE Home Inspections. Refundable
Estimates. Free Collection/Delivery
Service.
SPEAK TO Mac Humble.
SEE Furniture, Silver.

LONDON HOUSE ORIENTAL RUGS & CARPETS
9 Montpellier Parade, Harrogate, **North Yorkshire HG1 2TJ**
TEL   0423 567167
OPEN   10–5.30 Tue–Sat.
Specialise in restoring and repairing
Oriental rugs and carpets.
PROVIDE Free Estimates.
SPEAK TO Christian Ries
SEE **West Yorkshire.**

GORDON REECE GALLERY
Finkle Street, Knaresborough, **North Yorkshire HG5 8AA**
TEL   0423 866219
FAX   0423 868044
OPEN   10.30–5 Mon–Sat, closed Thur;
           2–5 Sun.
Specialise in restoring knotted Oriental
rugs and kilims.

PROVIDE Free Estimates. Free
Collection/Delivery Service.
SPEAK TO Gordon Reece or Jane Munro.

LONDON HOUSE ORIENTAL RUGS & CARPETS
238–240 High Street, Boston Spa, By
Wetherby, **West Yorkshire LS23 6AD**
TEL   0937 845123
OPEN   10–5.30 Tues–Sun.
Specialise in restoring and repairing
Oriental carpets and rugs.
PROVIDE Free Estimates.
SPEAK TO Martin or Inger Ries.
SEE **North Yorkshire.**

CHISHOLME ANTIQUES
5 Orrock Place, Hawick, **Borders TD9 0HQ**
TEL   0450 76928
OPEN   9–6 Mon–Fri.
Specialise in repairing and restoring
antique tapestry and beadwork chair
covers.
PROVIDE Home Inspections. Free
Estimates. Chargeable
Collection/Delivery Service.
SPEAK TO Mr. Roberts.
SEE Furniture.

JOHN MACLEAN
1A Cambridge Street, Edinburgh,
Lothian EH1 2DY
TEL   031 447 4225
OPEN   By Appointment.
Specialise in repairing and restoring
Oriental rugs and carpets.
PROVIDE Home Inspections. Free
Estimates. Free Collection/Delivery
Service.
SPEAK TO John Maclean.
Member of SSCR.

WHYTOCK & REID
Sunbury House, Belford Mews,
Edinburgh, **Lothian EH4 3DN**
TEL   031 226 4911
FAX   031 226 4595
OPEN   9–5.30 Mon–Fri; 9–12.30 Sat.

Specialise in restoring antique and 20th
century rugs and carpets.

PROVIDE Home Inspections. Free
Estimates. Free/Chargeable
Collection/Delivery Service.
SPEAK TO David Reid.

SEE Furniture.

Books, Manuscripts, Maps and Globes

Books occupy a special place in our culture and this has had a fundamental effect on the way we regard and treat them. As the means by which we transmit and record so much of our history, information, literature and art, there is reluctance to discard or destroy them but there is also an unwillingness to regard them as the historic artefacts which books of any age must also be. In addition, they survive in larger numbers than almost any other manufactured objects, and this vast mass of material has, with the exception of only the very rarest examples, discouraged the sort of individual care and attention which other museum objects are likely to command. Unlike museum collections, which are kept primarily for their beauty or antiquity, or both, books in libraries, whatever their age, are likely to be read, that is handled, by successive readers. Their repair has therefore to deal with two often irreconcilable aims. One is to return a damaged book to a state in which it can be read without further risk of damage and the other is to interfere as little as possible with its original structure and materials, all of which can contribute not only to our knowledge of the history of the individual book but also to our knowledge of the history of the book trade and the distribution of books (and thus learning) in earlier centuries.

Until comparatively recently (the damage to the libraries of Florence in the flood of 1966 was largely instrumental in forcing those involved to rethink the ways in which books were treated), the repair of books was almost solely concerned with returning them to a condition in which they could be read, without regard to preserving their original structure or even appearance where this was thought not sufficiently decorated or well preserved to merit it. Since then, increasing attention has been paid to repair work which disturbs as little as possible of what survives of the original materials of the book, so as to preserve the historical value of the artefact. Techniques are now practised by some conservators (as opposed to restorers) which can often make continued access to texts possible, given careful handling, without the wholesale disruption of their bindings and loss of damaged components. In many cases, especially for books in private hands, protective measures such as making fitted drop-spine boxes (not slip- or pull-off cases both of which often cause damage to books) for fragile material will avoid the need for repair altogether, or, where necessary, can be combined with very conservative non-intrusive repairs to secure loose or detached boards and covers. Every effort should be made to avoid taking books to pieces in order to repair them. It is both expensive in time (and therefore money) and affects the character and quality of the book.

Above all, it is important to remember that returning books to some imagined state of undamaged perfection can only be done by destroying much of their historical authenticity; the tidy mind is an enemy of the true preservation of our past. The replacement of missing endleaves, even covers, of old books with paper and boards taken from other books, is a form of forgery and must be avoided. Edges should never be trimmed or given new decoration. If gilt edges are required, a copy which already has them should be bought. The existing edges should not be destroyed. The materials used to repair books must be chosen both because of their aesthetic compatibility with the surviving parts of a damaged book and their physical durability and chemical stability. If poor quality materials are used, the repairs will not last and will probably cause further damage when they break down and have to be replaced. If the person who is asked to repair a book does not appear to know which materials are conservationally sound, the book should be taken to someone else. The repair of early books requires skills which are not always possessed by people trained to bind new books. Books with vellum leaves, for instance, require entirely different treatment from paper-leaved books, and most early books function better in the type of structure originally designed for them.

In any case, it will prove more useful in the long term to pay attention first to the conditions in which books are kept rather than repair damage caused by those conditions and then return the books to the same conditions. Excessive levels of light, heat, humidity and dryness will sooner or later cause irreparable damage. Excessive fluctuation, especially of heat and humidity levels, will wear books out, largely because they are composite objects, made up of different materials which react and move at different rates to changes in their environment. Relative humidity levels for bound books in leather, vellum or cloth should be kept at 55% RH; mould spores will germinate above 70% RH, and low levels will result in organic materials shrinking and becoming increasingly brittle. Modern paper (post 1870 as a rough guide), most of which is being gradually destroyed by increasing levels of acidity, should be kept at lower humidity levels (35–40% RH), as the rate of deterioration increases with higher levels of moisture. Where modern paper-leaved books are bound in leather or vellum a compromise level of humidity will be necessary, and advice from a conservator should be sought. The temperature, which has a direct effect on the relative humidity of a room, should be kept as low as possible without causing excessive humidity levels. It is often difficult to reconcile the safe storage of books with modern ideas of comfortable living conditions. Light levels should be kept as low as possible – total darkness is best for storage. 50 lux is the accepted level for exhibition, and ideally storage levels should be no higher – after all, books usually spend longer in storage on shelves than they do on display. Above all, direct sunlight has to be avoided, as well as fluorescent light which does most damage. Ultra-violet filters on window glass can do a lot to protect not only books but most of the other contents of a room.

There is little that private owners themselves can do to the books beyond keeping them free from dust (a soft brush will do this safely and efficiently) and away from insects, rodents (and dogs) and food and drink. Apart from being kept clean, the shelving should be sound, well ventilated behind the books, especially on outside walls (it should be added that glass-fronted cases can be a danger in damp houses) and free from projections or roughness which will damage the books. Leather dressing, often regarded as a magical cure-all, will only serve to keep sound leather in good condition (and then only if used sparingly) and improve the appearance of leather-bound books in general. It must not be used on vellum or parchment bindings. It will not 'restore' damaged and chemically deteriorated leather, and will often turn it black if used on it. It should never be put on books taken straight out of overly dry storage conditions, and should always be applied in the smallest quantities. Adequate humidity levels will do more to preserve the flexibility of leather than dressings, and excessive quantities of dressing, especially when applied to dry leather, will seal the fibres against moisture and thus accelerate their decay. It is safer to use simple dressings of neatsfoot oil, lanolin and wax, mixed to a creamy consistency, than liquid dressings with solvents and other often unnamed ingredients, which may well cause trouble. All self-adhesive tapes and synthetic adhesives should be avoided.

The conservation of globes is, if anything, even more complex than that of books. They are also composite objects, made up of wood, metal, papier-mâché, gesso, paper, pigments and varnish. As a result they require very even humidity and temperature levels, similar to those suggested for leather-bound books, and they must also be kept dust-free and away from bright light. They are very vulnerable to damage, especially the gesso used to give a perfect surface to the sphere, and are often large and awkward to handle; they should never be spun in their stands. The gores, the individual wedges of paper which are used to make up the map, have to be moulded over a compound curve in order to fit the globe, and it may prove exceptionally difficult to replace lifted pieces exactly as they were. Wherever possible, work should avoid lifting the gores, and only conservators with a proven track record in globe conservation should be asked to work on them.

Nicholas Pickwoad

GEORGE BAYNTUN
Manvers Street, Bath, **Avon BA1 1JW**
TEL   0225 466000
FAX   0225 482122
OPEN   9–1, 2–5.30 Mon–Fri; 9.30–1
       Sat – By Appointment only
Specialise in restoring rare books and
fine bindings.
PROVIDE Home Inspections. Free
Estimates. Postal Service.
SPEAK TO George Bayntun.

BRISTOL-BOUND BOOKBINDING
2nd Floor, 14 Waterloo Street, Clifton,
Bristol, **Avon BS8 4BT**
TEL   0272 238279
OPEN   10–6 Tue–Sat.
Specialise in restoring leather and cloth
bindings, fine bindings and leather
repairs.
PROVIDE Free Estimates. Chargeable
Collection/Delivery Service.
SPEAK TO Mrs. R. M. James.

CEDRIC CHIVERS
9 A/B Aldermoor Way, Longwell Green,
Bristol, **Avon BS15 7DA**
TEL   0272 352617
FAX   0272 618446
OPEN   8–4.30 Mon–Fri.
Specialise in refurbishment, repair and
rebinding of books and the repair and
conservation of paper.
PROVIDE Free Estimates. Chargeable
Collection/Delivery Service.
Have had 113 years' experience.

DAVID ENGLISH
225 Carter Street, Fordham, Ely,
Cambridgeshire CB7 SJU
TEL   0638 720216
OPEN   8–5 Mon–Sat.

Specialise in repairing and restoring
antiquarian books, new bindings in
cloth, vellum, leather and paper.
PROVIDE Free Estimates.
SPEAK TO David English.

ART WORKS
54b Church Street, Falmouth, **Cornwall
TR11 3DS**
TEL   0326 211238
OPEN   By Appointment.
Specialise in restoring antiquarian
books.
PROVIDE Home Inspections. Free
Estimates. Chargeable
Collection/Delivery Service.
SPEAK TO Suzanne Nunn.
SEE Oil Paintings.

**FRANCIS BROWN CRAFT
BOOKBINDER**
24 Camden Way, Dorchester. **Dorset
DT1 2RA**
TEL   0305 266039
OPEN   9–12.30, 2–5.30 Mon–Fri.
Specialise in all types of bookbinding and
restoration, gold blocking, edge gilding,
boxmaking design.
SPEAK TO Francis Brown.

**ACORN PRESS BOOKBINDING
SERVICES**
103 London Road, Stanway, Colchester,
Essex CO3 5AW
TEL   0206 46101
FAX   0206 571201
OPEN   9–5 Mon–Fri.
Specialise in the restoration and repair
of books and bindings
PROVIDE Home Inspections. Free
Estimates. Chargeable
Collection/Delivery Service.
SPEAK TO Brian Strudwick.
Members of the Guild of Master
Craftsmen.

BEELEIGH ABBEY BOOKS
Beeleigh Abbey, Maldon, **Essex**
CM3 4AD
TEL   0621 856308
FAX   0621 850064
OPEN   9–6 Mon–Thur; Fri by
         appointment.
Specialise in fine bindings.
PROVIDE Home Inspections. Free
Estimates. Free Collection/Delivery
Service.
SPEAK TO Alan Liddell.
Member of the ABA.

DAVID BANNISTER
26 Kings Road, Cheltenham,
Gloucestershire GL52 6BG
TEL   0242 514287
FAX   0242 513890
OPEN   By Appointment.
Specialise in restoring, colouring and
cataloguing maps.
PROVIDE Free Estimates. Chargeable
Collection/Delivery Service.
SPEAK TO David Bannister.
SEE Oil Paintings.

THE BOOKBINDERY
Saint Michael's Abbey, Farnborough,
Hampshire GU14 7NQ
TEL   0252 547573
OPEN   8.30–12, 1.30–5 Mon–Fri.
Specialise in hand-crafted bookbinding;
all types of bookbinding undertaken.
PROVIDE Free Estimates. Free
Collection/Delivery Service on large
consignments only.
SPEAK TO Mr. L. Prior.
Benedictine monastery, holding craft
certificates for the restoration of old
books.

THE PETERSFIELD BOOKSHOP
16a Chapel Street, Petersfield,
Hampshire GU32 3DS
TEL   0730 63438
FAX   0730 63438
OPEN   9–5.30 Mon–Sat.
Specialise in bookbinding repair.
PROVIDE Home Inspections by
arrangement. Free Estimates.
Collection/Delivery Service by
arrangement.
SPEAK TO Frank Westwood.
SEE Oil Paintings.

LEONORA WEAVER
6 Aylestone Drive, Hereford, **Hereford**
& Worcester HR1 1HT
TEL   0432 267816
OPEN   By Appointment.
Specialise in restoring and hand-
colouring maps.
PROVIDE Free Estimates.
Collection/Delivery Service sometimes
available.
SPEAK TO Leonora Weaver.
SEE Oil Paintings.

G. & D.I. MARRIN & SONS
149 Sandgate Road, Folkestone, **Kent**
CT20 2DA
TEL   0303 53016
FAX   0303 850956
OPEN   9.30–5.30 Mon–Sat.
Specialise in restoring antiquarian books
and maps.
PROVIDE Home Inspections. Chargeable
Estimates. Chargeable
Collection/Delivery Service.
SPEAK TO John or Patrick Marrin.
They are ABA and PBFA members.
SEE Oil Paintings.

THE OLD HOUSE GALLERY
13–15 Market Place, Oakham,
Leicestershire LE15 6DT
TEL   0572 755538
OPEN   10–5 Mon–Fri; 10–4 Sat; closed
Thur p.m.

Specialise in restoring antiquarian maps.
PROVIDE Home Inspections. Free Local
Collection/Delivery Service.
SPEAK TO Richard Clarke.
SEE Oil Paintings.

RILEY, DUNN & WILSON LTD
Pegasus House, 116–120 Golden Lane,
London EC1Y 0UD
TEL   071 251 2551
FAX   071 490 2338
OPEN   9–5 Mon–Fri.

Specialise in restoring antiquarian books
and paper conservation including
manuscripts, prints, drawings and maps.
Also rebind and repair bindings.
PROVIDE Home Inspections. Free
Estimates. Free Collection/Delivery
Service.
SPEAK TO the Office Manager.
SEE **West Yorkshire, Central.**

DON BAKER
3 Canonbury Park South, **London
N1 2JR**
TEL   071 226 2314
OPEN   By Appointment.

Specialise in repairing Islamic
manuscripts, Indian miniatures and
parchment.
PROVIDE Free Estimates.
SPEAK TO Don Baker.

JANE ZAGEL
31 Pandora Road, **London NW6 1TS**
TEL   071 794 1663
OPEN   9–6 Mon–Fri.

Specialise in restoring books.

PROVIDE Home Inspections. Refundable
Estimates. Chargeable
Collection/Delivery Service.
SPEAK TO Jane Zagel.
This workshop is included on the register
of conservators maintained by the
Conservation Unit of the Museums and
Galleries Commission.
SEE Oil Paintings.

SANGORSKI & SUTCLIFFE/ZAEHNSDORF LTD
175R Bermondsey Street, **London
SE1 3UW**
TEL   071 407 1244
FAX   071 357 7466
OPEN   9–4.30 Mon–Fri.

Specialise in restoring and repairing
bookbinding.
PROVIDE Home Inspections. Free
Estimates. Free Collection/Delivery
Service.
SPEAK TO Janet Blake.
Make visitors' books, game books, cellar
books and stationery items to individual
specification.
SEE **London W1.**

CATHERINE HODGSON
265 Croxted Road, **London SE21 8NN**
TEL   081 761 2567
OPEN   By Appointment.

Specialise in repairing both cloth and
leather books. Will also design and bind
presentation books.
PROVIDE Home Inspections. Free
Estimates. Chargeable
Collection/Delivery Service.
SPEAK TO Catherine Hodgson.

SHEPHERDS BOOKBINDERS LTD
76B Rochester Row, **London SW1P 1JU**
TEL   071 630 1184
FAX   071 931 0541
OPEN   9–5.30 Mon–Fri, 10–1 Sat.

Specialise in restoring bookbinding and
archive conservation.

PROVIDE Free Estimates.
SPEAK TO Mairi Salters.
SEE Oil Paintings.

BERNARD C. MIDDLETON
3 Gauden Road, **London SW4 6LR**
TEL   071 622 5388
OPEN   9–6 Mon–Fri.

Specialise in the restoration of antiquarian books and rebinding in period styles.

PROVIDE Free Estimates.
SPEAK TO Bernard Middleton.

CAROLINE BENDIX
14 Blake Gardens, **London SW6 4QB**
TEL   071 384 2407
OPEN   8.30–6.30 Mon–Fri.

Specialise in library conservation, advising on the treatment and housing of collections of books, training of volunteers in refurbishment.

PROVIDE Home Inspections. Free Estimates.
SPEAK TO Caroline Bendix.

BATES & BASKCOMB
191 St. John's Hill, **London SW11 1TH**
TEL   071 223 1629
OPEN   9.30–5.30 Mon–Fri and By Appointment.

Specialise in restoring works of art on paper including maps.

PROVIDE Local Home Inspections. Free/Chargeable Collection/Delivery Service.
SPEAK TO Debbie Bates or Camilla Baskcomb.
SEE Oil Paintings.

SANGORSKI & SUTCLIFFE/ZAEHNSDORF LTD
4th floor, 23 Albemarle Street, **London W1**
TEL   071 499 8579 (Tel 071 407 1244 to make appointment).
FAX   072 357 7466
OPEN   9–4.30 Mon–Fri by appointment only.

Specialise in bookbinding restoration and repair.

PROVIDE Home Inspections. Free Estimates. Free Collection/Delivery Service.
SPEAK TO Janet Blake.
SEE **London SE1**.

LYVER & BOYDELL GALLERIES
15 Castle Street, Liverpool, **Merseyside L2 4SX**
TEL   051 236 3256
OPEN   10–30–5.30 Mon–Fri; Sat by appointment.

Specialise in restoring and framing maps.

PROVIDE Home Inspections. Free Estimates.
SPEAK TO Paul or Gill Breen.
SEE Oil Paintings.

R. & S. LANE BOOKBINDING
Heath House, 2 Smiths Lane, Fakenham, **Norfolk NR21 8LG**
TEL   0328 862151
OPEN   By Appointment.

Specialise in all types of bookbinding, journals and theses, presentation copies and full restoration.

PROVIDE Home Inspections. Free Estimates. Free Collection/Delivery Service.
SPEAK TO Richard or Susan Lane.

ARTHUR & ANN RODGERS
7 Church Street, Ruddington,
Nottingham, **Nottinghamshire**
NG11 6HA
TEL   0602 216214
OPEN   9–5 Tues,Wed; 9–1 Thur, Fri; 9–
5 Sat.
Specialise in hand colouring, cleaning,
restoring and repairing of maps.
PROVIDE Home Inspections. Chargeable
Estimates. Free Collection/Delivery
Service.
SPEAK TO Arthur Rodgers.
SEE Oil Paintings.

KING'S COURT GALLERIES
54 West Street, Dorking, **Surrey**
RH4 1BS
TEL   0306 881757
FAX   0306 75305
OPEN   9.30–5.30 Mon–Sat.
Specialise in paper conservation and
restoration including antique maps.
PROVIDE Home Inspections. Free
Estimates.
SPEAK TO Mrs.J. Joel.

WEST DEAN COLLEGE
West Dean, Chichester,**West Sussex**
PO18 0OZ
TEL   0243 63 301
FAX   0243 63 342
OPEN   9–5 Mon–Fri.
Specialise in training conservators and
restorers in the field of early manuscripts
and rare books and will also undertake
restoration.
PROVIDE Local Home Inspections. Free
Estimates.
SPEAK TO Peter Sarginson.
SEE Furniture, Porcelain, Silver.

D.M. BEACH
52 High Street, Salisbury, **Wiltshire**
SP1 2PG
TEL   0722 333801
OPEN   9–5.30 Mon–Sat.
Specialise in restoring maps and
repairing bookbindings.
PROVIDE Home Inspections. Free
Estimates. Free Local Collection Service.
SEE Oil Paintings.

BOOTH'S ANTIQUE MAPS &
PRINTS
30 Edenvale Road, Westbury, **Wiltshire**
BA13 3NY
TEL   0373 823271
FAX   0373 858185
OPEN   By Appointment.
Specialise in restoring antique maps.
PROVIDE Home Inspections. Chargeable
Collection/Delivery Service.
SPEAK TO John Booth.
Mr Booth is a FRSA.
SEE Oil Paintings.

WINSTANLEY SALISBURY
BOOKBINDERS
213 Devizes Road, Salisbury, **Wiltshire**
SP2 9LT
TEL   0722 334998
OPEN   8.30–5.30 Mon–Fri.
Specialise in book restoration and paper
conservation.
PROVIDE Free Estimates. Chargeable
Collection/Delivery Service
SPEAK TO Alan Winstanley.
Mr. Winstanley also makes fine new
bindings to individual requirements.
SEE Oil Paintings.

ARTHUR HENRY FAIRHURST
23A Raincliffe Avenue, Scarborough,
North Yorkshire YO12 5BU
TEL   0723 372780
OPEN   10–5 Mon–Fri.

Specialise in bookbinding and restoring
and repairing books.

PROVIDE Home Inspections. Free
Estimates. Local Collection/Delivery
Service.

SPEAK TO Arthur Fairhurst.

RILEY, DUNN & WILSON LTD
Red Doles Lane, Leeds Road,
Huddersfield, **West Yorkshire HD2 1YE**
TEL   0484 534323
FAX   0484 435048
OPEN   8.15–3.45 Mon–Fri.

Specialise in the restoring, repairing and
rebinding of antiquarian books,
including paper conservation. Also
supply bookboxes.

PROVIDE Home Inspections. Free
Estimates. Free Collection/Delivery
Service.

SPEAK TO Geoff Crosland.

Member of the Society of Bookbinders
and the Institute of Paper Conservation.
SEE **London EC1, Stirling**.

RILEY, DUNN & WILSON LTD
Bellevue Bindery, Glasgow Road,
Camelon, Falkirk, **Central FK1 4HP**
TEL   0324 21591
FAX   0324 611508
OPEN   8.30–5 Mon–Fri.

Specialise in restoring antiquarian
books, repairing bindings and
rebinding. Paper conservation including
manuscripts, prints, drawings and maps.

PROVIDE Home Inspections. Free
Estimates. Free Collection/Delivery
Service.

SPEAK TO John Penman.

SEE **London EC1, W. Yorks**.

TOM VALENTINE
Caronvale Bindery, 18 The Main Street,
Larbert, Falkirk, **Central FK5 3AN**
TEL   0324 552247
OPEN   By Appointment.

Specialise in archival work, restoring
books and manuscripts, bookbinding,
paper conservation.

PROVIDE Home Inspections. Free
Collection/Delivery Service.

SPEAK TO Tom Valentine.

Mr. Valentine is a member of the Society
of Bookbinders.

Collectors' Items

FOUNTAIN PENS

Fountain pens are among the simplest of everyday items yet can cause frustration when they appear to fail for no apparent reason. Many fountain-pen manufacturers used to offer lifetime guarantees for their products against all but loss or wilful damage. Today they no longer do, but the premise that the pen can be repaired still holds true.

The earliest pens fill with an 'eyedropper' (pipette) and the pen barrel is also the ink reservoir. If your pen has no apparent cartridge, lever, button or plunger, then this is probably the filling system employed. Washing with cold water and a re-fill with new ink will put most pens in working order. 'Safety' pens with retractable nibs also fall into this category. When the cap is unscrewed the pen appears to have no nib – turning the end of the pen will reveal the nib for use.

Reservoir pens with a rubber sac filled by lifting a side lever, or depressing a button under a 'blind cap' at the end of the pen, are simple to repair. A new sac costs around £1 from a collector and a pen, shop will charge between £10 and £15 (in 1991 prices) for fitting a new sac along with general cleaning and overhaul.

Plunger-filled pens such as the De La Rue 'Onoto' and some Sheaffer pens can also be repaired but at greater expense. The same is true for the Parker Vacumatic, repairs often costing £30 or £40.

Spare parts can be found for many old pens – but at a price – as many can be obtained only by 'cannibalising' another pen. Parker 51 and 61 spares are readily available with repairers and most pen companies keeping enough parts to repair discontinued models for at least ten years after production ceases.

Pen repairers such as Classic Pens and Penfriend are able to regrind nibs to your requirement if a vintage pen is not ideal for your handwriting. Some common sense is needed as obviously a left-handed fine nib cannot be turned into a right-handed broad calligraphic nib.

Most problems can be swiftly put in order by qualified pen mechanics. If you are unable to contact a pen company or repairer, a good high-street stationer (such as W. H. Smith) will be able to do this for you.

CAMERAS

A camera at its simplest is a means of focusing light from a subject onto a light-sensitive surface. Collectors like their cameras to be in as close to working order as possible and different collectors/restorers are able to provide or make new parts for most vintage cameras. Early wooden and brass cameras are the simplest mechanically and fairly easy to return to a working state.

From 1910, led by the Eastman-Kodak company, there was mass production of cameras. It is often easier to buy a replacement camera than to undertake major restoration work.

Cameras which have been looked after and kept in a dry, moisture-free environment still offer excellent service and are prized for that little 'something' which they contribute towards the picture that the almost clinical precision of a modern 35mm SLR seems unable to provide.

Before you consider replacing a part or modifying your camera it is best to seek the advice of an expert restorer as each fault needs individual attention.

PHOTOGRAPHS

In the broadest of terms, photographs should be treated with similar care to watercolours. Particular attention should be paid to keep them away from dust (which scratches), tobacco smoke (which stains), sunlight (which fades), damp and heat. The natural oils in your fingertips will also stain photographic surfaces.

Paper photographs are a (comparatively) inexpensive art-form to display, and care will ensure a long life and, with luck, an increased value for your photograph. To this end, do not hang them in a room with wet paint, or in front of a window. Photographs should be mounted on acid-free board, glazed and sealed against dust. Because most photographs contain silver they should be kept away from sulphur, which is commonly found in newspaper, brown paper and cardboard.

Glass photographs such as Daguerreotypes and Ambrotypes which are usually displayed in leather and gilded frames must be looked after so that the chemical surface is not damaged. They should not be removed from these frames (which often bear the photographer's name) as they are easily scratched. The old wives' remedy of silver polish should never ever be used to clean a photograph!!

TEDDY BEARS

Teddy bears usually find a soft spot with most owners and are fairly simple to look after.

Dusty bears can be washed with a mild shampoo. This is not a difficult operation but it is important to prevent the insides of the bear from becoming damp at the same time as you are gently washing his fur. 'Care' is the watchword, and then place the bear in an airing cupboard to dry slowly and thoroughly.

There is little one can do if your Teddy is going bald – indeed owners feel that their bear looks more distinguished. However, should his stuffing leak it should be repaired straight away before the hole worsens and a limb – or more seriously the head – becomes mis-shaped. Your local dolls' hospital will be able to perform any operation beyond your own needlework skills. With the recent increase in value for Teddys over the last few years, and especially for German and Steiff bears, it is most important not to be too cavalier in any approach to repair. Remarkable results can be obtained by sewing together the edges of a wound/tear and patching with muslin. Always try to keep Teddy as near to original as possible – if one of his pads becomes 'holey' it is best to patch over the torn felt to the size of a new pad if needs be. This will keep the original shape of the bear as well as the original material. Noses should be resewn using the same colour wool. Keep single eyes in case a similar one turns up in a friend's button box or dolls' hospital. As an alternative, it is quite possible to make a black eyepatch giving your Teddy a very worldly-wise air!

If the worst happens and a bear becomes an involuntary home to insects drastic measures are called for. Keep the bear in a sealed plastic bag in a deep-freeze for three days as the sub-zero conditions should kill the wild life and their eggs. Watch out for signs of further life. Camphor (moth balls) is an effective deterrent against further attacks.

Not all bears have as traumatic a life as this. A clean, dry and (fairly) dust-free environment is all that is required of a loving owner by most bears.

METAL TOYS

If your treasured 'Flying Scotsman' has seized up with fluff in the electric motor – don't be alarmed, it can be dismantled and cleaned. Clockwork motors in trains, transport toys and penny toys are frequently over-wound and a friendly clock repairer should be able to restore motor power to your toy and probably enjoy the repair too!

Damaged paintwork and missing parts provoke the awkward question 'to restore or not'. Toy auctions show that the greatest demand is for 'mint' (i.e. unused) toys in their original boxes. However, repaired/rebuilt toys often fetch less than a similar example in a play-worn state. From the viewpoint of value it is probably not worth having a new roof/boiler/door built for your metal toy when a collector will be able to cannibalise a badly damaged example for spares. It may be worth repainting/retouching some toys. Before you consider this, it is worth contacting an auction house expert, museum or collector. Establish if you are about to obliterate the original paintwork of one of a handful of known examples of a rare Victorian tinplate battleship or similar rarity. As a general rule 'if in doubt – don't'. However, it is acceptable for an expert to retouch a scratch, and great fun to repaint distressed examples of common toys.

DOLLS

A good doll with the original wig and clothing is a wonderful period piece, be she seventeenth or twentieth century. The costume should be treated in a similar fashion to other antique textiles, especially if it is fragile silk, which was often treated with tin that hastens decay today. If your doll has no dress, you should consult reference books on fashion or visit museums to find a similar doll in her original costume to copy.

The bisque head of a doll can be washed using cotton wool, liquid soap and a little water and then wiped clean with a damp cloth. Abrasives should never be used and take care not to wash off eyelashes and eyebrows or to allow water inside the head.

Dolls' bodies should not be cleaned. Composition bodies deteriorate and it is difficult to clean kid and cloth bodies. Wooden dolls have their gessoed heads protected by varnish, and again this should not be washed off.

Restringing a bisque doll which has loose limbs is simple and can be carried out quickly by any dolls' hospital. Check that your doll is not restrung too tightly, as this can damage the head and body.

The bisque head of a doll contributes most towards her appeal. Hairline cracks and firing cracks may spread and can be 'held' with a small drop of glue. However, cracked heads which have been badly restored often return to the owner with an unpleasant high shine, quite unlike the subtleties of the original matte bisque. There are three courses of action with a damaged bisque head; firstly, reglue the old friendly face, cracks and all; secondly, buy another head (if the doll is a common one) and use this; thirdly, visit a good ceramic restorer. This will be expensive; great expertise and skill are necessary if a rare or valuable doll needs repair. It won't automatically increase the value, but the appearance may be enhanced as the best repairs are only visible under ultra-violet light.

Prevention is better than cure with most dolls. Wax and wooden dolls are fragile and should be kept away from humidity and temperature changes, and preferably not in a centrally heated room or (heaven forbid) a sunny window. All dolls should be wrapped in acid-free tissue paper when they are put away and bisque dolls with weighted (sleeping) eyes should be stored face downwards to prevent the eyes jamming.

Alexander Crum Ewing

BOWED INSTRUMENTS

The bowed instruments – violins, violas and cellos – are usually amongst the most valuable of all instruments in terms of money. Consequently, the art of restoring them is at an incredibly high level. A violin that has been chopped and smashed, seemingly unrepairable, can these days be completely restored.

Recently, a violin by Joseph Guarneri del Gesu of Cremona, circa 1740, with a pre-accident value of hundreds of thousands of pounds, was literally smashed into pieces, but after a whole year of careful restoration at the firm of Bein & Fushi of Chicago it was almost impossible to see where the instrument was damaged.

Looking after valuable instruments is fairly easy as long as you do not drop them. Keep them in a good case when not in use. Try to make sure that the room temperature is fairly constant, neither too dry nor too humid. This applies to all instruments, and bowed instrument cases with a humidity gauge can be purchased.

Always clean an instrument after use with a soft cloth. When travelling with an instrument ensure that when put into the case it does not move at all. *Never* try to repair any instrument yourself. Always seek the advice of a professional. In most cases where the instrument has been 'repaired' at home, terrible damage has been inflicted and it can take the restorer many more hours of work to 'fix'. One of the most common forms of home repair is re-varnishing. Just a lick or two to smarten up the appearance usually destroys the value of an instrument. Plucked instruments should always have the tension reduced after use, particularly the antique instruments. Constant tension will result in a warped neck. The same applies to bows; these can be re-cambered but are never really quite as good as before.

Make sure that your instruments are insured at their full value. British Reserve are the biggest insurers of musical instruments and have a special branch for this purpose (see Musicians' Union Handbook).

Peter Horner

Cameras

LES FRANKHAM
166 Westcote Drive, Leicester,
Leicestershire LE3 0SP
TEL   0533 550825
OPEN   9–4 Mon–Fri.

Specialise in restoring classic cameras,
Zeiss–Ikon, Voigtlander, Rollex and all
cameras post-1890.
SPEAK TO Les Frankham.
Mr. Frankham is a Fellow of the Royal
Photographic Society.

T. A. CUBITT
240 Torbay Road, Harrow, **Middlesex
HA2 9QE**
TEL   081 866 9289
OPEN   8.30–5.30 Mon–Fri.

Specialise in restoring vintage cameras.
PROVIDE Free Estimates.
SPEAK TO Mr. Cubitt.

Dolls and Dolls' Houses

**EUROOM INTERNATIONAL (UK)
LTD**
Vine House, Reach, **Cambridgeshire
CB5 0JD**
TEL   0638 741989
FAX   0638 743239
OPEN   By Appointment.

Specialise in restoring dolls.
PROVIDE Home Inspections. Free
Estimates. Free Collection/Delivery
Service.
SPEAK TO Mr. A. Dudley.

Members of the Guild of Master
Craftsmen and the Association of
Master Upholsterers.
SEE Collectors (Toys), Furniture.

**THE TEXTILE RESTORATION
STUDIO**
20 Hargreaves Road, Timperley,
Altrincham, **Cheshire WA15 7BB**
TEL   061 904 9944
FAX   061 903 9144
OPEN   9.30–5 Mon–Fri.

Specialise in cleaning, conserving and
repairing antique dolls.
PROVIDE Home Inspections. Free
Estimates. Collection/Delivery Service
by arrangement.
SPEAK TO Jacqueline Hyman.
SEE Carpets, Silver.

D. C. BLAIR
12 Columbia Street, Cheltenham,
Gloucestershire GL52 2JR
TEL   0242 222795
OPEN   8–6 Mon–Sat.

Specialise in restoring period dolls, dolls'
houses and toy castles.
PROVIDE Home Inspections. Chargeable
Collection/Delivery Service.
SPEAK TO D. C. Blair.

**LILIAN MIDDLETON'S ANTIQUE
DOLL SHOP**
Days Stable, Sheep Street, Stow-on-the-
Wold, **Gloucestershire GL54 1AA**
TEL   0451 30381
OPEN   9–5 Mon–Sat; 11–5 Sun.

Specialise in providing a comprehensive
dolls' hospital service. Make bisque
dolls' heads on the premises (180
different types).
PROVIDE Home Inspections. Free
Estimates. Free Collection/Delivery
Service.
SPEAK TO Lilian Middleton
SEE **Wiltshire**.

THE LILLIPUT MUSEUM OF ANTIQUE DOLLS AND TOYS
High Street, Brading, **Isle of Wight PO36 0DJ**
TEL   0983 407231
OPEN   1–5 Winter, 9.30–9.30 Summer
       Sun–Sat; closed mid Jan–mid
       March.
Specialise in restoring all types of dolls and dolls' houses
PROVIDE Free Estimates.
SPEAK TO G. K. Munday.
Member of the Guild of Master Craftsmen.

CAROLINE J. BOOTH TEXTILE CONSERVATOR
Fold Farm, Higher Eastwood,
Todmorden, **Lancashire OL14 8RP**
TEL   0706 816888
OPEN   10–5 Mon–Fri.
Specialise in a full range of services for historic textiles both woven and embroidered, including materials for dolls' houses and costumes for dolls and automata. Condition and conservation reports provided and advice given on handling, storage and display. Ms. Booth uses traditional conservation techniques so that any work done is reversible.
PROVIDE Home Inspections. Chargeable Estimates. Chargeable Collection/Delivery Service.
SPEAK TO Caroline Booth.
SEE Carpets.

MARCELLA FLETCHER
24–26 Leyland Road, Penwortham,
Preston, **Lancashire PR1 9XS**
TEL   0772 744970
OPEN   By Appointment.
Specialise in dolls' hospital service for Victorian and Edwardian dolls.

PROVIDE Home Inspections. Free Estimates. Chargeable Collection/Delivery Service.
SPEAK TO Marcella Fletcher.

CHELSEA LION
Chenil Galleries, 181–183 Kings Road, **London SW3 5EB**
TEL   071 351 9338
OPEN   11–5 Mon–Sat.
Specialise in restoring dolls.
PROVIDE Free Estimates.
SPEAK TO Steve Clark.
SEE Collectors (Toys).

THE DOLLS' HOSPITAL
16 Dawes Road, **London SW6 7EN**
TEL   071 385 2081
OPEN   9.30–5 Mon–Tues, Fri; 10–4 Sat.
Specialise in repairing and restoring antique dolls.
PROVIDE Free Estimates.
SPEAK TO Mr. J. Smith

FAITH S. EATON
16 Clifton Gardens, **London W9 1DT**
TEL   071 289 2359
Specialise in wax restoration and conservation of dolls and dolls' houses. She also advises on security and display.
PROVIDE Home Inspections if expenses paid. Refundable Estimates. Chargeable Collection/Delivery Service.
SPEAK TO Faith Eaton.

MARGARET GLOVER
42 Hartham Road, Isleworth, **Middlesex TW7 5ES**
TEL   081 568 4662
OPEN   By Appointment.
Specialise in restoring wax dolls of every kind.
PROVIDE Free Estimates.
SPEAK TO Margaret Glover.
SEE Collectors (Musical, Wax).

SARAH BROMILOW
180 Reading Road, Henley-on-Thames,
Oxfordshire RG9 1EA
TEL   0491 577001
FAX   0491 410735
OPEN   9–5 Mon–Fri.

Specialise in repairing and restoring dolls' houses, rocking horses and other wooden toys.

PROVIDE Verbal Estimates over the telephone. Chargeable Collection/Delivery Service
SPEAK TO Sarah Bromilow.

PETER STRANGE
'The Willows', Sutton, Oxford,
Oxfordshire OX8 1RU
TEL   0865 882020
OPEN   By Appointment Only.

Specialise in china doll restoration, especially the invisible repairing of broken and damaged bisque dolls' heads and bisque figurines, as well as sleeping eyes and lashes.

PROVIDE Home Inspections. Free Estimates. Chargeable Collection/Delivery Service.
SPEAK TO Peter Strange.

WEAVES & WAXES
53 Church Street, Bloxham, Banbury,
Oxfordshire OX15 4ET
TEL   0295 721535
FAX   0295 271867

Specialise in restoring dolls.

PROVIDE Home Inspections. Free/Chargeable Estimates. Chargeable Collection/Delivery Service.
SPEAK TO Laurie Grayer.
SEE Furniture.

RECOLLECT STUDIOS
(C. JACKMAN)
The Old School, London Road, Sayers
Common, **West Sussex BN6 9HX**
TEL   0273 833314
OPEN   10–5 Tues–Sat.

Specialise in restoring antique and modern collectors' dolls, wax doll making, porcelain heads, composition parts, bodies. (Antique dolls not accepted by post.)
PROVIDE Free Estimates.
SPEAK TO Mrs. Carol Jackman or Mr. Paul Jago.

Member of the Doll Artisan Guild, the Guild of Master Craftsmen and the UKIC. Also teach doll restoration.

SECOND CHILDHOOD
20 Byram Arcade, Westgate,
Huddersfield, **West Yorkshire HD1 1ND**
TEL   0484 530117 or 603854
OPEN   10.30–3.30 Tues–Sat.

Specialise in restoring antique dolls and related items; dolls' hospital.

PROVIDE Free Estimates. Local Free Collection/Delivery Service.
SPEAK TO Michael or Elizabeth Hoy.
SEE Collectors (Toys).

LILIAN MIDDLETON'S DOLL SHOP
5 Brown Street, Salisbury, **Wiltshire SP1 10N**
TEL   0722 333303
OPEN   9–5 Mon–Sat.

Specialise in a dolls' hospital service.

PROVIDE Home Inspection. Free Estimates. Free Collection/Delivery Service.
SPEAK TO Joyce Heard.
SEE **Gloucestershire**.

DAPHNE FRASER
Glenbarry, 58 Victoria Road, Lenzie,
Glasgow, **Strathclyde G66 5AP**
TEL   041 776 1281
OPEN   By Appointment.
Specialise in restoring dolls and dolls'
houses.
PROVIDE Free Estimates.
SPEAK TO Daphne Fraser.
SEE Collectors (Toys), Furniture, Oil
Paintings.

Hair

CHARLES CLEMENTS
4–5 Burlington Arcade, Piccadilly,
London W1V 9A13
TEL   071 493 3923
OPEN   9–5.30 Mon–Fri; 9–4.30 Sat.
Specialise in rebristling hairbrushes,
replacing mirrors and combs.
PROVIDE Free Estimates.
SPEAK TO Charles Clements.

Mechanical Music

VINTAGE WIRELESS CO. LTD
Tudor House, Cossham Street,
Mangotsfield, Bristol, **Avon BS17 3EN**
TEL   0272 565472
FAX   0272 575442
OPEN   9.30–1.30 Sat; Mon–Fri mail
        order only.
Specialise in components and service
information on Vintage Valve hi–fi
radios.
SPEAK TO T. G. Rees.
They do not offer a restoration service at
present.

S. J. BIRT & SON
21 Windmill Street, Brill, Aylesbury,
Buckinghamshire HP18 9TG
TEL   0844 237440
OPEN   By Appointment.
Specialise in restoring musical boxes.
PROVIDE Home Inspections. Free
Estimates. Free Collection/Delivery
Service.
SPEAK TO Mr. S. J. Birt.
SEE Furniture.

**J. V. PIANOS & CAMBRIDGE
PIANOLA CO.**
The Limes, Landbeach, Cambridge,
Cambridgeshire CB4 4DR
TEL   0223 861408 or 861348 or 861507
FAX   0223 441276
OPEN   By Appointment.
Specialise in complete rebuilding of
player–pianos, pianolas and
nickelodeons.
PROVIDE Home Inspections. Chargeable
Estimates. Chargeable
Collection/Delivery Service.
SPEAK TO F. T. Poole.
SEE Musical Instruments.

MILL FARM ANTIQUES
50 Market St, Disley, Stockport,
Cheshire SK12 2DT
TEL   0663 764045
OPEN   9–6 Mon–Sat.
Specialise in restoring cylinder- and
disc-playing musical boxes.
PROVIDE Home Inspections. Free
Estimates. Free Collection/Delivery
Service.
SPEAK TO F. E. Berry.
SEE Furniture.

MAURICE YARHAM
Holly Cottage, Birdsmoorgate, Paynes Downe, Nr. Bridport, **Dorset DT6 5PL**
TEL   02977 377
OPEN   7–7 Mon–Fri.

Specialise in repairing, restoring and conserving antique musical boxes.
PROVIDE Home Inspections. Free Estimates. Chargeable Collection/Delivery Service.
SPEAK TO Maurice Yarham.
SEE Furniture.

GEORGE WORSWICK
108–110 Station Road, Bardney, **Lincolnshire LN3 5UF**
TEL   0526 398352
OPEN   By Appointment.

Specialise in restoring and repairing mechanisms of antique musical boxes of the cylinder type and music combs of disc–playing music boxes.
PROVIDE Free Estimates.
SPEAK TO George Worswick.
Fellow of BHI.

DAVID NEWELL
55 Shelton Street, **London WC2H 9HE**
TEL   071 836 1000
OPEN   10–6 Mon–Fri By Appointment.

Specialise in restoring musical boxes and automata.
PROVIDE Free Estimates in shop.
SPEAK TO David Newell.
Fellow of BHI.
SEE Furniture.

MARGARET GLOVER
42 Hartham Road, Isleworth, **Middlesex TW7 5ES**
TEL   081 568 4662
OPEN   By Appointment.

Specialise in re–dressing automata in exact reproduction of original dress using antique materials.
PROVIDE Free Estimates.
SPEAK TO Margaret Glover.
SEE Collectors (Dolls, Wax).

WICKENDEN CLOCKS
53 Gorse Rd, Thorpe St. Andrew, Norwich, **Norfolk NR7 0AY**
TEL   0603 32179
OPEN   9–5 Sun–Sat.

Specialise in restoring music boxes.
PROVIDE Home Inspections. Free Estimates. Free Local Collection/Delivery Service.
SPEAK TO Eric Wickenden.
SEE Furniture.

JOHN COWDEROY ANTIQUES
42 South Street, Eastbourne, **East Sussex BN21 4XB**
TEL   0323 20058
FAX   0323 410163
OPEN   9.30–1, 2.30–5 Mon, Tues, Thur, Fri; 9.30–1 Wed, Sat.

Specialise in restoring musical boxes.
PROVIDE Home Inspections. Free Estimates. Chargeable Collection/Delivery Service.
SPEAK TO Ruth Cowderoy.
SEE Furniture.

T. P. BROOKS
Sycamores, School Lane, Lodsworth, Petworth, **West Sussex GU28 9DH**
TEL   07985 248

Specialise in restoring musical boxes and automata.
PROVIDE Home Inspections. Free Estimates. Free Collection/Delivery Service.
SPEAK TO Mr. T. P. Brooks.

Member of UKIC. This workshop is included on the register of conservators maintained by the Conservation Unit of the Museums and Galleries Commission.

TIME RESTORED & CO.
18–20 High Street, Pewsey, **Wiltshire SN9 5AQ**
TEL   0672 63544
FAX   0672 63544
OPEN   By Appointment.
Specialise in restoring musical boxes and automata.
PROVIDE Home Inspections. Free Estimates. Free Collection/Delivery Service.
SPEAK TO J. H. Bowler–Reed.
SEE Furniture.

DAVID GAY
23 Taypark, 30 Dundee Road, West Ferry, Dundee, **Tayside DD5 1LX**
TEL   0382 739845
OPEN   By Appointment.
Specialise in restoring barrel organs and automata.
PROVIDE Free Estimates.
SPEAK TO David Gay.

Paper

D. A. ROGERS CORDELL ANTIQUES
13 St.Peter's Street, Ipswich, **Suffolk IP1 1FX**
TEL   0473 219508 and 230685
FAX   0473 230685 (Att. Rogers)
OPEN   10–4 Mon–Fri.
Specialise in restoring paper objects, quill work, box-lining, puzzle pieces, Victorian scraps.
PROVIDE Local Home Inspections. Free Estimates. Local Chargeable Collection/Delivery Service.
SPEAK TO D. A. Rogers.

Pens

JASMIN CAMERON
Antiquarius J6, 131–141 Kings Road, **London SW3 5ST**
TEL   071 351 4154
OPEN   10.15–5.30 Tues–Sat.
Specialise in restoring vintage and collectors' fountain pens.
PROVIDE Free Estimates.
SPEAK TO Jasmin Cameron.

PENFRIEND (LONDON) LTD
Bush House Arcade, Bush House, Strand, **London WC2B 4PH**
TEL   071 836 9809
OPEN   9.30–5.30 Mon–Fri.
Specialise in restoring fountain pens and pencils.
PROVIDE Free Estimates.
SPEAK TO Mr. P. Woolf.

Scientific Instruments

PETER D. BOSSON
10B Swan St, Wilmslow, **Cheshire SK9 1HE**
TEL   0625 525250 and 527857
OPEN   10–12.45, 2.15–5 Tues–Sat.
Specialise in restoring scientific instruments.
PROVIDE Home Inspections. Free Estimates. Free Collection/Delivery Service within 50 miles.
SPEAK TO Peter Bosson.
SEE Furniture.

OLD ROPERY ANTIQUES
East Street, Kilham, Nr. Driffield, **North Humberside YO25 0ST**
TEL   026282 233
OPEN   9.30–5 Mon–Sat.
Specialise in restoring scientific instruments.

PROVIDE Home Inspections. Chargeable
Estimates. Chargeable
Collection/Delivery Service.
SPEAK TO John Butterfield.
SEE Furniture.

PROVIDE Home Inspections. Free
Estimates. Chargeable Collection/
Delivery Service.
SPEAK TO James Layte.
SEE Furniture.

HENNELL SILVER LTD
12 New Bond Street, **London W1Y OH6**
TEL   071 629 6888
FAX   071 493 8158
OPEN   9.30–5.30 Tues–Sat.
Specialise in restoring antique medical
instruments.
PROVIDE Home Inspections. Free
Estimates. Free Collection/Delivery
Service.
SPEAK TO A. C. Kaufmann.
SEE Silver.

RELCY ANTIQUES
9 Nelson Road, **London SE10 9JB**
TEL   081 858 2812
FAX   081 293 4135
OPEN   10–6 Mon–Sat.
Specialise in restoring scientific and
nautical instruments.
PROVIDE Home Inspections.
Free/Chargeable Estimates.
Collection/Delivery Service by
arrangement.
SPEAK TO Robin Challis.
SEE Furniture, Oil Paintings, Silver.

HUMBLEYARD FINE ART
3 Fish Hill, Holt, **Norfolk NR25 6BD**
TEL   0263 713362
OPEN   10–5 Mon–Thur; 10–5 Sat.
Specialise in repairing and restoring
scientific, medical and nautical
instruments.

PETER WIGGINS
Raffles, Southcombe, Chipping Norton,
Oxfordshire OX7 5QH
TEL   0608 642652
OPEN   9–6 Mon–Fri.
Specialise in restoring scientific
instruments.
PROVIDE Home Inspections. Free
Estimates. Chargeable
Collection/Delivery Service.
SPEAK TO Peter Wiggins.
SEE Furniture.

NIDD HOUSE ANTIQUES
Nidd House, Bogs Lane, Harrogate,
North Yorkshire HG1 4DY
TEL   0423 884739
OPEN   9–5 Mon–Fri or By
         Appointment.
Specialise in restoring scientific
instruments.
PROVIDE Home Inspections. Free Local
Estimates. Chargeable
Collection/Delivery Service.
SPEAK TO Mr. D. Preston.
Members of the Guild of Master
Craftsmen, UKIC. This workshop is
included on the register of conservators
maintained by the Conservation Unit of
the Museums and Galleries
Commission.
SEE Furniture, Porcelain, Silver.

NOLF & MANN
29 Breadalbane Terrace, Wick, **Highland
KW1 5AT**
TEL   0955 4284
OPEN   By Appointment.
Specialise in restoring scientific
instruments.

197

PROVIDE Home Inspections.
Free/Chargeable Estimates. Chargeable
Collection/Delivery Service.
SPEAK TO T. Nolf.
SEE Collectors (Arms and Armour).

Taxidermy

ANN & JOHN BURTON
Natural Craft Taxidermy, 21 Main
Street, Ebrington, Nr. Chipping
Camden, **Gloucestershire GL55 6NL**
TEL   038678 231
OPEN   By Appointment.

Specialise in taxidermy commissions and
restoration work.

PROVIDE Home Inspections. Chargeable
Estimates. Chargeable
Collection/Delivery Service.
SPEAK TO Ann or John Burton.

GET STUFFED
105 Essex Road, **London N1 2SL**
TEL   071 226 1364
OPEN   10.30–4 Mon–Wed, Fri; 10.30–1
          Thur; 11–4 Sat.

Specialise in all aspects of taxidermy and
also supply glass domes.

PROVIDE Free Estimates. Chargeable
Collection/Delivery Service.
SPEAK TO Robert Sinclair.

HEADS' N' TAILS
Bourne House, Church Street,
Wiveliscombe, **Somerset TA4 2LT**
TEL   0984 23097
OPEN   By Appointment.

Specialise in fine taxidermy including
restoration, particularly cased fish.

PROVIDE Home Inspections. Free
Estimates. Chargeable
Collection/Delivery Service.
SPEAK TO D. McKinley.

Toys and Rocking Horses

JOHN MARRIOTT ROCKING
HORSES
86 Village Road, Bromham,
Bedfordshire MK43 8HU
TEL   02302 3173
OPEN   8–8 daily.

Specialise in manufacturing and
restoring traditionally styled rocking
and carousel horses.

PROVIDE Free/Chargeable Home
Inspections. Free/Chargeable Estimates.
Free Local Collection/Delivery Service.
SPEAK TO John Marriott.

MICHAEL BARRINGTON
The Old Rectory, Warmwell,
Dorchester, **Dorset DT2 8HQ**
TEL   0305 852104
OPEN   8.30–5.30 or By Appointment.

Specialise in restoring model steam
engines.

PROVIDE Free Local Estimates.
Free/Chargeable Collection/Delivery
Service.
SPEAK TO Michael Barrington.
SEE Collectors (Musical Instruments),
Furniture.

BEARWOOD MODELS
20 Westminster Road, Malvern Wells,
Hereford & Worcester WR14 4EF
TEL   0684 568977
OPEN   By Appointment.

Specialise in repairing and restoring old
toys, particularly clockwork repairs to
model railway locomotives.

PROVIDE Free Estimates.
SPEAK TO R. W. Chester–Lamb
SEE Furniture.

J. & D. WOODS
180 Chorley Road, Westhoughton,
Bolton, **Lancashire BL5 3PN**
TEL   0942 816246
OPEN   By Appointment.
Specialise in constructing and restoring
all types of rocking horses. They also
supply accessories and are one of the few
companies able to restore and make
skin-covered horses.
PROVIDE Home Inspections. Free
Estimates. Chargeable
Collection/Delivery Service.
SPEAK TO John Woods.

CHELSEA LION
Chenil Galleries, 181–183 Kings Road,
London SW3 5EB
TEL   071 351 9338
OPEN   11–5 Mon–Sat.
Specialise in restoring Teddy bears and
rocking horses.
PROVIDE Free Estimates.
SPEAK TO Steve Clark.
SEE Collectors (Dolls).

WEAVES & WAXES
53 Church Street, Bloxham, Banbury,
Oxfordshire OX15 4ET
TEL   0295 721535
FAX   0295 271867
Specialise in restoring Teddy bears.
PROVIDE Home Inspections.
Free/Chargeable Estimates. Chargeable
Collection/Delivery Service.
SPEAK TO Laurie Grayer.
SEE Collectors (Dolls), Furniture.

ANTHONY DEW
The Rocking Horse Shop, Old Road,
Holme upon Spalding Moor, York,
North Yorkshire YO4 4AB
TEL   0430 860563
FAX   0430 860563
OPEN   9–5 Mon–Sat By Appointment.

Specialise in restoring and making
rocking horses. He will supply all parts
and accessories and makes tailor-
made-to-measure kits for restorers.
PROVIDE Home Inspections. Free
Estimates. Collection/Delivery Service
by arrangement.
SPEAK TO Pat Dew.
Anthony Dew will also take
commissions for other carving work.

SECOND CHILDHOOD
20 Byram Arcade, Westgate,
Huddersfield, **West Yorkshire HD1 1ND**
TEL   0484 530117 or 603854
OPEN   10.30–3.30 Tues–Sat.
Specialise in specialist Teddy bear
repairs.
PROVIDE Free Estimates. Local Free
Collection/Delivery Service.
SPEAK TO Michael or Elizabeth Hoy.
SEE Collectors (Dolls).

DAPHNE FRASER
Glenbarry, 58 Victoria Road, Lenzie,
Glasgow, **Strathclyde G66 5AP**
TEL   041 776 1281
OPEN   By Appointment.
Specialise in restoring rocking horses.
PROVIDE Free Estimates.
SPEAK TO Daphne Fraser.
SEE Collectors (Dolls), Furniture, Oil
Paintings.

Wax

MARGARET GLOVER
42 Hartham Road, Isleworth, **Middlesex
TW7 5ES**
TEL   081 568 4662
OPEN   By Appointment.
Specialise in restoring all types of wax
artefacts including wax portraits and
small sculptures.

PROVIDE Free Estimates.
SPEAK TO Margaret Glover.
SEE Collectors (Dolls, Mechanical Music).

Musical Instruments

J.V. PIANOS & CAMBRIDGE PIANOLA CO.
The Limes, Landbeach, Cambridge, **Cambridgeshire CB4 4DR**
TEL   0223 861408 or 861348 or 861507
FAX   0223 441276
OPEN   By Appointment.

Specialise in complete rebuilding of pianos.

PROVIDE Home Inspections. Chargeable Estimates. Chargeable Collection/Delivery Service.
SPEAK TO F. T. Poole

JOHN DIKE
The Manse, Gold Street, Stalbridge, **Dorset DT10 2LX**
TEL   0963 62285
OPEN   9–5 Mon–Fri; 9–12.30 Sat.

Specialise in restoring instruments and bows of the violin family.

PROVIDE Home Inspections. Free Estimates. Collection/Delivery Service by arrangement.
SPEAK TO John Dike.

PAXMAN (CASES) LTD
3 Tudor Court, Harold Court Road, Romford, **Essex RM3 OAE**
TEL   04023 45415
OPEN   10–6 Mon–Fri.

Specialise in restoring musical instrument cases and brass, string and woodwind instruments.

PROVIDE Free Estimates.
SPEAK TO Peter Robinson.
SEE **London WC2.**

N. P. MANDER LTD.
St. Peter's Close, Warner Place, Hackney Road, **London E2 7AF**

Specialise in construction and repair of pipe organs.

PROVIDE Home Inspections. Refundable Estimates (normally £100.00). Free Collection/Delivery Service.
SPEAK TO Mr. J. P. Mander

JOSEPH MALACHI O'KELLY
Luthier, 2 Middleton Road, **London E8 4BL**
TEL   071 254 7074
OPEN   By Appointment.

Specialise in restoring plucked–string musical instruments. He works with wood, ivory and tortoisehell on both Western and Islamic instruments.

PROVIDE Chargeable Home Inspections. Chargeable Collection/Delivery Service.
SPEAK TO Joseph O'Kelly.

Also give estimates on restoration for instruments in auction.

BRIDGEWOOD & NEITZERT
Ilex Works, 10 Northwold Road, **London N16 7HR**
TEL   071 249 9398
FAX   071 249 9398
OPEN   9–6 Mon–Sat.

Specialise in repairing and restoring violins, violas, cellos, double basses and bows particularly of the baroque and classical periods.

PROVIDE Home Inspections. Free Estimates. Chargeable Collection/Delivery Service.
SPEAK TO Gary Bridgewood or Tom Neitzert.

This workshop is included on the register of conservators maintained by the Conservation Unit of the Museums and Galleries Commission.

ROBERT MORLEY & CO. LTD
34 Engate Street, **London SE13 7HA**
TEL   081 318 5838
FAX   081 297 0720
OPEN   9–5 Mon–Sat.

Specialise in repairing and restoring pianos, harpsichords, celestes, spinets, virginals and clavichords, both antique and modern.
PROVIDE Home Inspections. Free Local Estimates. Free Local Collection/Delivery Service.
SPEAK TO John Morley.

J. & A. BEARE LTD
7 Broadwick Street, **London W1V 1FJ**
TEL   071 437 1449
FAX   071 439 4520
OPEN   9–12.15, 1.30–5 Mon–Fri.

Specialise in restoring violins, violas, cellos and bows.
PROVIDE Free Estimates.
SPEAK TO Mr. Beare.

J. R. GUIVIER & CO. LTD
99 Mortimer Street, **London W1N 7TA**
TEL   071 580 2560
FAX   071 436 1461
OPEN   9–5 Mon–Fri.

Specialise in restoring and repairing violins, violas, cellos.
PROVIDE Free Estimates.
SPEAK TO Mr. Wilks.

PHIL PARKER LTD
26 Chiltern Street, **London W1M 1PH**
TEL   071 486 8206
OPEN   10–5.30 Mon–Wed, Fri; 10–4 Thur; 10–3 Sat.

Specialise in restoring brass instruments.
PROVIDE Free Estimates.
SPEAK TO Dave Woodhead.

THE LONDON HARPSICHORD WORKSHOP
130 Westbourne Terrace Mews, **London W2 6QG**
TEL   071 723 9650
OPEN   By Appointment.

Specialise in repairing and restoring harpsichords, spinets and virginals.
SPEAK TO Mark Ransom.

PAXMAN (CASES) LTD
116 Longacre, **London WC2**
TEL   071 240 3642
OPEN   9–5 Mon–Fri; 10–5 Sat.

Specialise in restoring musical instrument cases and brass, string and woodwind instruments.
PROVIDE Free Estimates.
SPEAK TO Bob Paxman.
SEE **Essex**.

J. G. TREVOR-OWEN
181–193 Oldham Rd, Rochdale, **Greater Manchester OL16 5QZ**
TEL   0706 48138
OPEN   1.30–7 Mon–Fri or By Appointment.

Specialise in restoring violins.
PROVIDE Home Inspections. Refundable Estimates.
SPEAK TO J. G. Trevor-Owen.
SEE Furniture, Oil Paintings.

MARTIN BLOCK INSTRUMENT REPAIRS
12 Elm Park, Stanmore, **Middlesex HA7 4BJ**
TEL   081 954 4347
OPEN   9–6 Mon–Fri (24-hour answering service).

Specialise in repairing and restoring saxophones and clarinets.
PROVIDE Free Estimates.

SPEAK TO Martin Block.

Mr. Block is a Member of the Institute of Musical Instrument Technology.

DAVID LEIGH c/o LAURIE LEIGH ANTIQUES
36 High Street, Oxford, **Oxfordshire OX1 4AN**
TEL   0865 244197 or 0608 810607
OPEN   By Appointment.
Specialise in restoring early keyboard instruments including spinets, harpsichords, pre-1820 square pianos and pre-1825 grand pianos.
SPEAK TO David Leigh.
Mr Leigh is a professional classical soloist.

PAUL NEVILLE, HARPSICHORDS & FORTEPIANOS
C.K.S. Workshop, 74 The Street, Blundeston, Lowestoft, **Suffolk NR32 5AB**
TEL   0502 730356
OPEN   By Appointment after 6 p.m.
Specialise in structural, musical and decorative restoration of harpsichords and fortepianos. Also supply specialist materials.
PROVIDE Home Inspections. Refundable Estimates. Chargeable Collection/Delivery Service.
SPEAK TO Paul Neville.
Member of the Guild of Master Craftsmen. This workshop is included on the register of conservators maintained by the Conservation Unit of the Museums and Galleries Commission.

SHARON McCALLUM
Workshop, 27 Lesbourne Road, Reigate, **Surrey RH2 7BU**
TEL   0737 223481
OPEN   By Appointment.

Specialise in repairing and restoring brass instruments, especially trombones.
PROVIDE Free Estimates.
SPEAK TO Sharon McCallum.

JOHN PAUL
Parkway, Waldron, Heathfield, **East Sussex TN21 0RH**
TEL   0435 86 2525
OPEN   By Appointment.
Specialise in restoring early keyboard instruments and early pianos up to 1840.
PROVIDE Home Inspections. Free Estimates. Chargeable Collection/Delivery Service.
SPEAK TO John Paul.

GRANT O'BRIEN
St. Cecilia's Hall, Niddry Street, Edinburgh, **Lothian EH1 1LJ**
TEL   031 667 7853 and 650 2805
OPEN   By Appointment.
Specialise in restoring keyboard instruments.
PROVIDE Home Inspections. Free/Chargeable Estimates. Collection/Delivery Service by arrangement.
SPEAK TO Grant O'Brien.

SAN DOMENICO STRINGED INSTRUMENTS
175 Kings Road, Cardiff, **South Glamorgan CF1 9DF**
TEL   0222 235881
FAX   0222 344510
OPEN   10–4.30 Mon–Fri; 10–1 Sat.
Specialise in restoring violins, violas, cellos and bows.
PROVIDE Home Inspections. Free Estimates. Free Collection/Delivery Service.
SPEAK TO Howard Morgan.

Arms and Armour and Sporting Equipment

ARMS AND ARMOUR

JASON ABBOT GUNMAKERS LTD
1–3 Bell Street, Princes Risborough,
Buckinghamshire P17 OAD
TEL   08444 6677
FAX   0844 274155
OPEN   By Appointment.
Specialise in restoring fine quality
English guns.
PROVIDE Free Estimates.
Free/Chargeable Collection/Delivery
Service.
SPEAK TO Jason Abbot.

**TERENCE PORTER ANTIQUE
ARMS**
The Old Forge, High Street, North
Marston, **Buckinghamshire MK18 3PD**
TEL   029667 422 or 029673 8255
FAX   029667 448
OPEN   9.30–5 Mon–Fri.
Specialise in restoration work on all
American and European arms and
armour.
PROVIDE Home Inspections. Free
Estimates. Chargeable
Collection/Delivery Service.
SPEAK TO Sandra Garner or Terry Porter.

H. S. GREENFIELD & SON
4–5 Upper Bridge Street, Canterbury,
Kent CT1 2NB
TEL   0227 456959
FAX   0227 765030
OPEN   8.30–5.30 Mon–Sat.
Specialise in repairing vintage shotguns
and fishing tackle.
PROVIDE Home Inspections. Chargeable
Estimates. Chargeable
Collection/Delivery Service.
SPEAK TO T. S. Greenfield.

ST. PANCRAS ANTIQUES
150 St.Pancras, Chichester, **West Sussex
PO19 1SH**
TEL   0243 787645
OPEN   9.30–5 Mon–Sat; 9.30–1 Thur.
Specialise in restoring European arms
and armour.
PROVIDE Home Inspections. Free
Estimates.
SPEAK TO Ralph Willatt.

D. W. DYSON (ANTIQUE WEAPONS)
Wood Lea, Shepley, Huddersfield, **West Yorkshire HD8 8ES**
TEL   0484 607331
FAX   0484 607331
OPEN   By Appointment.

Specialise in restoration of all types of arms including pistols, guns and swords.

PROVIDE Home Inspections. Free Estimates. Collection/Delivery Service can be arranged.

SPEAK TO David Dyson.

Also manufacture miniature arms and presentation pieces to customers' specifications. Experienced in working with precious metals.

TONY PTOLOMEY
Comlongon Castle, Clarencefield, **Dumfries & Galloway DG1 4NA**
TEL   038 787 283
OPEN   By Appointment.

Specialise in restoring European and Oriental armour.

PROVIDE Free Estimates.

SPEAK TO Tony Ptolomey.

THE BARON OF EARLSHALL
Earlshall Castle, Leuchars, by St. Andrews, **Fife KY16 0DP**
TEL   0334 839205
OPEN   By Appointment.

Specialise in restoring antique arms and armour. The Baron is a specialist in Scottish weapons.

PROVIDE Home Inspections. Free Estimates. Free Collection/Delivery Service.

SPEAK TO The Baron of Earlshall.

NOLF & MANN
29 Breadalbane Terrace, Wick, **Highland KW1 5AT**
TEL   0955 4284
OPEN   By Appointment.

Specialise in restoring firearms.

PROVIDE Home Inspections. Free/Chargeable Estimates. Chargeable Collection/Delivery Service.

SPEAK TO T. Nolf.

SEE Collectors (Scientific Instruments).

THE HIGHLAND SHOP
Blair Atholl, **Tayside PH18 5SG**
TEL   079 681 303
OPEN   9–5 Sun–Sat (Summer); 9–5 Tues–Sat (Winter).

Specialise in restoring antique weapons, individual and collections, edged and firearm.

PROVIDE Home Inspections. Free Estimates. Chargeable Collection/Delivery Service.

SPEAK TO Edward H. Slaytor.

Mr. Slaytor is an indentured gunsmith (London).

NEIL LIVINGSTONE
3 Old Hawkhill, Dundee, **Tayside DD1 5EU**
TEL   0382 25517
OPEN   9–5 Mon–Fri.

Specialise in restoring firearms.

PROVIDE Free Estimates. Chargeable Collection/Delivery Service.

SPEAK TO Neil Livingstone.

SEE Furniture, Oil Paintings, Silver.

HERMITAGE ANTIQUES
10 West Street, Fishguard, **Dyfed SA65 9AE**
TEL   0348 873037 and 872322
OPEN   9.30–5.30 Mon–Sat; 9.30–1 Wed and Sat.

Specialise in antique arms restoration, especially 16th and 17th century.
PROVIDE Home Inspections. Free

Estimates. Chargeable
Collection/Delivery Service.
SPEAK TO J. B. Thomas.

SPORTING EQUIPMENT

Billiards

HAMILTON & TUCKER BILLIARD CO. LTD
Park Lane, Knebworth, **Hertfordshire SG3 6PJ**
TEL   0438 811995
FAX   0438 814939
OPEN   9–5 Mon–Fri.

Specialise in restoring period billiard tables and associated accessories.
PROVIDE Home Inspections. Free Estimates. Chargeable Collection/Delivery Service.
SPEAK TO Hugh Hamilton.

MALLARD RESTORATIONS
Unit 6, The Dove Centre, 109 Bartholomew Road, **London NW5 2BJ**
TEL   071 267 7547
OPEN   9–6 Mon–Fri.

Specialise in restoring billiard and snooker tables.
PROVIDE Home Inspections. Free Estimates. Chargeable Collection/Delivery Service.
SPEAK TO Jeff Walkden.

Golf

OLD ST. ANDREWS GALLERY
9 Albany Place, St. Andrews, **Fife KY16 9HH**
and 10 Golf Place, St. Andrews, **Fife KY16 9JA**
TEL   0334 7840 and 0334 78712
OPEN   10–5 Mon–Sat.

Specialise in advice on care of antique golf clubs.
PROVIDE Home Inspections. Free Estimates. Free Collection/Delivery Service.
SPEAK TO Mr. or Mrs. Brown.
SEE Silver.

Riding

TRENT SADDLERS WORKSHOP
Unit 10, Chaucer Court Workshops, Chaucer Street, Nottingham, **Nottinghamshire NG1 5LO**
TEL   0602 473832
OPEN   9.30–6 Mon–Fri.

Specialise in servicing, repair and refurbishment of saddlery and bridlework and associated leatherwork.
PROVIDE Chargeable Home Inspections. Free Estimates. Chargeable Collection/Delivery Service.
SPEAK TO Christopher or Clare Beswick.

Security and Insurance

SECURITY

'But we thought it would never happen to us!' is the cry most often heard from the recently burgled. In 1990 over 60,000 works of art and antiques, each with a worth of over £5,000, were stolen in Europe. Each year in Britain alone an estimated 5,000 paintings are stolen. The profits made from the illicit dealing in stolen fine art and antiques are second only to those achieved from dealing in narcotics. It is too late to presume that such thefts only happen to other people.

The criminals concerned are becoming more sophisticated in their planning and execution of thefts, and their knowledge of which items are worth taking is becoming expert. In more than one case a book describing the different hallmarks used by silversmiths has been left behind by thieves at the scene of a crime.

The private person can, however, take basic precautions which will reduce the likelihood of burglary or robbery. Before attempting to secure one's house it is advisable to call in an expert to ascertain the weaknesses inherent in the house. Rather than pay vast amounts of money initially for a security company to vet the premises, try a telephone call to your local police station and ask for a visit from their Crime Prevention Officer. These officers are primarily concerned with crime prevention and since burglary, in particular, is rife at the present time, a reduction would save the police thousands of man hours. The simple expedient of good window locks in the right places, adequate locks on front and back doors and a routine of securing the house before bed or before leaving the house will drastically reduce the likelihood of being burgled by the opportunist thief.

A burglar alarm is another protection worth considering although an inefficient system is worse than useless. The police can often suggest a number of companies from their own experience who could be contacted. There are a number of 'cowboy' firms in existence which do not provide the proper cover one imagines to be there when an alarm system is installed.

Of course, the security in a home is only efficient if it is used! So many cases of burglary are made that much easier for the thief if, for instance, the window locks are not properly secured or the alarm is left switched off at night when someone is on the premises. Take good advice on security in the home and use the systems properly when they have been professionally installed.

If your alarm system was not operative and you were burgled you may not be able to claim on your insurance policy. I hear you say, 'I can't afford to insure my fine art and antiques, it will be far too expensive.' This may be true but first of all you must find out what your possessions are actually worth. Many family collections of fine art and antiques are built up over generations, the monetary worth never being considered. Some poor victims only discover the true value of an item *after* it has been stolen. Even if you are not considering insurance it does pay to have your precious possessions valued by a professional.

A good photograph is worth a thousand words of description to someone trying to identify a stolen work of art or antique. The police have almost despaired at the lack of photographic records kept by people who own beautiful and valuable items. It is not always necessary to employ a professional photographer to take the pictures, although the results are often well worth the expense. Photographs taken with natural light and a good 35mm camera are much better than none at all.

A good valuation and photographs provide a basis for insurance. With fine art and antiques in your possession you need a policy designed for such items. A normal household policy will probably not be specific enough. There are a number of brokers offering policies custom-built for different clients. Collectors, dealers, families with heirlooms and artists themselves all have to be considered as separate special cases. The premiums may appear high initially but, taking into consideration the value of the items concerned and the fact that you may be able to replace them if they are insured, it is well worth looking into the different options before making a final decision.

What happens after a burglary has occurred and your treasured possessions have gone? Information is sent to the Force Crime Intelligence Bureau of the police force concerned and they in turn circulate the details by telex to other forces in the United Kingdon. If the items are likely to go abroad then information is sent through Interpol to a central computer in Lyon, France. One hundred and fifty-four countries have access to this database and can use it to help track down specific items if they are recovered outside the country where the theft originated, and the database also records details on international criminals and their modus operandi.

Another avenue open to the loser of stolen fine art and antiques is advertising the loss. A number of publications provide illustrations of items which have been stolen along with descriptions. The *Antiques Trade Gazette* is a weekly newspaper with a large circulation among the trade, especially for those dealers and collectors attending fairs and markets, and information about forthcoming auctions is also published. They carry advertisements for stolen goods and have been successful in recovering a number of items. Another monthly magazine, *Trace*, is the only specialist magazine which shows illustrations and gives descriptions of stolen works of art and antiques. The pages in the magazine are split into sections (pictures, silver, clocks, furniture, sculpture, etc.) and a pull-out six-monthly index is printed to enable specialist dealers, the different departments of auction houses, museums and art galleries to concentrate on their own sections. Records on works are retained on a database until the items are recovered. Over £7,500,000 worth of insured items alone have been recovered in the first three years of the magazine's life.

The Antiques Loss Register is a computer database which records details and photographs of stolen items and has two prime functions: one, it allows dealers and other clients to contact it and search its database to find out whether prospective purchases are there or not; two, it will check against the major auction rooms' catalogues of sales to see whether any of the stolen goods entered on the computer match any of the items entered for sale. The latter system has only just begun its operation but should prove effective.

If one of your stolen items turns up in an antiques shop or an auction room, what is your position regarding recovering the piece? In English law, a stolen item remains the property of the original owner no matter how many hands the piece has gone through. There is one exception to this and this is the 'market overt'. On certain market sites within England, if a stolen piece is sold by a trader who usually deals in such work, from a regular stall between the hours of dawn and dusk, then good title to the stolen item does pass. This is quite rare, however, and usually any dispute regarding title to a stolen item goes to court as a civil case, the original owner standing an excellent chance of retaining good title to their goods.

If you purchase a stolen work of art or antique in good faith abroad then the ownership of the goods is a very different matter. The law changes with each country. If a number of transactions involving the stolen item have taken place in different countries then it is extremely difficult for the original owner to recover their possessions. If an amount of time has elapsed between the theft and discovery of the stolen works, then each individual country's statutes of limitations must also be considered. These are time limits beyond which good title remains with the purchaser. They differ from as little as two years in Japan to as much as 30 or more in England

If one wishes to avoid purchasing stolen fine art and antiques, as the majority of people do, it is far better to buy items through the large and specialist auction rooms or to buy from antique dealers who are members of trade organisations such as the British Antique Dealers Association (BADA) or the London and Provincial Antique Dealers Association (LAPADA), both of which self-regulate their members, keeping all transactions to a very high standard and offering a purchaser their money back should there not be good title to an item bought.

Naturally, professional dealers, auction houses and collectors will wish to avoid the complications of purchasing stolen items in good faith, and they will make sure they regularly peruse the stolen columns in the *Antiques Trade Gazette* and *Trace* magazine, always checking with the police and other organisations who keep records of stolen works if they are in doubt about the provenance or ownership of an item.

Philip Saunders

VALUATION

In order for satisfactory insurance arrangments to be made it is essential to agree a valuation. While this usually presents no problem with buildings, cars, household appliances and so on, as these are all items which have an ascertainable price, the valuation of works of art is, as has often been said, more art than science.

There is no such thing as a fixed value for a work of art. Two identical items may fetch dramatically different prices in different places on the same day, depending on who is buying, the mood of the auction room, and even the weather or the state of air traffic control that morning! What is more, there are different levels of valuation: the basic market price, equivalent perhaps to the auction reserve; the open market price, equivalent to the actual saleroom price (subject to the remarks above); and the full replacement price, being the figure asked in an appropriate dealer's gallery.

Despite these difficulties, an experienced valuer can generally produce a list which will satisfy both the owner and the insurance company. Whether the insurance is based on agreed individual values or not, it is essential for any collector to maintain an inventory, with values updated every year or two. It is surprising how difficult it can be to make a list of items in even the most familiar room in the house – try doing it with your eyes shut and see what you leave out! After a burglary or a fire it will be even harder, and you will have to convince the loss adjuster of exactly what is missing.

How should you go about obtaining a valuation? Obviously, you can do it yourself, by keeping all your original invoices, checking sale results and prowling round the shops lifting tickets, but it is probably more realistic to employ a qualified specialist valuer. Such a person will have a 'feel' for the prices resulting from constant exposure to the actuality of the market place, and will be able to back his judgement or fill in any gaps by research in the literature, sale catalogues and so on. All of the larger auction houses maintain specialised valuation departments, usually staffed by trained general valuers who will be able to tackle most things found in the average home. One advantage of dealing with large firms is that their valuers will also have access to highly specialised knowledge in the expert departments, as well as to superb reference libraries and internal records. Many dealers offer valuation services, and clearly if the valuation required is within the field of the dealer's experience, you will be in safe hands. However, if a furniture dealer comes across a piece of Polynesian art or a Rembrandt etching, he will often be flummoxed. There are also specialist valuation companies, often staffed by ex-auction house staff, who will bring an expert eye to the job.

How much should you expect to pay for a valuation? Although all firms publish tariffs, generally based on a percentage of the values taken, this should be regarded as a starting-point for negotiation. Indeed, most large firms charge on a time basis, generally about £250 per valuer per day, plus expenses. It clearly pays to employ a speedy valuer and not to keep him or her talking too long about your prized possessions! As in all professional matters, you should get an estimate in writing before proceeding. Auction houses are generally very keen to undertake interesting valuations, as they build their businesses on long-term relationships, so you can often negotiate a very favourable rate. The Bonhams Valueplan system, which incorporates automatic updating over a period of years at a very low fee, is an attractive new service.

What will you get for your money? The finished inventory will describe in detail all your more valuable possessions above a pre-set level, generally £500, but this may vary according to your own or your insurance company's requirements. Less valuable items can be listed without values, and 'lumped together' into a sum for general contents. You can expect two copies of the inventory, one for yourself and one for the insurance company. The valuers will, of course, keep a file copy and the information is also held on computer disk. For security purposes you should certainly expect the valuers to keep your name and address physically separate from the file copy held by them and for that copy to be identified by a code. Obviously, you should keep your own copy securely, preferably in a separate place such as the office, or in a safe at the bank or in a solicitor's office. There are all sorts of horror stories about burglaries taking place shortly after a valuation has been deposited with the insurance company, but I have never known of an actual, provable incident.

Lastly, it is also increasingly good sense (and easy) to keep a photographic record of your possessions. The task of the police and others in tracing stolen goods is made immeasurably easier if photographs exist, as is proving that the items were actually yours if anything is recovered.

Diddi Malek

TOWRY LAW (GENERAL INSURANCE) LIMITED
Godolphin Court, Stoke Poges Lane,
Slough, **Buckinghamshire SL1 3PB**
TEL   0753 821241
FAX   0753 70881
OPEN   9–5 Mon–Fri.
Specialise in household insurance for collectors of fine art and antiques.
PROVIDE Home Inspections. Free Estimates.
SPEAK TO Roger Parkinson.

FRIZZELL FINE ART INSURANCE
Frizzell House, 14–22 Elder Street,
London E1 6DF
TEL   071 247 6595
FAX   071 377 9114
OPEN   9–5 Mon–Fri.
Specialise in insurance for art dealers and collectors.
PROVIDE Security Surveys, Free Estimates.
SPEAK TO Mr. M. J. Dheehan or Mrs. P. Gwennap.

SNEATH KENT & STUART LTD
Stuart House, 53–55 Scrutton Street,
London EC2A 4QQ
TEL   071 739 5646
FAX   071 739 6467 or 2656
OPEN   9.00–5.30 Mon–Fri.
Specialise in insurance for collectors and dealers.
SPEAK TO Geoffrey Sneath, Stephen Brown, David Smith or David Ezzard.
They are official brokers to LAPADA and the Fine Art Trade Guild.

CAMERON RICHARD & SMITH INSURANCE SERVICES LTD
Boundary House, 7–17 Jewry Street,
London EC3N 2HP
TEL   071 488 4554
FAX   071 481 1406
OPEN   9.30–5.30 Mon–Fri.

Specialise in fine art insurance including furniture, jewellery, objets d'art and classic cars.
PROVIDE Home Inspections by arrangement.
SPEAK TO Charles Williams.

CROWLEY COLOSSO LIMITED
Ibex House, Minories, **London
EC3N 1JJ**
TEL   071 782 9782
FAX   071 782 9783
OPEN   9–6.30 Mon–Fri.
Specialise in fine arts and antiques insurance for private collectors, museums, galleries, shippers/packers, auction houses and restorers/conservators.
PROVIDE Free Estimates.
SPEAK TO Robert Read or Dominic Hepworth.

THOMAS R. MILLER & SON (HOME) LIMITED
Dawson House, 5 Jewry Street, **London
EC3N 2EX**
TEL   071 488 2345
FAX   071 481 3651
OPEN   9.30–5.30 Mon–Fri.
Specialise in insurance broking and risk management of fine art and antiques for collectors and dealers.
PROVIDE Home Inspections. Free Estimates.
SPEAK TO David Needham, Andrew Jobson or Marcus Elwes.

RICHARDS LONGSTAFF (INSURANCE) LTD
Battlebridge House, 97 Tooley Street,
London SE1 2RF
TEL   071 407 4466
FAX   071 403 3610
OPEN   9.30–5.30 Mon–Fri.

Specialise in fine art insurance.
PROVIDE Home Inspections.
SPEAK TO Ian Hill-Wood.

PROVIDE Home Inspections. Free
Estimates.
SPEAK TO M. A. Hill.

HANOVER INSURANCE BROKERS
13 Relton Mews, Knightsbridge, **London
SW7 1ET**
TEL   071 581 1477
FAX   071 225 1411
OPEN   9–5 Mon–Fri.
Specialise in insurance particularly for
collectors of fine art, jewellery and
antiques. They can tailor-make policies
for individual clients.
PROVIDE Home Inspections. Free
Estimates.
SPEAK TO Barbara Hollis.

PENROSE FORBES
27–30 Horsefair, Banbury, **Oxfordshire
OX16 ONE**
TEL   0295 259892
FAX   0295 269968
OPEN   9–5.30 Mon–Fri.
Specialise in fine art insurance.
PROVIDE Free Estimates.
SPEAK TO Michael Forbes.

STERLING SECURITY SYSTEMS
Sterling House, 305–307 Chiswick High
Road, **London W4 4HH**
TEL   081 747 0072
FAX   081 994 4394
OPEN   8.30–6 Mon–Fri.
Specialise in intruder alarms, access
control systems and c.c.t.v. systems.

S. G. D. SECURITY/ELECTRICAL
26–28 Dalcross Street, Roath, Cardiff,
South Glamorgan CF2 4UB
TEL   0222 464120
OPEN   By Appointment.
Specialise in security systems including
alarms, door access, video and closed
circuit television.
PROVIDE Home Inspections. Free
Estimates.
SPEAK TO G. S. Whitty.

Lighting, Display and Suppliers Including Specialist Booksellers

UTILITARIAN FOLDING
BOOKCASES
4 Wrenwood, Welwyn Garden City,
Hertfordshire. AL7 1QG
TEL   0707 332965
OPEN   By Appointment.

Specialise in folding bookcases and
display stands.

PROVIDE Home Inspections. Free
Estimates. Chargeable Delivery Service.
SPEAK TO Nicky Tutt.

ANTIQUE RESTORATIONS
The Old Wheelwright's Shop, Brasted
Forge, Brasted, Westerham, **Kent
TN16 1JL**
TEL   0959 563863
FAX   0959 561262
OPEN   9–5 Mon–Fri; 10–1 Sat.

Specialise in brass castings including
handles and mounts. Anything not in
their catalogue can be cast by special
order.

PROVIDE Refundable Estimates. 28-Day
Postal Service.
SPEAK TO Raymond Konyn.

Members of BAFRA.
SEE Furniture.

C. & A. J. BARMBY
68 Judd Road, Tonbridge, **Kent
TN9 2NJ**
TEL   0732 356479
OPEN   Mail Order only.

Specialise in display stands, ultra–violet
lamps, magnifiers, metal-testers, digital
scales, swing balances, Chelsea filters.

PROVIDE Home Inspections. Chargeable
Collection/Delivery Service.
SPEAK TO Chris Barmby.

ST. JOHN A. BURCH
Myrtle House, Headcorn Road, Grafty
Green, **Kent ME17 2AR**
TEL   0622 850381
FAX   0622 850381
OPEN   By Appointment.

Specialise in conservation lighting for
organic materials including
watercolours, oils and manuscripts.

PROVIDE Home Inspections. Chargeable
Estimates.
SPEAK TO St. John Burch

Mr. Burch is a chartered designer,
FRSA.

LIBERON WAXES LTD
Mountfield Industrial Estate, Learoyd Road, New Romney, **Kent TN28 8XU**
TEL   0679 67555
FAX   0679 67575
OPEN   9–5.30 Mon–Fri.

Specialise in antique restoration and care products for staining and dyeing.
PROVIDE Chargeable Collection/Delivery Service.
SPEAK TO Isabelle Haumont.

RANKINS (GLASS) COMPANY LIMITED
The London Glass Centre, 24–34 Pearson Street, **London E2 8JD**
TEL   071 729 4200
FAX   071 729 7135
OPEN   8–5.50 Mon–Fri.

Specialise in non-reflective safety glass for paintings, custom-made display cabinets and anti-bandit and bullet-resistant glass.
PROVIDE Chargeable Estimates. Free/Chargeable Collection/Delivery '
Service.
SPEAK TO Mr. K. Hussein or Mr. C. Clifford.

CHATSWORTH COMMERCIAL LIGHTING
6 Highbury Corner, **London N5 1RD**
TEL   071 609 9829
FAX   071 700 4804
OPEN   9–6 Mon–Fri (24-hour answering service).

Specialise in picture and gallery lighting from domestic and professional gallery sector to museums.
PROVIDE Home Inspections. Free Estimates.
SPEAK TO John Khan.

PICREATOR ENTERPRISES LTD
44 Park View Gardens, **London NW4 2PN**
TEL   081 202 8972
OPEN   By Appointment.

Specialise in supply of materials for professional restoration and conservation of fine art objects. Manufacture 'Renaissance' wax polish and other own–brand restoration products. Mail order.
SPEAK TO John Lawson.

AIR IMPROVEMENT CENTRE
23 Denbigh Street, **London SW1V 2HF**
TEL   071 834 2834
FAX   071 821 8485
OPEN   9.30–5.30 Mon–Fri; 10–1 Sat.

Specialise in humidity control. Advise on and supply humidifiers, dehumidifiers and hygrometers.
PROVIDE Local Home Inspections. Free Estimates. Free Delivery Service.
SPEAK TO Valerie Taplin.

ABSOLUTE ACTION LIMITED
Mantle House, Broomhill Road, Wandsworth. **London SW18 4JQ**
TEL   081 871 5005
FAX   081 877 9498
OPEN   8.30–6 Mon–Fri.

Specialise in fibre optic lighting systems for display and conservation.
PROVIDE Home Inspections. Free Estimates. Chargeable Collection/Delivery Service.
SPEAK TO Phillip Reddiough.

PICTURE PLAQUES
142 Lambton Road, **London SW20 0TJ**
TEL   081 879 7841
OPEN   By Appointment.

215

Specialise in hand-finished wooden picture plaques in gold leaf or white gold leaf.
PROVIDE Free Estimates.
SPEAK TO Kate Sim.

Specialise in courses throughout the year (maximum of four students per course) in French polishing, wax and ornamental finishes.
SPEAK TO Alfred Fry.

DAUPHIN DISPLAY CABINET CO.
118A Holland Park Avenue, **London W11 4PA**
TEL   071 727 0715
FAX   071 221 8371
OPEN   9–5.30 Mon–Fri; 9.30–1 Sat.
Specialise in display stands and cabinets for the antique and collectors' market.
PROVIDE Home Inspections. Free Estimates. Chargeable Collection/Delivery Service.
SPEAK TO John Harrison-Banfield.

JUSTIN F. SKREBOWSKI
82E Portobello Road, **London W11 2QD**
TEL   071 792 9742
OPEN   1–6.30 Tues–Fri; 7am–6pm Sat.
Specialise in stands, easels, browsers, folio stands.
PROVIDE Chargeable Estimates. Chargeable Collection/Delivery Service.
SPEAK TO Justin Skrebowski.

TURNROSS & CO.
130 Pinner Road, Harrow, **Middlesex HA1 4JE**
TEL   081 863 5036
OPEN   9–5 Thur–Sat.
Specialise in upholstery supplies, brass castors and fittings.
PROVIDE Free Estimates.
SPEAK TO A. R. Rosman.

MIDLAND SCHOOL OF FRENCH POLISHING
18A Mansfield Road, Eastwood, **Nottinghamshire NG16 3AQ**
TEL   0773 531157 or 715911
OPEN   8.45–5 Mon–Thur.

BERKELEY STUDIO
The Old Vicarage, Castle Cary, **Somerset BA7 7EJ**
TEL   0963 50748
FAX   0963 51107
OPEN   9–5 Mon–Fri By Appointment Only.
Specialise in making picture plaques and display cabinets.
PROVIDE Home Inspections. Free Estimates. Free Collection/Delivery Service.
SPEAK TO John Harries.

SUFFOLK BRASS
Thurston, Bury St.Edmunds, **Suffolk IP31 3SN**
TEL   0359 30888 and 0379 898670
OPEN   9–6 Mon–Fri; 9–12 Sat.
Specialise in casting brass by the hot wax or sand process from original brassware for furniture fittings. Also make hand-forged iron fittings.
PROVIDE Free Estimates. Free Collection/Delivery Service (same day).
SPEAK TO Mark Peters or Thane Meldrum.

ALBERT PLUMB
31 Whyke Lane, Chichester, **West Sussex PO19 2JS**
TEL   0243 788468
OPEN   9.30–5 Mon–Sat.
Specialise in supplying waxes and other items for restoration. Brass fittings, handles, upholstery fittings.

PROVIDE Home Inspections. Free
Estimates. Chargeable
Collection/Delivery Service.
SPEAK TO Albert Plumb.
SEE Furniture.

ALAN MORRIS (WHOLESALE)
10 Coughton Lane, Alcester,
Warwickshire B49 5HN
TEL   0789 762800
OPEN   By Appointment or Mail Order.
Specialise in supplying display stands for
ceramics, dolls and pictures as well as
wire and disc plate-hangers. Also
provide peelable price labels and strung
tickets.
SPEAK TO Alan Leadbeater.

ROD NAYLOR
208 Devizes Road, Hilperton,
Trowbridge, **Wiltshire BA14 7QP**
TEL   0225–754497
OPEN   By Appointment.
Specialise in supplying hard-to-find
items for restorers such as three-
dimensional copying machines,
embossed lining paper.
PROVIDE Home Inspections. Free Local
Estimates. Free Local
Collection/Delivery Service.
SPEAK TO Rod Naylor.
SEE Furniture, Porcelain.

SPECIALIST BOOKSELLERS

REFERENCE WORKS
12 Commercial Road, Swanage, **Dorset
BH19 1DF**
TEL   0929 424423
FAX   0929 422597
OPEN   By Appointment; Telephone
            Orders 9–5.30 Mon–Sat.
Specialise in books on ceramics of all
countries.
PROVIDE Mail Order Service.
SPEAK TO Barry Lamb.

PHILLIPS OF HITCHIN
The Manor House, Hitchin,
Hertfordshire SG5 1JW
TEL   0462 432067
FAX   0462 459405
OPEN   9–5.30 Mon–Sat.
Specialise in reference books on
antiques, particularly furniture.
SPEAK TO Jerome Phillips.
SEE Furniture.

C. & A. J. BARMBY
68 Judd Road, Tonbridge, **Kent
TN9 2NJ**
TEL   0732 356479
OPEN   Mail Order only.
Specialise in antique reference books.
PROVIDE Chargeable Collection/Delivery
Service.
SPEAK TO Chris Barmby.

THOMAS HENEAGE
42 Duke Street, **London SW1Y 6DJ**
TEL   071–930–9223
FAX   071–839–9223
OPEN   10–6 Mon–Fri.
Specialise in books on the fine and
decorative arts.
SPEAK TO Thomas Heneage.

ST. GEORGE'S GALLERY BOOKS LTD
8 Duke Street, St.James's, **London SW1Y 6BN**
TEL   071 930 0935
FAX   071 976 1832
OPEN   10–6 Mon–Fri.

Specialise in books and exhibition catalogues on all aspects of the fine and decorative arts.
SPEAK TO Jo Walton.

SIMS REED LTD
58 Jermyn Street, **London SW1Y 6LX**
TEL   071 493 5660
FAX   071 493 8468
OPEN   10–6 Mon–Fri.

Specialise in monographs, art reference and modern illustrated books.

PROVIDE Home Inspections. Free/Chargeable Estimates. Chargeable Collection/Delivery Service.
SPEAK TO Nina Lyndsay.

CAROL MANHEIM
31 Ennismore Avenue, **London W4 1SE**
TEL   081 994 9740
FAX   081 995 5396
OPEN   Mail Order Service.

Specialise in 19th and 20th century British and Continental out-of-print art reference books and catalogues, including sculpture, fashion and photography.

PROVIDE Free Book Search Service.
SPEAK TO Carol Manheim.

ZWEMMER ART BOOKS
24 Litchfield Street, **London WC2H 9NJ**
TEL   071 379 7886
FAX   071 836 7049
OPEN   9.30–6 Mon–Wed; 10–6 Thur & Sat.

Specialise in books on the fine and decorative arts including out-of-print and foreign language books.
SPEAK TO Christopher Goodyear.
Established in 1921.

JOHN IVES BOOKSELLER
5 Normanhurst Drive, Twickenham, **Middlesex TW1 1NA**
TEL   081 892 6265
OPEN   By Appointment.

Specialise in scarce and out–of–print books on antiques and collecting, costume and needlework and architecture.

PROVIDE Mail Order Service.
SPEAK TO John Ives.

THE CERAMICS BOOK CENTRE
Three Gables, The Drive, Wonersh Park, Guildford, **Surrey GU5 0QW**
TEL   0483 892152
OPEN   Mail Order Service.

Specialise in new and out-of-print books on ceramics.

PROVIDE A complimentary search service.
SPEAK TO Susan Gerry.

NICHOLAS MERCHANT
3 Promenade Court, Promenade Square, Harrogate, **North Yorkshire HG1 2PJ**
TEL   0423 505370
FAX   0423 506183
OPEN   By Appointment.

Specialise in reference books on all aspects of the decorative arts, including antiques, fine art, architecture and interior design.

PROVIDE Mail Order Service.
SPEAK TO Nicholas Merchant.

POTTERTON BOOKS
The Old Rectory, Sessay, Thirsk, **North Yorkshire YO7 3LZ**
TEL   0845 401218
FAX   0845 401439
OPEN   9.30–4.30 Mon–Fri or By
         Appointment.

Specialise in books on the fine and decorative arts, including interior design and decoration. Also supply library accessories.
SPEAK TO Clare Jameson.

Transport and Packing

A.B.C. PACKAGING SUPPLIES
45 St John's Road, Moggerhanger,
Bedfordshire MK44 3RJ
TEL   0767 40777
OPEN   By Appointment.
Specialise in wrapping and labels of all kinds in 'small user' quantities.
PROVIDE Postal Service.
SPEAK TO Mrs. Harvey.

ALAN FRANKLIN TRANSPORT
Unit 8, 27 Blackmoor Road, Ebblake Industrial Estate, Verwood, **Dorset BH31 6BE**
TEL   0202 826539
FAX   0202 827337
OPEN   8.30–6 Mon–Fri; 8–2 Sat.
Specialise in transporting antiques and works of art throughout Europe, air freight and containerised shipments worldwide. Storage facilities in United Kingdom and France.
SPEAK TO Alan Franklin or James Scollen.

GEO. COPSEY & CO. LTD
Danes Road, Romford, **Essex RM7 0HL**
TEL   081 592 1003
FAX   0708 727305
OPEN   8–5 Mon–Fri.
Specialise in packing and removal of fine art and antiques.

PROVIDE Home Inspections. Free Estimates.
SPEAK TO Barry Tebbutt.

ALBAN SHIPPING LTD
43 Hatfield Road, St. Albans,
Hertfordshire AL1 4JE
TEL   0727 41402
FAX   0727 46370
OPEN   8–5.30 Mon–Fri.
Specialise in the collection, packaging and export or delivery of antiques and collectors' items.
PROVIDE Home Inspections. Free Estimates.
SPEAK TO Andrew Jackman.

C. R. FENTON & COMPANY
Beachy Road, Old Ford, **London E3 2NX**
TEL   081 533 2711
FAX   081 985 6032
OPEN   9–5.30 Mon–Fri.
Specialise in fine art packing, shipping and storage.
PROVIDE Home Inspections. Free Estimates.
SPEAK TO Brian Bath.
Members of the British International Freight Association.

MOMART PLC
199–205 Richmond Road, **London E8 3NJ**
TEL 081 986 3624
FAX 081 533 0122
OPEN By Appointment.
Specialise in fine art handling, including transportation worldwide, case making and packing, exhibition installation and storage.
PROVIDE Home Inspections. Free Estimates.
SPEAK TO Richard Chapman, Transport Director
or Kevin Richardson, Shipping Director.

LOCKSON SERVICES LTD
29 Broomfield Street, Poplar, **London E14 6BX**
TEL 071 515 8600
FAX 071 515 4043
OPEN 9–6 Mon–Fri.
Specialise in fine art, antique and general packing and shipping and transportation within the U.K.
PROVIDE Free Estimates.
SPEAK TO David Armitage Snr.

L. J. ROBERTON LTD
Marlborough House, Cooks Road, **London E15 2PW**
TEL 081 519 2020
FAX 081 519 8571
OPEN 9–5 Mon–Fri.
Specialise in export packing and shipping of antiques and fine art, including a countrywide collection service.
SPEAK TO Mr. J. Tebbutt.
Member of LAPADA.

WINGATE AND JOHNSTON LTD
78 Broadway, **London E15 1NG**
TEL 081 555 8123
FAX 081 519 8115
OPEN 9–5.30 Mon–Fri.
Specialise in packing and shipping of antiques and fine art.
PROVIDE Home Inspections. Free Estimates.
SPEAK TO Paul Brecht.

STEPHEN MORRIS SHIPPING LTD
Manor Warehouse, 318 Green Lanes, **London N4 1BX**
TEL 071 354 1212
FAX 081 802 4110
OPEN 8–6 Mon–Fri.
Specialise in packing and shipping fine art and antiques.
PROVIDE Home Inspections. Free Estimates.
SPEAK TO Stephen Morris or John Holser.

PITT & SCOTT LTD
20–24 Edengrove, **London N7 8ED**
TEL 071 607 7321
FAX 071 607 0566
OPEN 8–5 Mon–Fri.
Specialise in international packing and shipping of fine art, domestic moving and storing.
PROVIDE Home Inspections. Free Estimates.
SPEAK TO Anthony Roberts.

KUWAHARA LIMITED
Unit 5, Bittacy Business Centre, Bittacy Hill, **London NW7 1BA**
TEL 081 349 7744
FAX 081 349 2916
OPEN 9–5.30 Mon–Fri.
Specialise in packing and shipping and are international removers.

PROVIDE Home Inspections.
SPEAK TO S. Kuwahara or K. Blair.

ANGLO–PACIFIC (FINE ART) LIMITED
Unit 2, Bush Industrial Estate, Standard Road, Nortn Acton, **London NW10 6DF**
TEL   081 965 0667
FAX   081 965 4954
OPEN   8–6 Mon–Fri.

Specialise in security storage, packing and shipping of fine art and antiques, packing for hand-carrying, insurance.
PROVIDE Free Estimates.
SPEAK TO Phyllis Kearns.

HEDLEYS HUMPERS LTD
Units 3 & 4, 97 Victoria Road, North Acton, **London NW10 6ND**
TEL   081 965 8733
FAX   081 965 0249
OPEN   7–7 Mon–Fri.

Specialise in worldwide packing and shipping.
PROVIDE Home Inspections. Free Estimates.
SPEAK TO Cliff Williams.

TRANS EURO WORLDWIDE
Fine Art Division, Drury Way, Brent Park, **London NW10 OJN**
TEL   081 784 0100
FAX   081 451 6419
OPEN   9–5.30 Mon–Fri; 10–4 Sat.

Specialise in export packing and worldwide freighting by road, sea and air, full door-to-door service. Insurance arranged from single pieces to complete container loads.
PROVIDE Home Inspections. Free Estimates.
SPEAK TO Gerry Ward or Richard Edwards.

EUROPE EXPRESS
125 Sydenham Road, **London SE26 5HB**
TEL   081–776–7556 and mobile 0860 239660
FAX   081 776 7606
OPEN   9–6 Mon–Fri.

Specialise in road transport removals to Europe, including Sardinia and Sicily.
SPEAK TO Tony Morgan.

FEATHERSTON SHIPPING LTD
24 Hampton House, 15/17 Ingate Place, **London SW8 3NS**
TEL   071 720 0422
FAX   071 720 6330
OPEN   8–6 Mon–Fri.

Specialise in packing and shipping fine art and antiques.
PROVIDE Home Inspections. Free Estimates.
SPEAK TO Caedmon Featherston.

THE PACKING SHOP LTD
Units K & L, London Stone Business Estate, Broughton Street, **London SW8 3QR**
TEL   071 627 5605
FAX   071 622 7740
OPEN   9–6 Mon–Fri.

Specialise in same-day shipment of small consignments, as well as airfreight, seafreight and packing.
PROVIDE Home Inspections. Free Estimates.
SPEAK TO Karen Bagot.
SEE **London SW10**.

T. ROGERS & CO. (PACKERS) LTD
PO Box 8, 1A Broughton Street, **London SW8 3QL**
TEL   071 622 9151
FAX   071 627 3318
OPEN   8–5 Mon–Fri.

Specialise in transporting, packing, warehousing and shipping of fine art and antiques as well as security storage and picture hanging.
PROVIDE Home Inspections. Free Estimates.
SPEAK TO Michael Evans.

THE PACKING SHOP LTD
535 Kings Road, **London SW10 OSZ**
TEL　　071 352 2021
FAX　　071 351 7576
OPEN　9–6 Mon–Fri; 10–1 Sat.

Specialise in fine art and antique packing and shipping with emphasis on same-day collection and 2/3-day delivery worldwide.
PROVIDE Home Inspections. Free Estimates.
SPEAK TO Eileen Abbas.
SEE **London SW8**.

PANTECHNICON GROUP LTD
Unit 3, The Gate Centre, Syon Gate Way, Great West Road, Brentford, **Middlesex TW8 9DD**
TEL　　081 568 6195
FAX　　081 847 3126
OPEN　8.30–5 Mon–Fri.

Specialise in UK, European and international removals of furniture, effects and antiques. They have regular services to France, Belgium and Spain. Storage facilities are available.

PROVIDE Home Inspections. Free Estimates.
SPEAK TO Stephen Bonner.

VULCAN INTERNATIONAL SERVICES
Unit 8, Ascot Road, Clockhouse Lane, Feltham, **Middlesex TW14 8QF**
TEL　　0784 244152
FAX　　0784 248183
OPEN　8.30–5.30 Mon–Fri.

Specialise in packing, storing, forwarding by air, sea and road of antiques and fine art including a full import/export service.

PROVIDE Home Inspections. Free Estimates. Chargeable Collection/Delivery Service.
SPEAK TO Dennis Jarvis.

GANDER & WHITE SHIPPING LTD
New Pound, Wisborough Green, Nr. Billingshurst, **West Sussex RH14 0AY**
TEL　　0403 700044
FAX　　0403 700814
OPEN　9–6 Mon–Fri.

Specialise in packing, moving and shipping fine art, antiques and household removals.

PROVIDE Home Inspections. Free Estimates.
SPEAK TO Maureen De'Ath.

223

Glossary and Useful Addresses

ABA	Antiquarian Booksellers Association Suite 2 26 Charing Cross Road London WC2 Tel. 071 379 3041
ABPR	Association of British Picture Restorers Station Avenue Kew Middlesex TW9 3QA Tel. 081 948 5644
	Association of Master Upholsterers Unit One Clyde Road Works Clyde Road Wallington Surrey SM6 8PZ Tel. 081 773 8069. Fax. 081 773 8103
BADA	British Antique Dealers' Association 20 Rutland Gate London SW7 1BD Tel. 071 589 4128
BAFRA	British Antique Furniture Restorers Association (Executive Administrator) 37 Upper Addison Gardens Holland Park London W14 8AJ Tel. 071 603 5643

BHI	British Horological Institute
CMBHI	Upton Hall
MBHI	Upton, Newark
	Notts.
	Tel. 0636 813795

BWCMG	British Watch and Clockmakers Guild
	West Wick
	Marsh Road
	Burnham-on-Crouch
	Essex CMO 8NE
	Tel. 0621 783104

City and Guilds of London Institute
46 Britannia Street
London WC1Y 9RG
Tel. 071 278 2468. Fax. 071 278 9460

The Conservation Unit of the Museums and Galleries
   Commission
16 Queen Anne's Gate
London W1H 9AA
Tel. 071 233 3683. Fax. 071 233 3686

GA	Gemmological Association of Great Britain
	27 Greville Street
	London EC1N 8SU
	Tel. 071 404 3334

GADR	Guild of Antique Dealers and Restorers
	23 Belle Vue Road
	Shrewsbury
	Shropshire SY3 7LN
	Tel. 0743 271 852

LAPADA	London and Provincial Antique Dealers' Association
	535 Kings Road
	Chelsea
	London SW10 OSZ
	Tel. 071 823 3511

RSA	Royal Society of Arts
	8 John Adams Street
	London WC2N 6EZ
	Tel. 071 930 5115

Royal Society of Miniature Painters
(Membership Secretary, Mrs S Burton)

15 Union Street
Wells
Somerset BA5 2PU
Tel. 0749 74472

(Formerly) Rural Development Commission
CoSIRA   (Headquarters)
141 Castle Street
Salisbury
Wiltshire
SP1 3TP
Tel. 0722 336 255

SSCR   Scottish Society for Conservation and Restoration
(The Membership Secretary, Fiona Butterfield)
Overhall
Kirkfieldbank
Lanark ML11 9TZ

Worshipful Company of Clockmakers
St Dunstans House
Carey Lane
London EC2V 8AA
Tel. 071 606 2366

Worshipful Company of Goldsmiths
Goldsmiths' Hall
Foster Lane
London EC2U 6BN
Tel. 071 606 8971